D1504276

MERCY

SHAKE THE WORLD

MERCY

SHAKE THE WORLD

WRITTEN BY J. M. DEMATTEIS
ILLUSTRATED BY PAUL JOHNSON
AFTERWORD BY ART YOUNG

DOVER PUBLICATIONS, INC.
MINEOLA, NEW YORK

Bibliographical Note

This Dover edition, first published in 2015, is an unabridged republication of the work originally published by DC Comics, New York, in 1993. The Dover edition adds new introductory text by J. M. DeMatteis and Paul Johnson, an Afterword by Art Young, and selected script excerpts, page layouts, and production art.

International Standard Book Number

ISBN-13: 978-0-486-79905-6
ISBN-10: 0-486-79905-0

Manufactured in the United States by Courier Corporation
79905001   2015
www.doverpublications.com

CONTENTS

About Mercy: Shake The World

A Conversation Between Writer
J. M. DeMatteis and Artist Paul Johnson

PJ: Hi Marc, it's great to be able to pull out what remains of the development art-work from *Mercy* and see it in print for the first time! I really felt that I was hitting my stride as a comic book artist with this project; it has always been my favorite comic that I drew. *Mercy* was and still is very special to me—a comic strip that looks beyond the normal boundaries of comics.

JMD: I think it was special project for both of us. How did you end up illustrating it? You'd been working for DC, right?

PJ: With my early American comic book work, I bounced back and forth between DC and Marvel. Art Young had been the assistant editor on *The Books of Magic,* and when he was approached to start up a new (but never to appear) line of com-ics for Disney to be called *Touchmark,* he asked if I might be interested in doing a project with J. M. DeMatteis. Of course I said, "Yes!" straight away.

JMD: Art was Karen Berger's assistant at DC and a superb editor in his own right. I worked with him very closely on *Doctor Fate* (Karen edited the first six issues of my run, and Art did the rest) and we had a great relationship. When he asked me to create something new for the *Touchmark* line, I jumped at the chance.

PJ: Your books *Moonshadow* and *Blood* had really had an impact on me as they moved away from the typical American comic book idioms. Not only did they look fantastic, but they felt different. Very different. So for me it was a no-brainer, I jumped at the opportunity. I'd read some of your more mainstream comics too. I've always been impressed by the breadth of your work, Marc. You seem to have covered all the bases from the most extreme personal stories to the most main-stream of licensed characters. That's quite an achievement!

JMD: Thanks, Paul. One of the things I've tried to do in my career (intuitively, at first, and then very consciously) is be as varied as I can. I've written creator-owned projects, mainstream superheroes, comedy, kid-friendly material, autobiography. Done television and film. Novels. It's a way not to get locked into any one thing, to keep things fresh and challenging. People like to pigeonhole writers and artists. It's our job to keep moving, to escape the pigeon holes.

PJ: Just an aside about *Touchmark*—Art Young was approached by Disney who wanted to create a serious, thoughtful line of comics aimed at a more mature audience. By hiring Art they knew they would have access to some of comics' most interesting creators—Marc, Grant Morrison, Pete Milligan, Duncan Fegredo, etc. It ended up being a bizarre setup in the end, though—the moment they saw the first couple of pages of Morrison and Fegrado's *Enigma,* they knew they could never put material that adult out under a Disney imprint! So all of the titles that were going to launch *Touchmark—Enigma, Sebastian O,* and *Mercy* became early titles for *Vertigo,* DC's mature reader imprint. Not that you would know it though, as *Mercy* has been airbrushed out of the history of *Vertigo* because as creator-owners, we asked for (and got) our creative rights back!

JMD: The *Touchmark* situation was kind of crazy. They flew a bunch of us out to San Diego for Comic Con, there was much ballyhoo, a big panel announcing the line and then Disney pulled the plug. Which ended up being a good thing, because it was wonderful to be part of the *Vertigo* launch.

Question for you: How did you get into the business?

PJ: I kind of came into mainstream comics sideways. I'd wanted to draw comics as a teenager, but after going to art school I was doing pretty off-the-wall stuff, mixing influences from printmaking, advertising, video, etc. Some of the stuff was large scale work in charcoal, several feet high, whilst other stuff was more reproducible and made it into various self-published compilations that were sold through small press outlets and art galleries. The success of Gaiman and McKeans' *Violent Cases* was a turning point for me because James Robinson persuaded me that we could pitch a similarly personal project to Titan Books over here in the UK. That became *London's Dark,* a book which was based in part on the conversations my parents had around the Sunday dinner table about their experiences in wartime London.

JMD: Interesting. I met James at a convention back in the 80s and I remember him giving me a graphic novel he'd written. I think it was *London's Dark*—which means I was familiar with your work when we started in on *Mercy.* Which is odd, because my memory is that Art was the one who first showed me your work. Maybe I read *London's Dark* and didn't file your name away.

PJ: I was a huge fan of the European (and South American) *bande dessinée,* and really hoped that you could come up with something of similar weight. I was starting to get typecast as a horror artist, and although I found that kind of stuff easy, it wasn't really what I wanted to do. I wanted something life-affirming. Something without fisticuffs, big muscles, and guns. Don't get me wrong, that stuff can be great, but there was a lot of it around at the time and little else. I can't remember exactly how the idea for *Mercy* started. Can you, Marc?

JMD: *Mercy* was another attempt to stretch myself creatively, to do something new and different. It was first and foremost an attempt to write a story about compassion; about the fact that the universe around us, which can seem cold and unfeeling, is really our greatest support. I'd certainly injected those themes into other works, but *Mercy* tackled them more directly and with a main character who was very much the embodiment of a Divine Idea. But, of course, Divine Ideas need to be rooted in the very real lives of real people, which is what the story tried to do: illustrate the way the Divine and the human intersect and show the love, the compassion, at the core of the universe. The older I get the more I believe that compassion is the single most important quality of life.

One of my favorite quotes ever is from Buddha: "That which is most needed is a loving heart." And that, at its core, is what *Mercy* is about. The compassion that flows from God to man, from man back to God, and from one human heart to the next.

PJ: I've still got the original script that you wrote for the project, Marc. I can see from the preamble that I must have already done some development artwork because you make comments on it and talk about going with the blue-skinned version of Mercy that resonated with the color of Hindu gods.

JMD: Yes. I wanted her to have that feeling. Krishna blue, evoking something both ancient and eternal.

PJ: What you wrote was essentially an outline, giving me as much space as possible to play with layout and pace. That was a great experience to have! It meant that I was able to do a lot of things I'd have liked to do elsewhere but hadn't been able to—collage, full-page illustrations, second-by-second storytelling, semi-abstract art. I had a ball! *Mercy* still remains my favorite project from those days. I remember you saying at the time that you found my *Mercy* artwork hard to put dialogue to. Was my storytelling that bad?

JMD: I don't remember saying that and, if I did, perhaps I meant that the pages were so beautiful I just wanted to leave them alone. (And, remember, I'm a writer who loves to run off at the mouth.) I do remember being very excited to be working with you. The work of yours that Art showed me had just the right mixture of cosmic grandeur and human intimacy that the story needed. And you could *really paint*. It takes a lot of skill to do painted comics and still keep the storytelling clear, the characters definitive. I've been lucky enough to work with guys like you, Jon J Muth and Kent Williams, who know how to do painted stories without losing the essential elements that make it a *comic book*.

As I recall, we hit it off creatively right from the start. I wouldn't have written a plot that had as much room for you to play with if I hadn't trusted you and your ability to tell the story clearly and well. Looking back, I'm amazed at how loose that plot is. I'm usually pretty anal about it: page by page, panel by panel, camera angles, the works. I must have *really* trusted you and wanted your input.

PJ: I worked your script into a series of breakdowns—did you get to see these at the time, Marc?

JMD: I'm sure I did. Probably went over them with Art and then we sent you notes.

PJ: I then set about gathering reference material. In those pre-Google days a lot of the fun of drawing was doing the research—like hunting down a picture of Guanyin, the East Asian goddess of mercy. I was a pretty consistent worker—three pages a week, so I guess the project must have taken me about six months to complete. I can't remember; did you start scripting it as we went along, or did you wait until all the art was in at the end?

JMD: I suspect I wrote it in sections as the work came in. By the time all the art was in, it would have been too late in the process for me to do all the scripting without rushing it.

PJ: Our collaboration was all Fedex and phone calls, I remember; it was pre-Internet days, so we couldn't email back and forth. I don't think I even saw a lettered version before the printed item arrived.

JMD: Since we didn't have the Internet, we didn't miss it!

One of the great things about working from an outline, as opposed to a full script, is that you, as the artist, get to play with the story in ways I wouldn't necessarily expect, and then I get to react to that art and it inspires *me* to do unexpected things with the story. This way of working really creates sparks…but only if there's genuine creative chemistry between the writer and artist. If there's no chemistry, this kind of collaboration can be deadly. But we had that creative click right from the start. Another blessing from *Mercy*.

I have a memory of going over the final lettered pages at the DC offices, making last minute changes to the copy. Art, an editor who always let me do things my own way, never tried to impose his own vision on mine, looked at a couple of pages (I don't recall which ones) and said, "I think we should reverse the copy on these two pages. The sequence will play better that way." And he was absolutely right, proving what a smart, intuitive guy he was (and remains). We switched the pages and that sequence was helped immeasurably. He could see what I couldn't—and that's the mark of a superb editor.

PJ: I knew the project was in safe hands, plus we weren't being rushed to meet a production schedule. I remember that you came over to London for a comic convention around that time and you were in a room in the Hotel Russell that had some prints of Kandinsky paintings on the walls and they reminded you of the concentric circle motif from the end of *Mercy*. You saw that as some kind of positive omen!

JMD: That rings a bell. I absolutely remember meeting with you in London. I think I was on my honeymoon on the way to India.

PJ: I've been away from the comics scene for ages. Have you done anything since *Mercy* in a similar vein?

JMD: Well, projects like *The Last One, Seekers Into the Mystery, Brooklyn Dreams, Abadazad, Augusta Wind* (among others that followed) all have that personal, experimental, literary feeling to them—accenting the "book" in comic book—that *Mercy* had. And many of them also were rooted in a spiritual exploration of our lives.

But *Mercy* was so direct, so magical. It was almost like a contemporary version of an ancient religious myth, a way to infuse those fundamental beliefs into a contemporary landscape. So, in that way, it was unique. It's a project I hold near and dear to my heart. I'm so delighted that it's back in print and that we got to talk about it and reconnect in the process. Another gift from our blue-skinned goddess.

MERCY

SHAKE THE WORLD

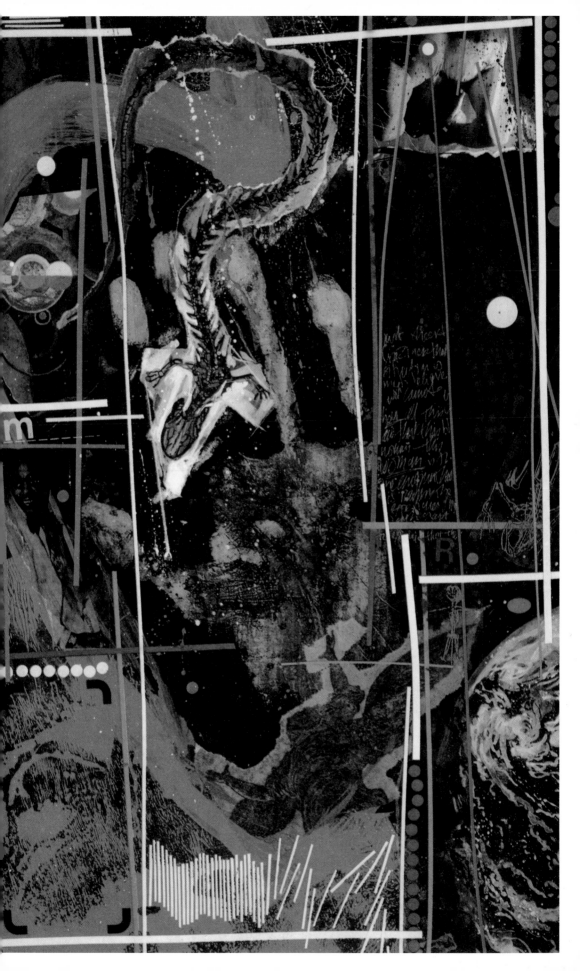

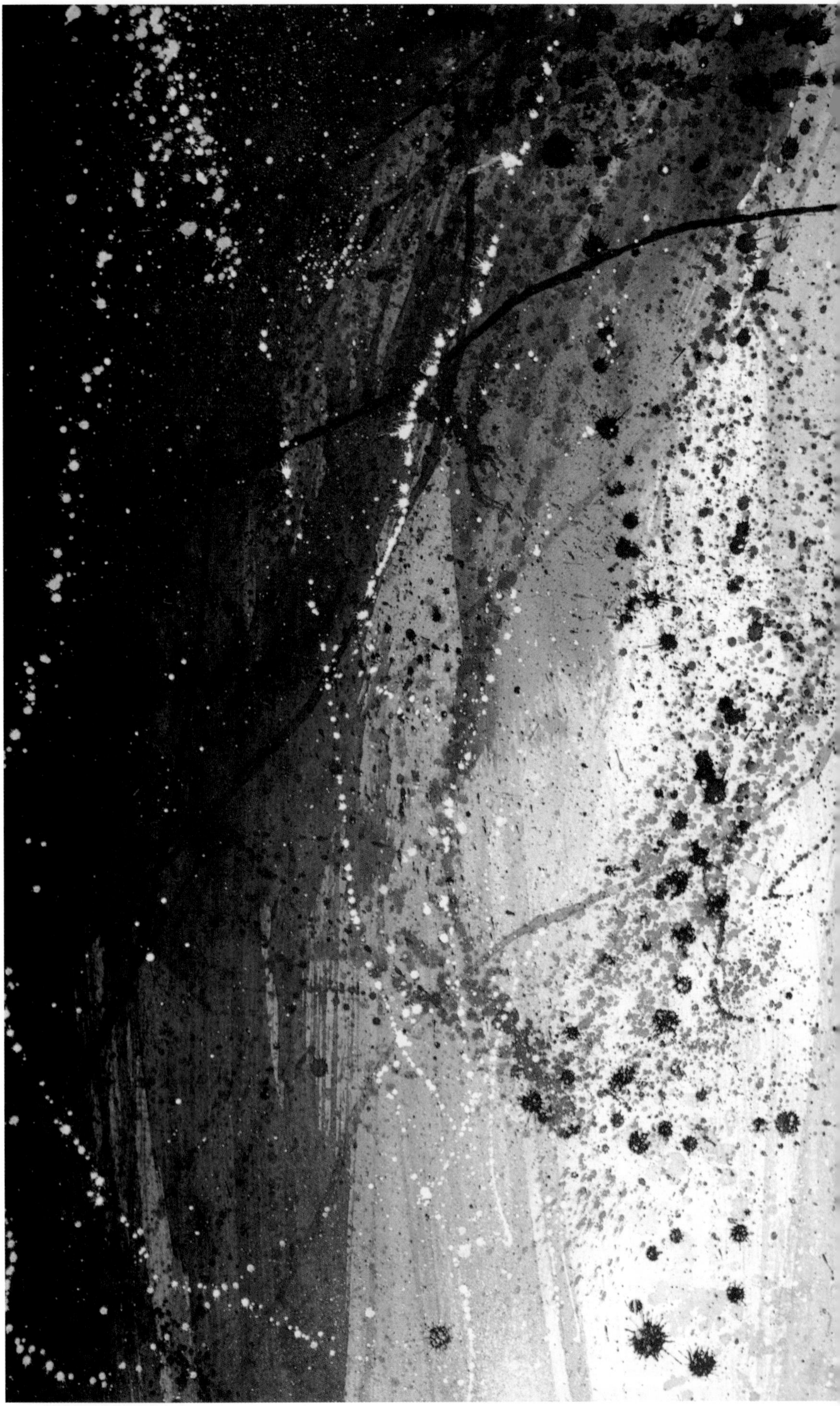

They're working so hard.

NO SM

Tubes and wires and medications and ministrations.

They scurry, like brainless little ants, intent on their task.

ROSE, JOSH

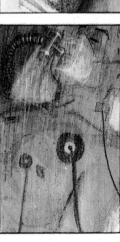

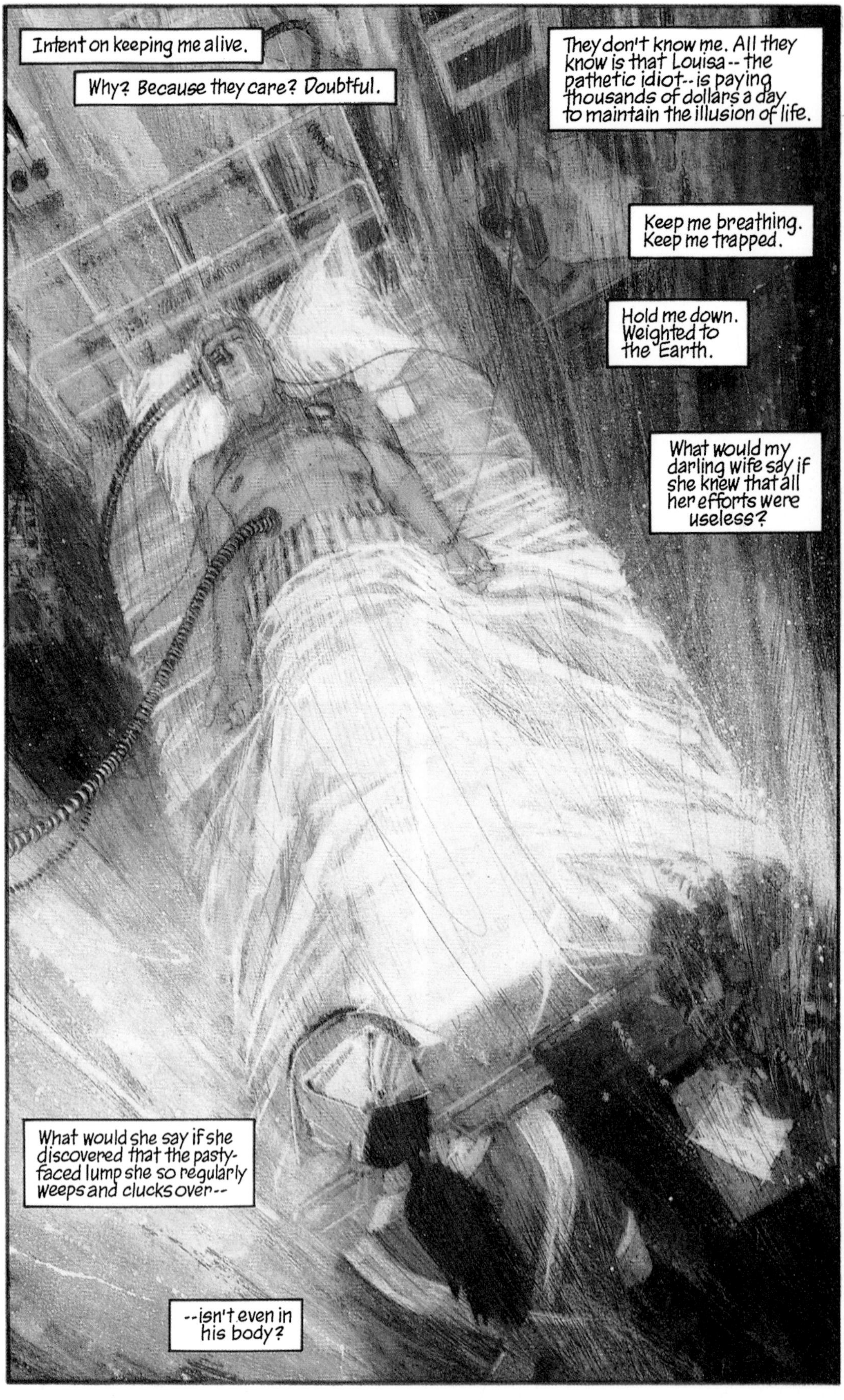
Intent on keeping me alive.
Why? Because they care? Doubtful.
They don't know me. All they know is that Louisa -- the pathetic idiot -- is paying thousands of dollars a day to maintain the illusion of life.
Keep me breathing. Keep me trapped.
Hold me down. Weighted to the Earth.
What would my darling wife say if she knew that all her efforts were useless?
What would she say if she discovered that the pasty-faced lump she so regularly weeps and clucks over--
--isn't even in his body?

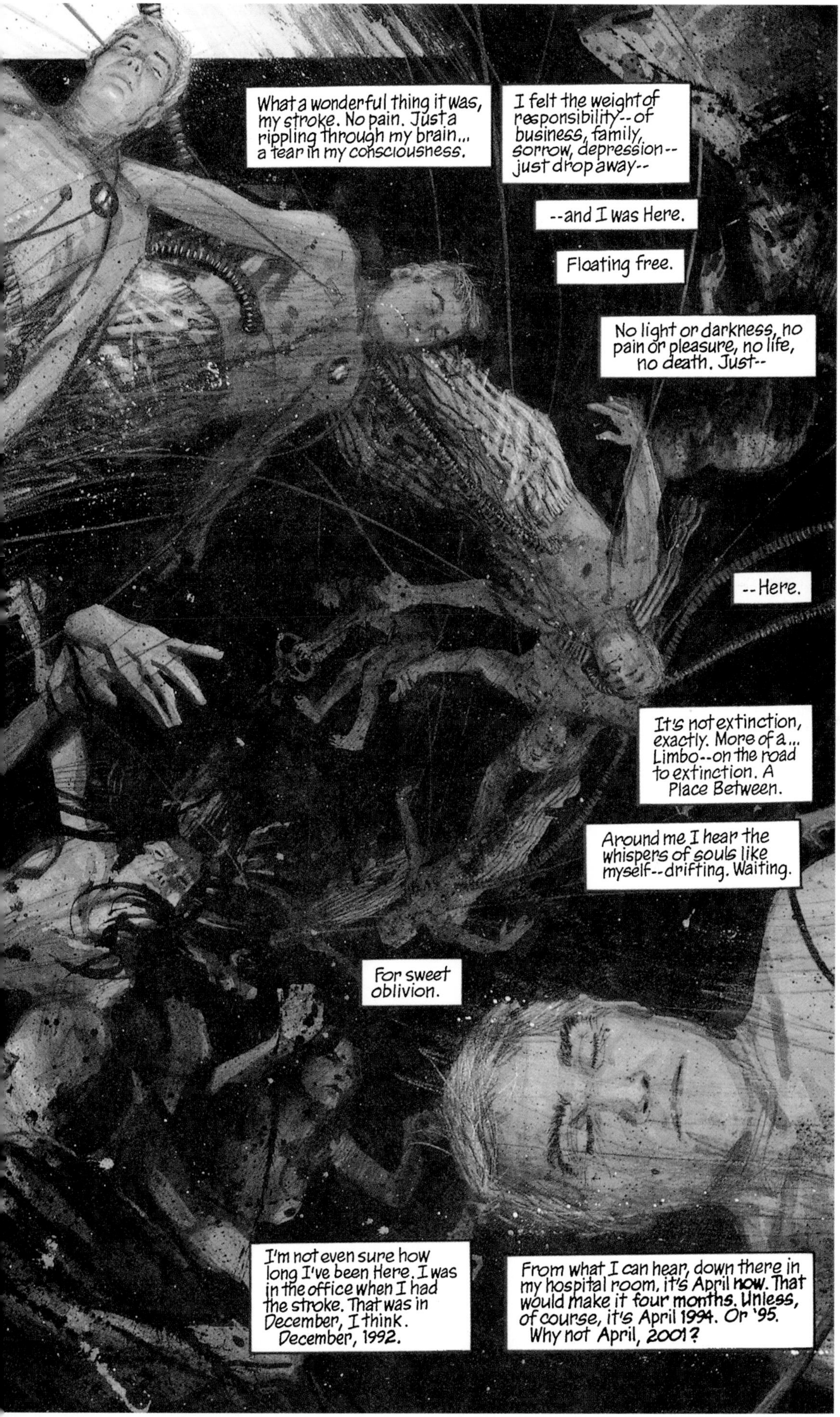
What a wonderful thing it was, my stroke. No pain. Just a rippling through my brain... a tear in my consciousness.
I felt the weight of responsibility--of business, family, sorrow, depression--just drop away--
--and I was Here.
Floating free.
No light or darkness, no pain or pleasure, no life, no death. Just--
--Here.
It's not extinction, exactly. More of a... Limbo--on the road to extinction. A Place Between.
Around me I hear the whispers of souls like myself--drifting. Waiting.
For sweet oblivion.
I'm not even sure how long I've been Here. I was in the office when I had the stroke. That was in December, I think. December, 1992.
From what I can hear, down there in my hospital room, it's April now. That would make it four months. Unless, of course, it's April 1994. Or '95. Why not April, 2001?

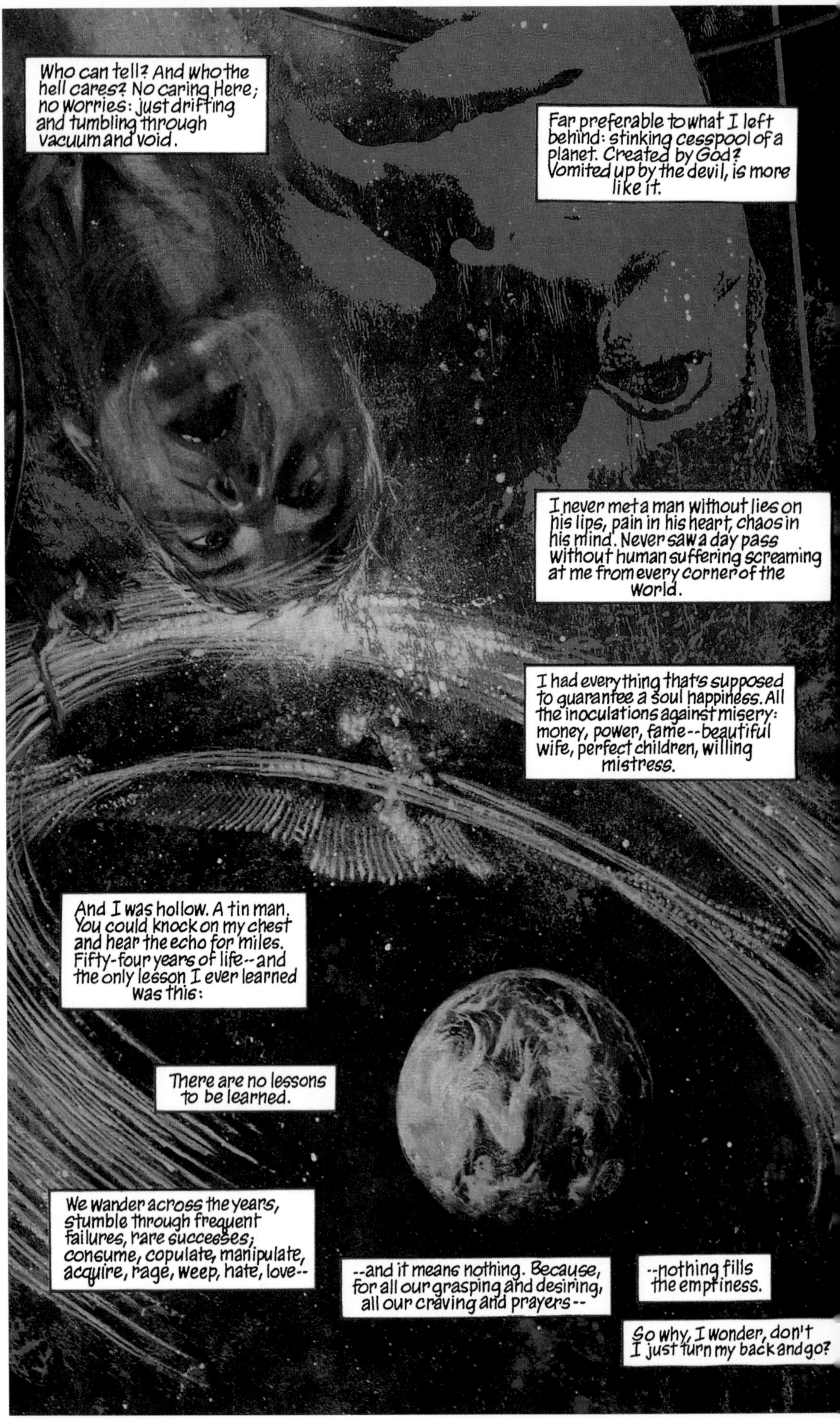
Who can tell? And who the hell cares? No caring Here; no worries: just drifting and tumbling through vacuum and void.
Far preferable to what I left behind: stinking cesspool of a planet. Created by God? Vomited up by the devil, is more like it.
I never met a man without lies on his lips, pain in his heart, chaos in his mind. Never saw a day pass without human suffering screaming at me from every corner of the world.
I had everything that's supposed to guarantee a soul happiness. All the inoculations against misery: money, power, fame--beautiful wife, perfect children, willing mistress.
And I was hollow. A tin man. You could knock on my chest and hear the echo for miles. Fifty-four years of life--and the only lesson I ever learned was this:
There are no lessons to be learned.
We wander across the years, stumble through frequent failures, rare successes; consume, copulate, manipulate, acquire, rage, weep, hate, love--
--and it means nothing. Because, for all our grasping and desiring, all our craving and prayers--
--nothing fills the emptiness.
So why, I wonder, don't I just turn my back and go?

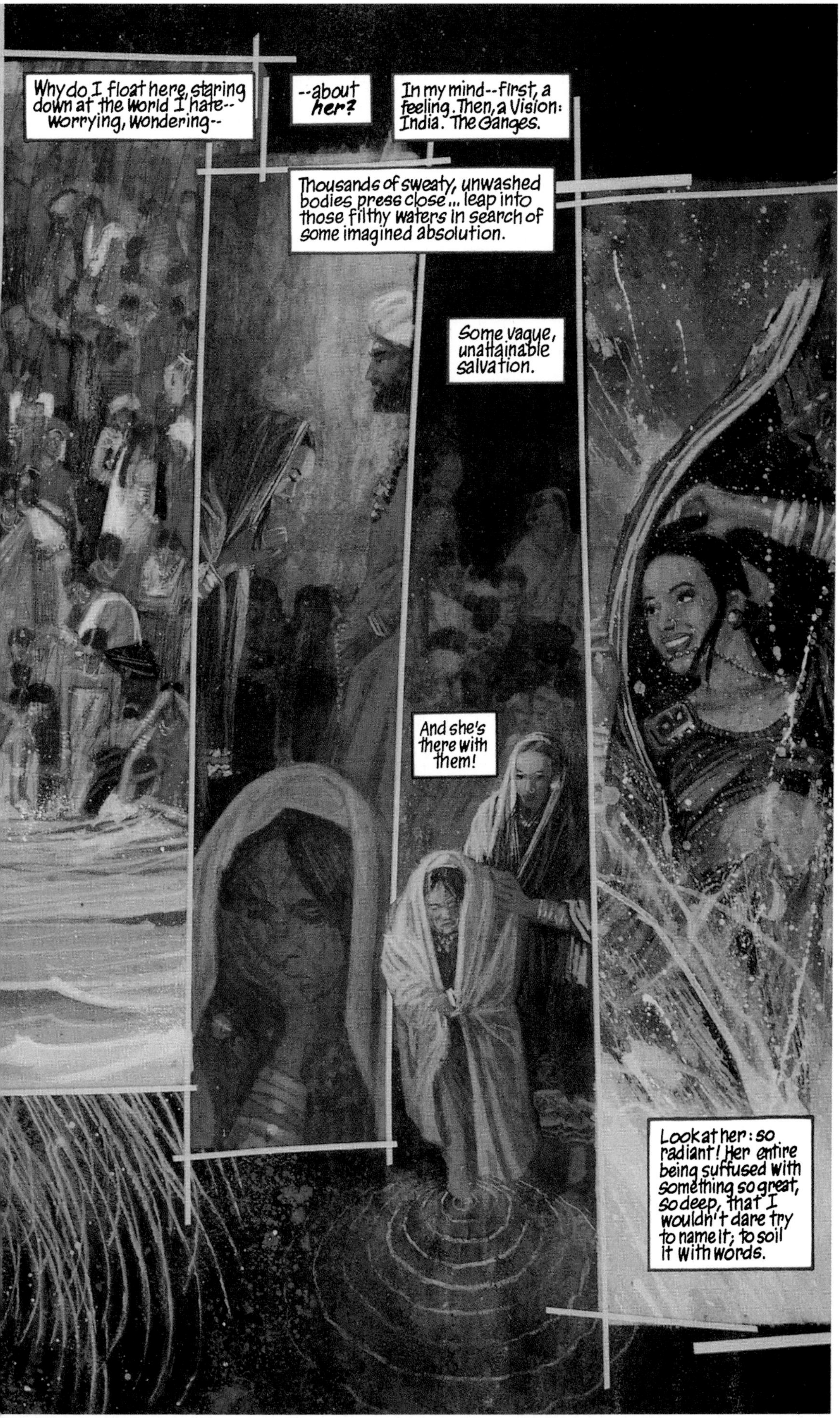
Why do I float here, staring down at the world I hate--worrying, wondering--
--about *her?*
In my mind--first, a feeling. Then, a Vision: India. The Ganges.
Thousands of sweaty, unwashed bodies press close... leap into those filthy waters in search of some imagined absolution.
Some vague, unattainable salvation.
And she's there with them!
Look at her: so radiant! Her entire being suffused with something so great, so deep, that I wouldn't dare try to name it; to soil it with words.

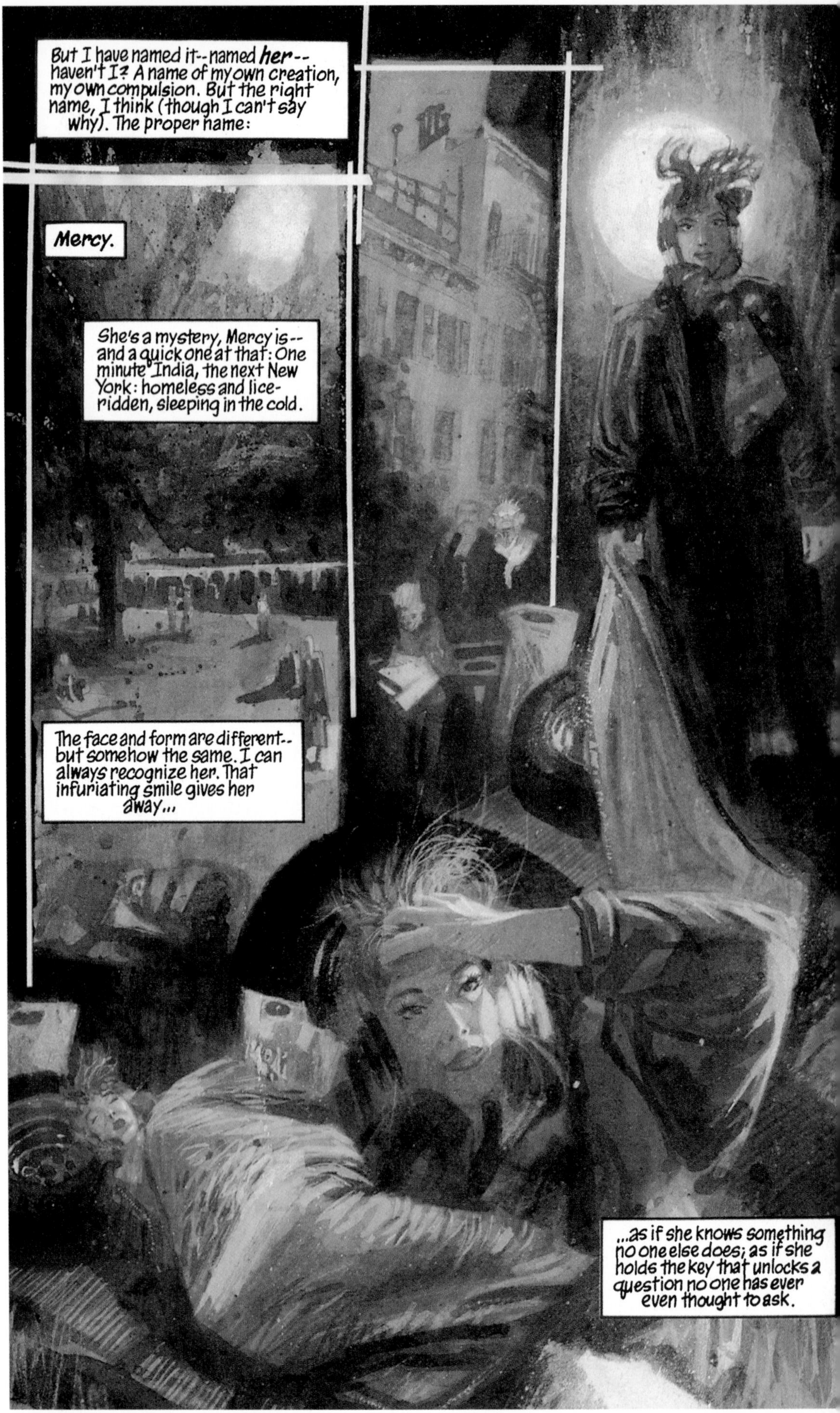
But I have named it--named **her**--haven't I? A name of my own creation, my own compulsion. But the right name, I think (though I can't say why). The proper name:
Mercy.
She's a mystery, Mercy is--and a quick one at that: One minute India, the next New York: homeless and lice-ridden, sleeping in the cold.
The face and form are different--but somehow the same. I can always recognize her. That infuriating smile gives her away...
...as if she knows something no one else does; as if she holds the key that unlocks a question no one has ever even thought to ask.

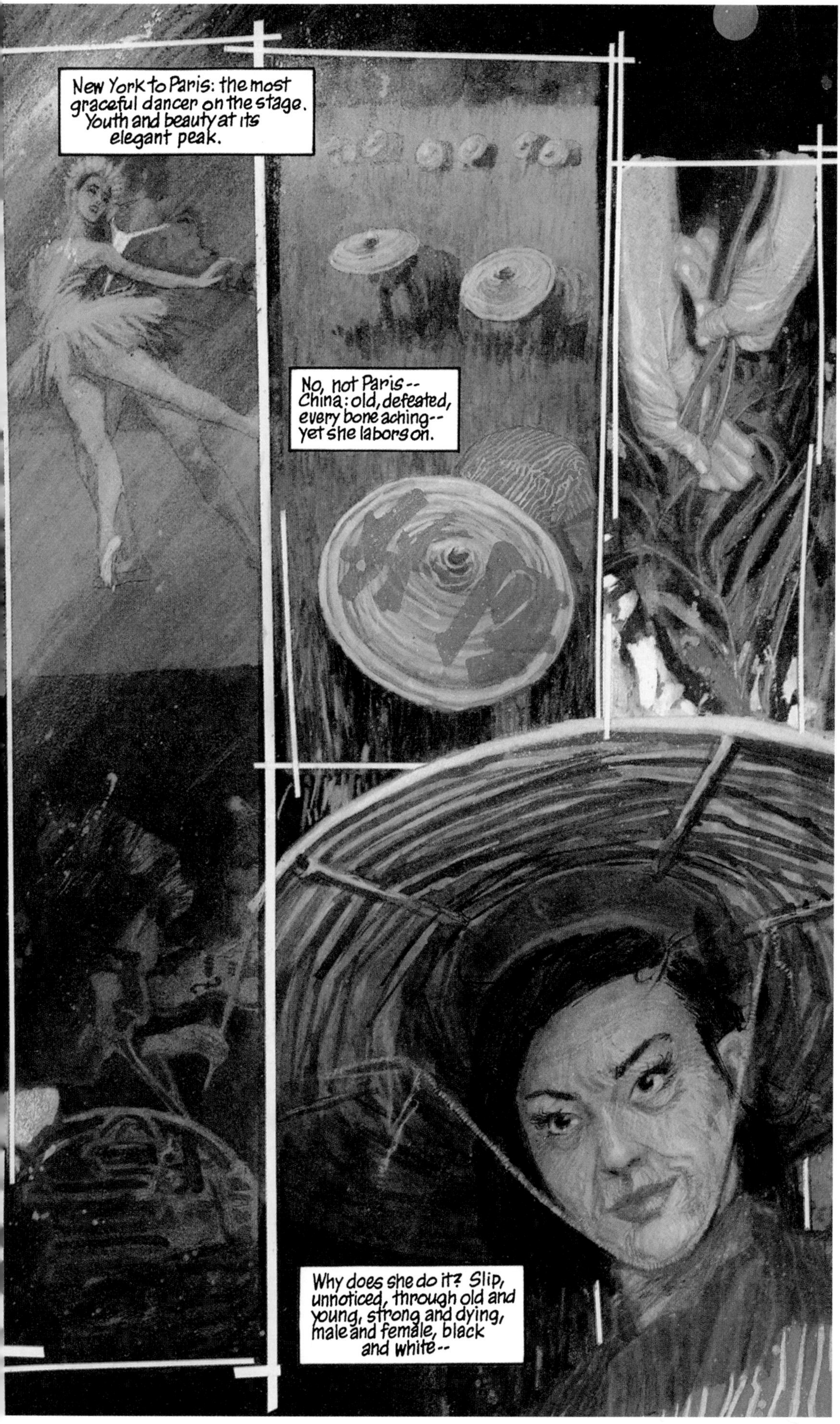
New York to Paris: the most graceful dancer on the stage. Youth and beauty at its elegant peak.
No, not Paris-- China: old, defeated, every bone aching-- yet she labors on.
Why does she do it? Slip, unnoticed, through old and young, strong and dying, male and female, black and white--

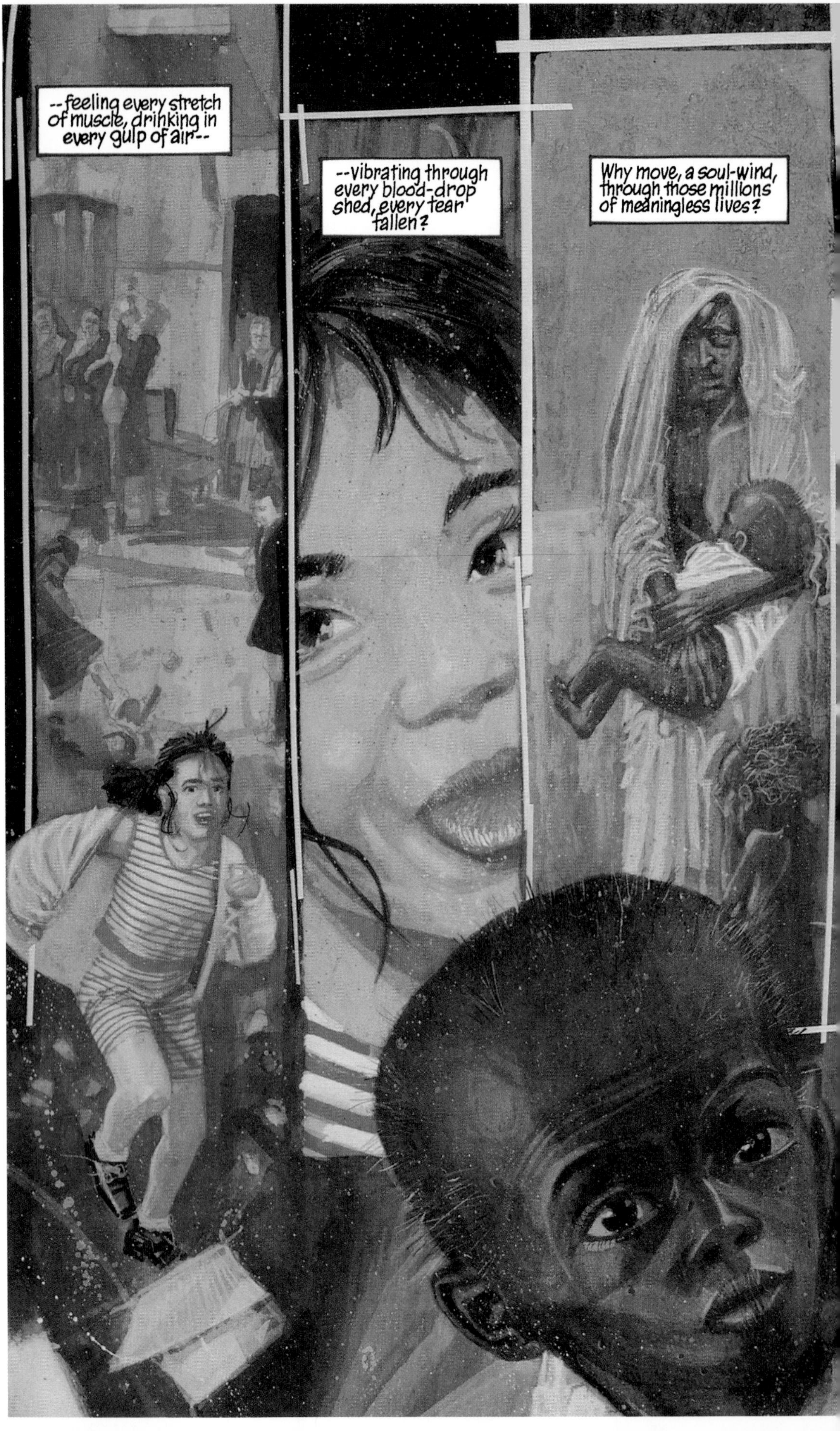
--feeling every stretch of muscle, drinking in every gulp of air--
--vibrating through every blood-drop shed, every tear fallen?
Why move, a soul-wind, through those millions of meaningless lives?

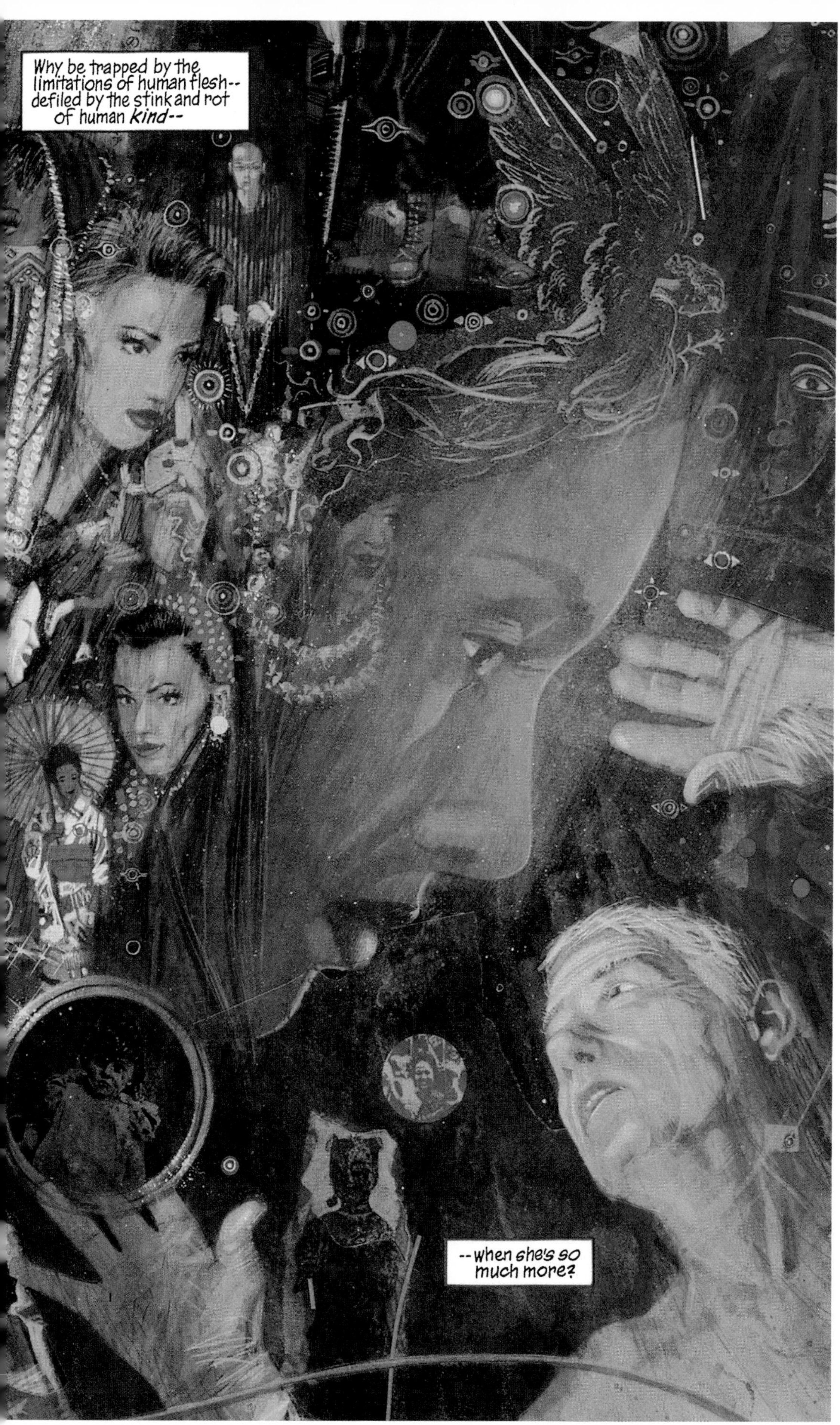
Why be trapped by the limitations of human flesh-- defiled by the stink and rot of human *kind*--
--when she's so much more?

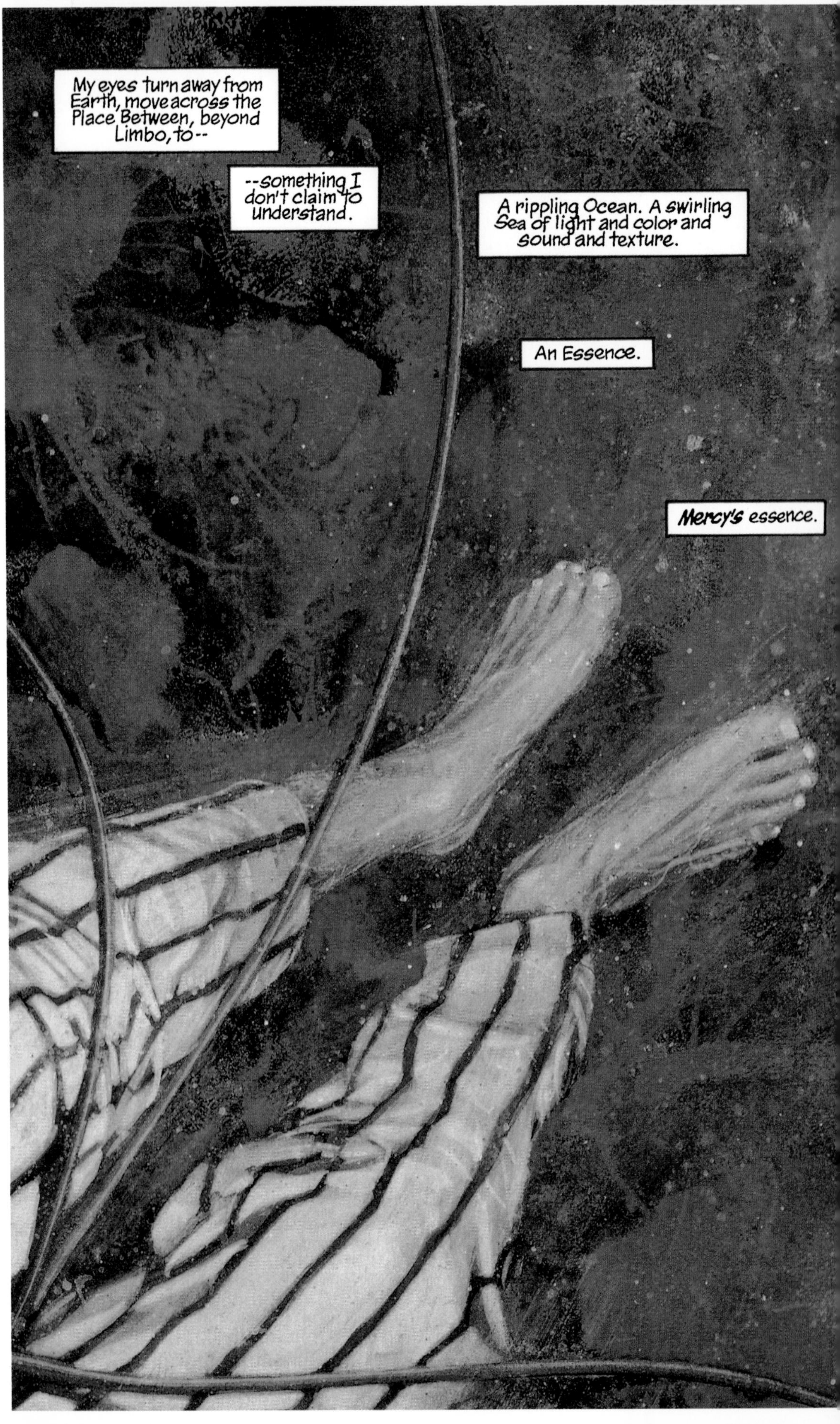
My eyes turn away from Earth, move across the Place Between, beyond Limbo, to--
--something I don't claim to understand.
A rippling Ocean. A swirling Sea of light and color and sound and texture.
An Essence.
Mercy's essence.

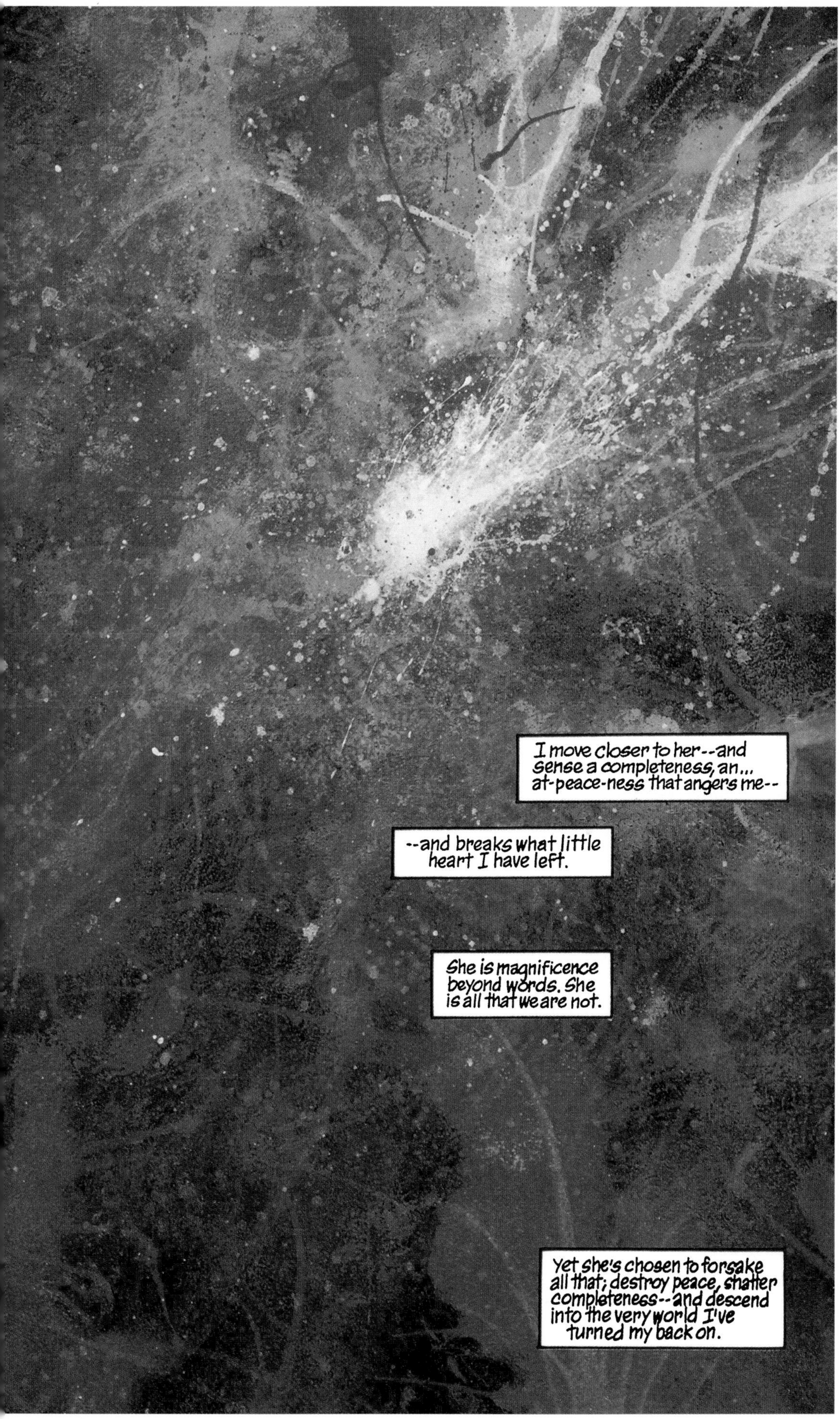
I move closer to her--and sense a completeness, an... at-peace-ness that angers me--
--and breaks what little heart I have left.
She is magnificence beyond words. She is all that we are not.
Yet she's chosen to forsake all that; destroy peace, shatter completeness--and descend into the very world I've turned my back on.

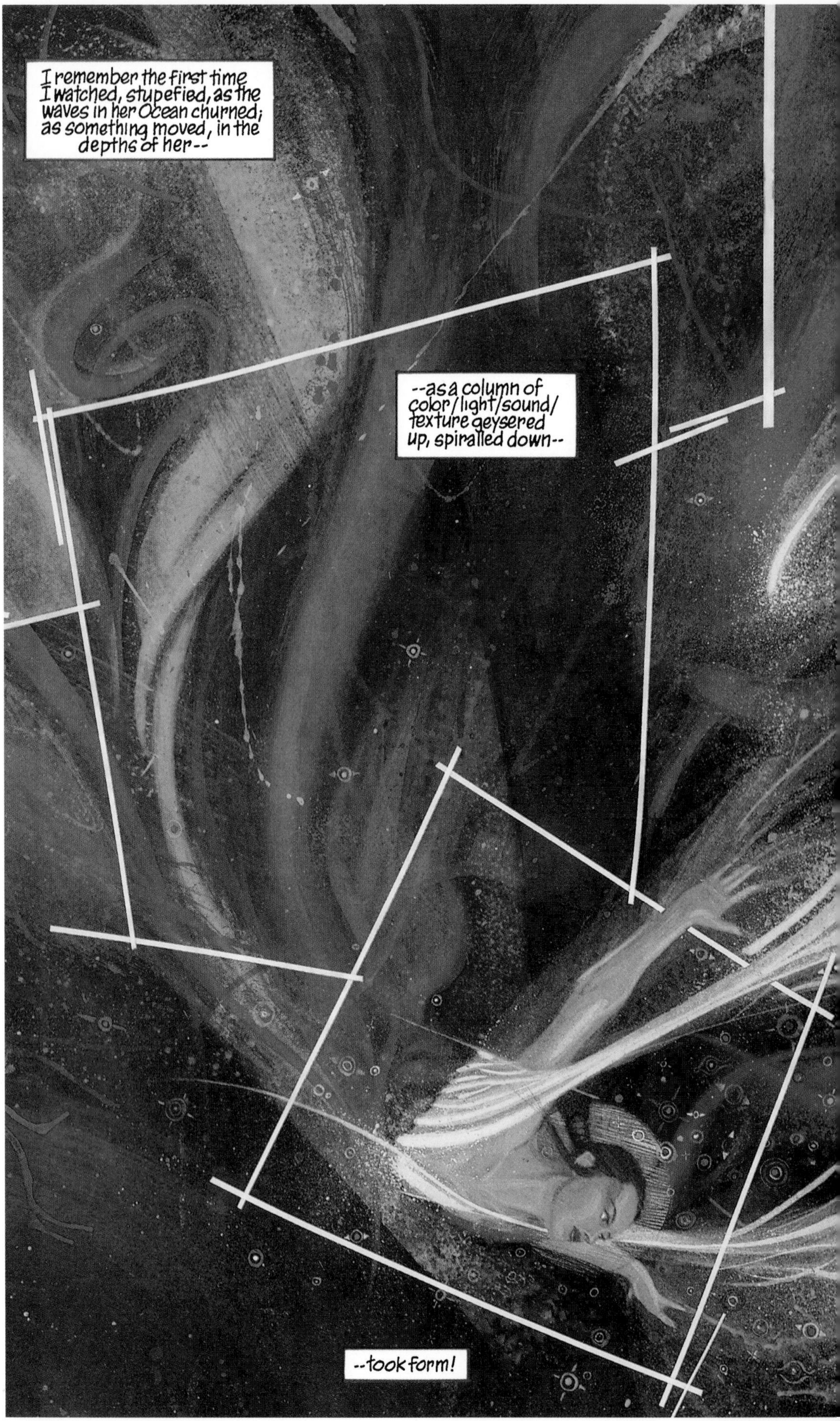
I remember the first time I watched, stupefied, as the waves in her Ocean churned; as something moved, in the depths of her--
--as a column of color/light/sound/texture geysered up, spiralled down--
--took form!

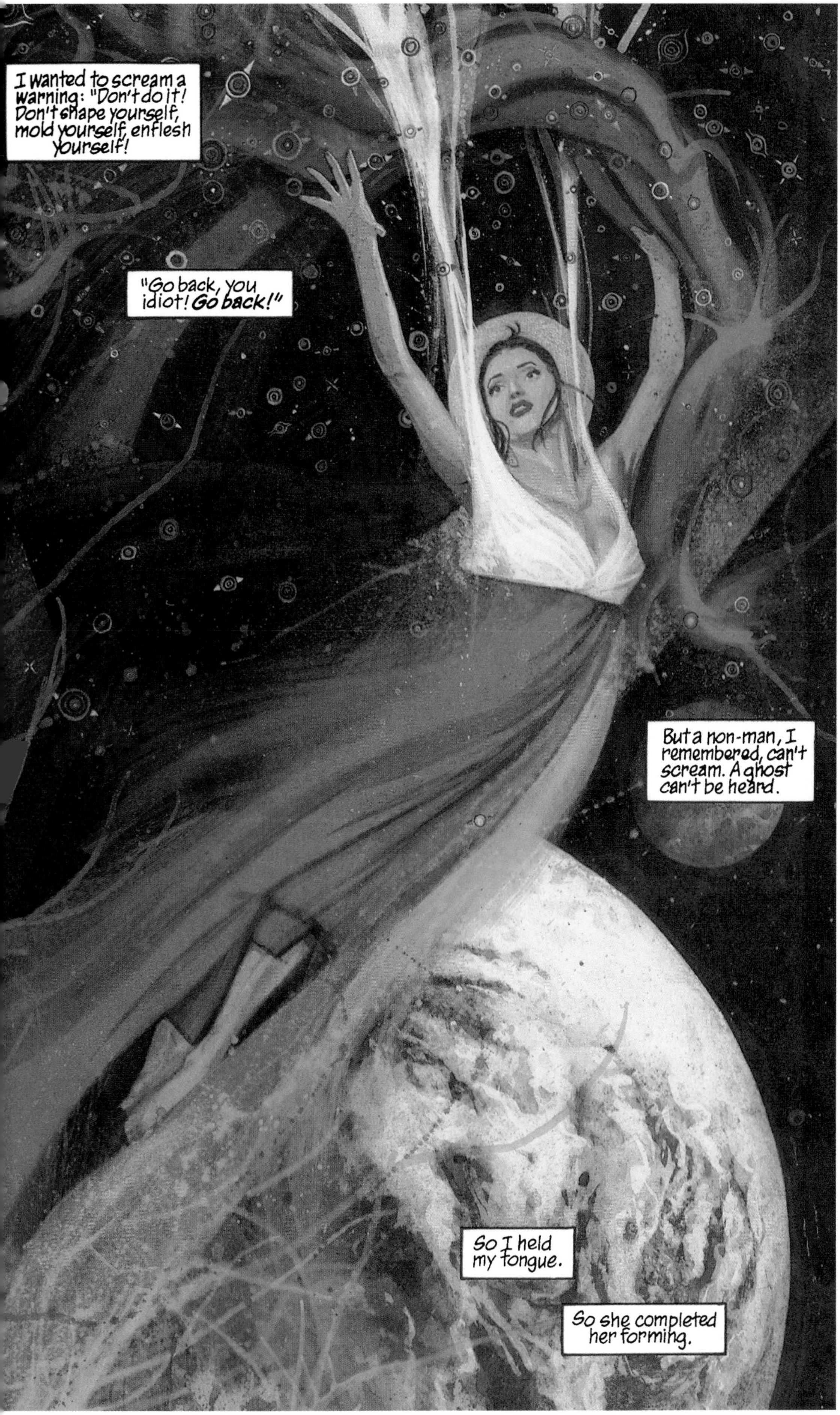
I wanted to scream a warning: "Don't do it! Don't shape yourself, mold yourself, enflesh yourself!
"Go back, you idiot! Go back!"
But a non-man, I remembered, can't scream. A ghost can't be heard.
So I held my tongue.
So she completed her forming.

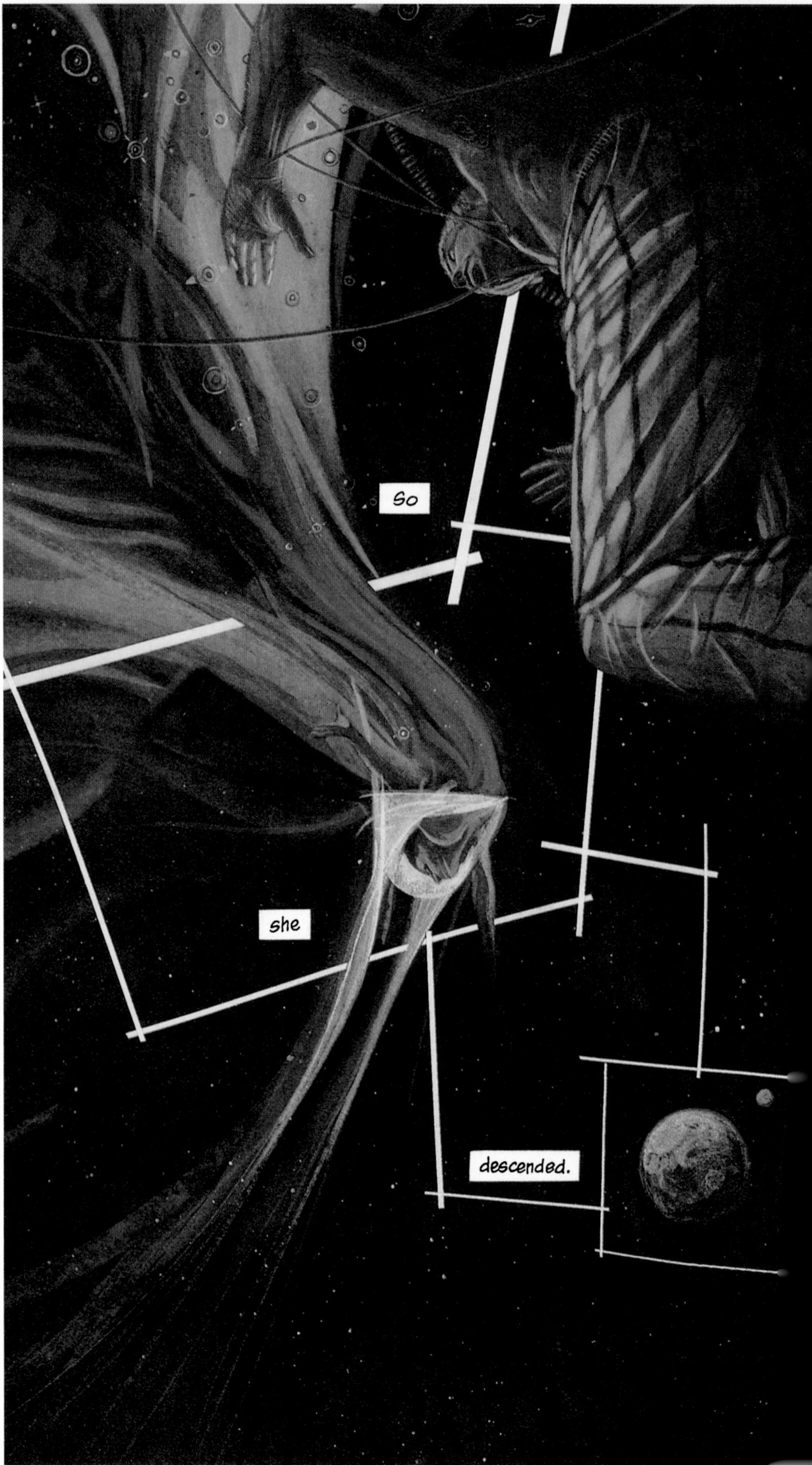
So
she
descended.

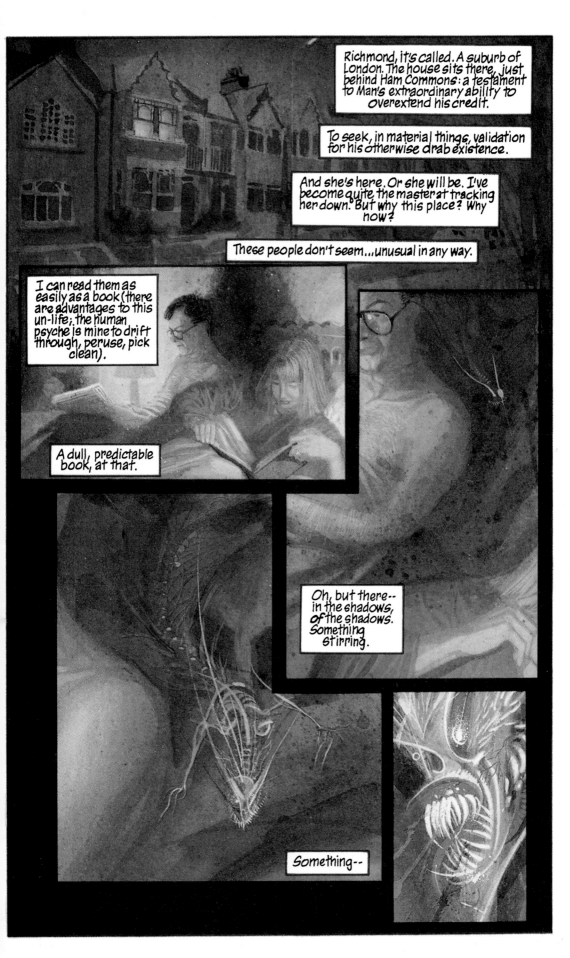

Richmond, it's called. A suburb of London. The house sits there, just behind Ham Commons: a testament to Man's extraordinary ability to overextend his credit.

To seek, in material things, validation for his otherwise drab existence.

And she's here. Or she will be. I've become quite the master at tracking her down. But why this place? Why now?

These people don't seem...unusual in any way.

I can read them as easily as a book (there are advantages to this un-life; the human psyche is mine to drift through, peruse, pick clean).

A dull, predictable book, at that.

Oh, but there-- in the shadows, of the shadows. Something stirring.

Something--

The thing--

--which hovers now, over her bed: a girl no older than my own daughter. And just as angry, if that engraved scowl is any indication.

What is it that makes them like that? Full of bile and rebellion? They start out so innocent...and then the hormones kick in and they go insane.

But the thing *likes* the girl's sleeping madness. Feeds on it. Fuels it. Descends on her unconscious, grabs at stray thoughts-- *worldterribleworldmight- aswellenditallmightaswell- die*--and magnifies it: *DieyesdieohenditallDIE!*

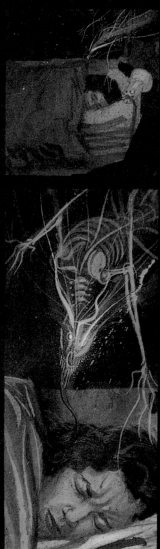

It's gone, now. No, not gone: shifted. I feel it... black and pulsing...somewhere in the house.

I start after the thing--but I'm caught, suddenly, in a crossfire of thoughts.

Muted thoughts, when I first arrived. Full of the boredom and longing, confusion and resentment, that permeate every marriage.

But now:

Buffoon, she thinks. Weak. Coarse. Unattentive. This can't be the man I married.

But now:

Witch, he thinks. Cold. Distant. Cruel. This can't be the woman I married.

Were these thoughts always there? Or did the thing call them out? Invoke them? Create them?

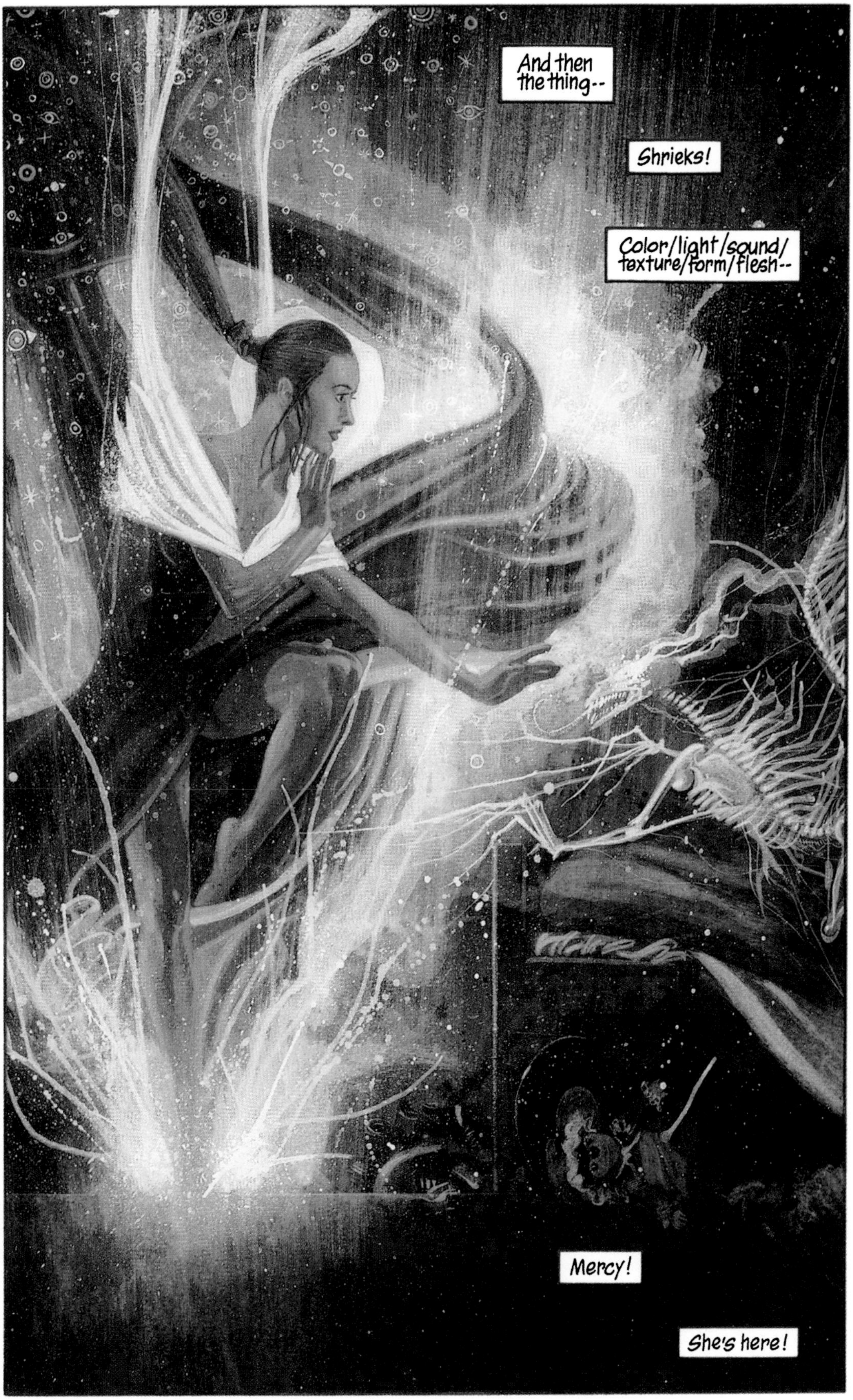
And then the thing--
Shrieks!
Color/light/sound/texture/form/flesh--
Mercy!
She's here!

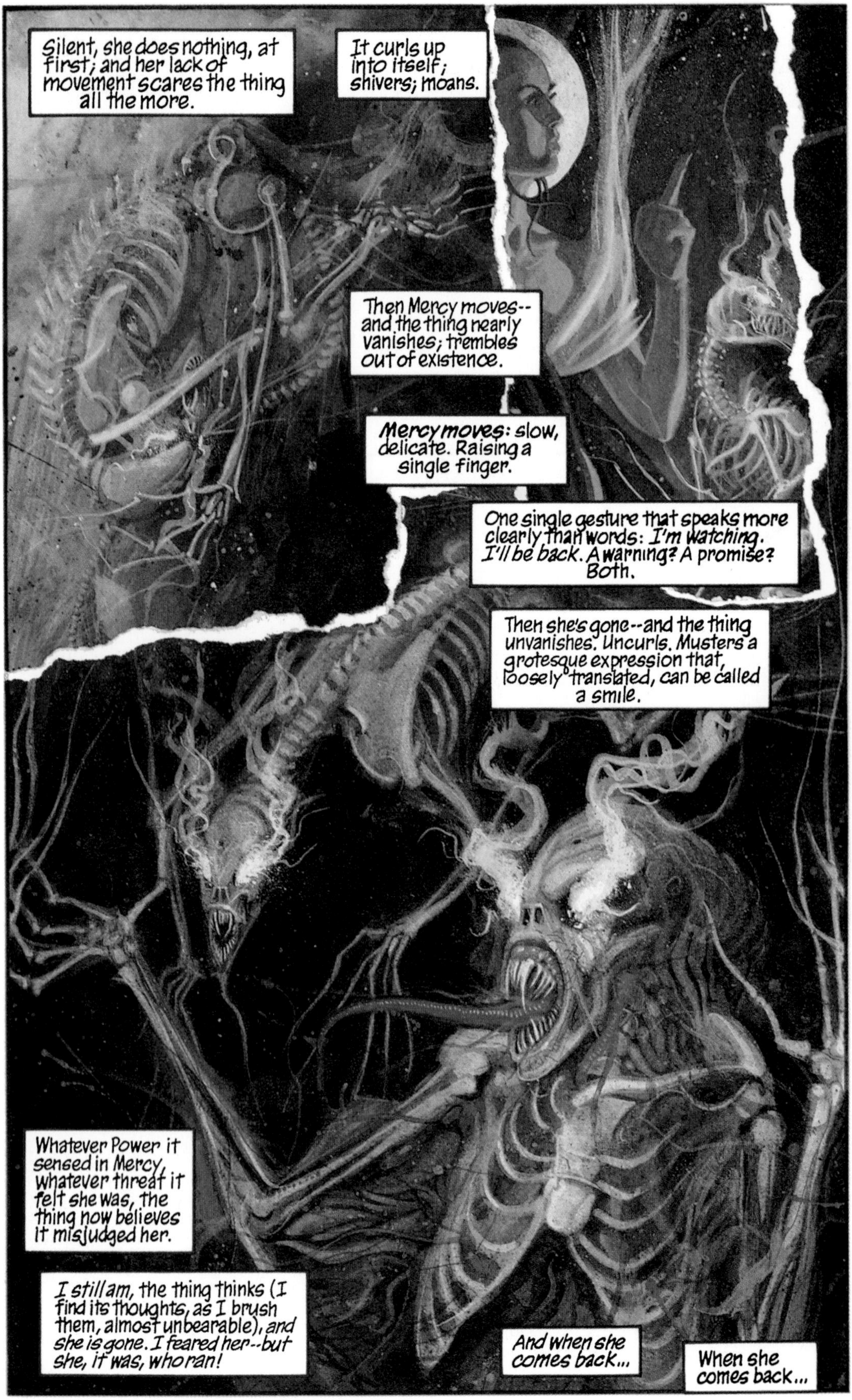

Silent, she does nothing, at first; and her lack of movement scares the thing all the more.
It curls up into itself; shivers; moans.
Then Mercy moves--and the thing nearly vanishes; trembles out of existence.
Mercy moves: slow, delicate. Raising a single finger.
One single gesture that speaks more clearly than words: I'm watching. I'll be back. A warning? A promise? Both.
Then she's gone--and the thing unvanishes. Uncurls. Musters a grotesque expression that, loosely translated, can be called a smile.
Whatever Power it sensed in Mercy, whatever threat it felt she was, the thing now believes it misjudged her.
I still am, the thing thinks (I find its thoughts, as I brush them, almost unbearable), and she is gone. I feared her--but she, it was, who ran!
And when she comes back...
When she comes back...

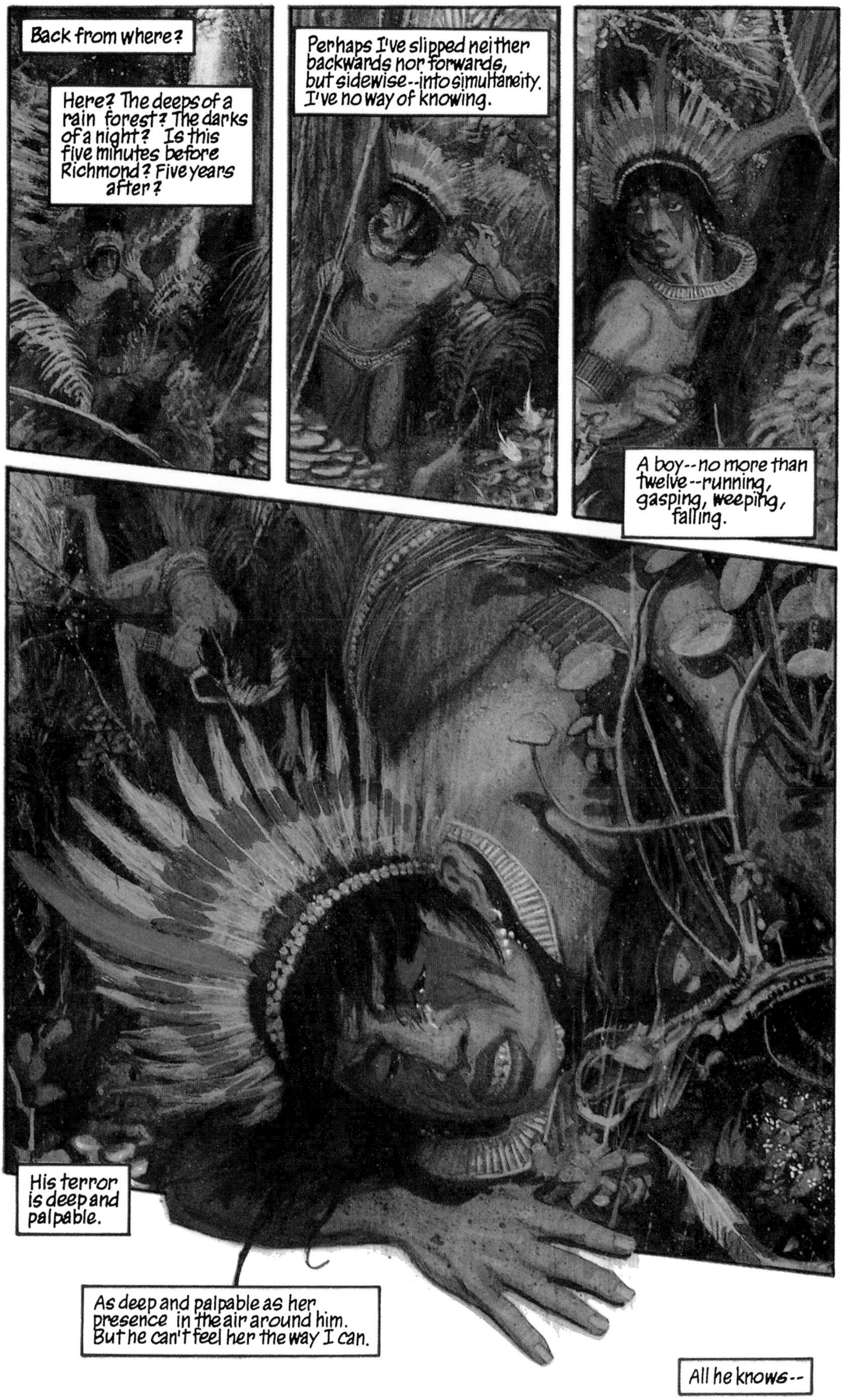
Back from where?
Here? The deeps of a rain forest? The darks of a night? Is this five minutes before Richmond? Five years after?
Perhaps I've slipped neither backwards nor forwards, but sidewise--into simultaneity. I've no way of knowing.
A boy--no more than twelve--running, gasping, weeping, falling.
His terror is deep and palpable.
As deep and palpable as her presence in the air around him. But he can't feel her the way I can.
All he knows--

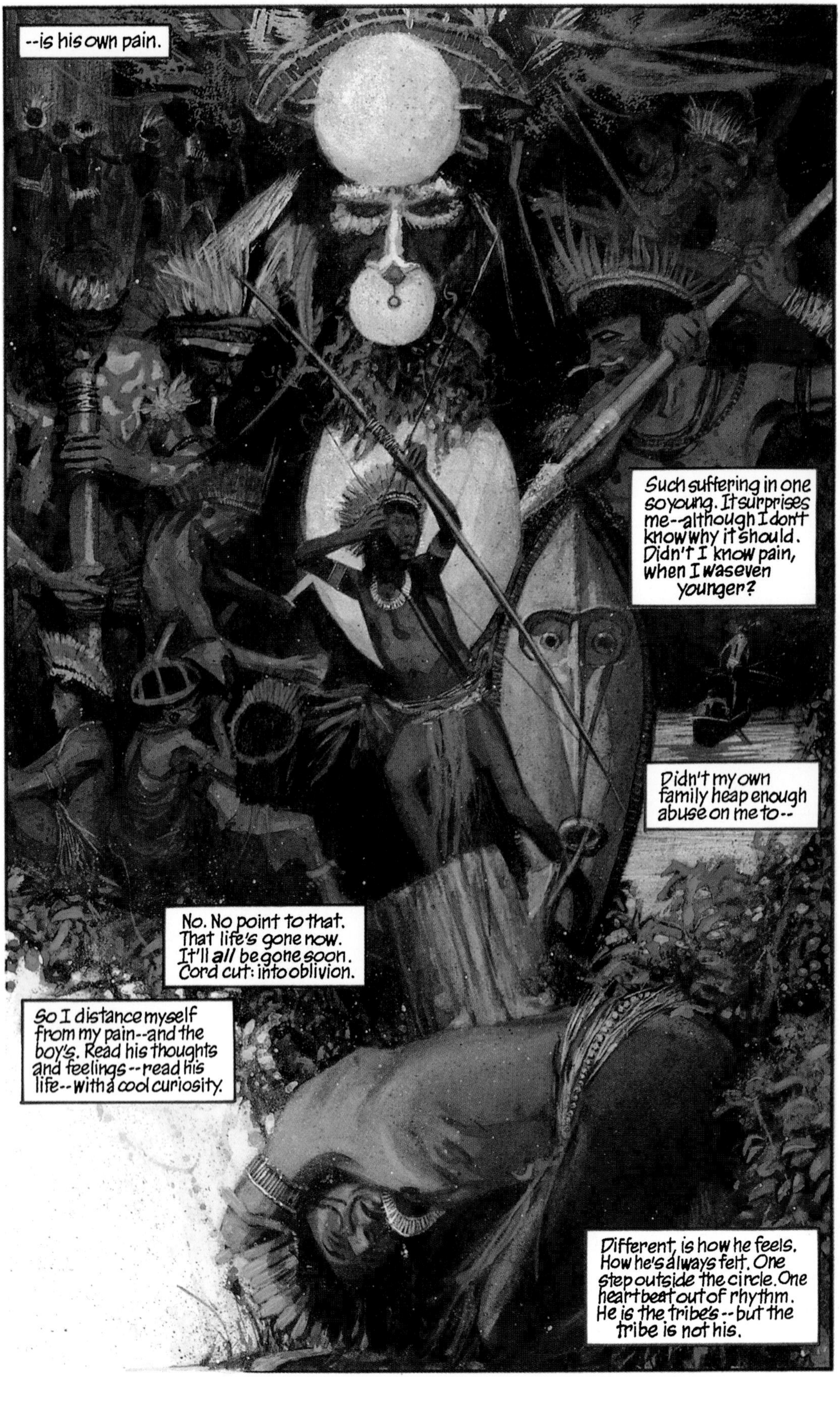
--is his own pain.
Such suffering in one so young. It surprises me--although I don't know why it should. Didn't I know pain, when I was even younger?
Didn't my own family heap enough abuse on me to--
No. No point to that. That life's gone now. It'll *all* be gone soon. Cord cut: into oblivion.
So I distance myself from my pain--and the boy's. Read his thoughts and feelings--read his life--with a cool curiosity.
Different, is how he feels. How he's always felt. One step outside the circle. One heartbeat out of rhythm. He is the tribe's--but the tribe is not his.

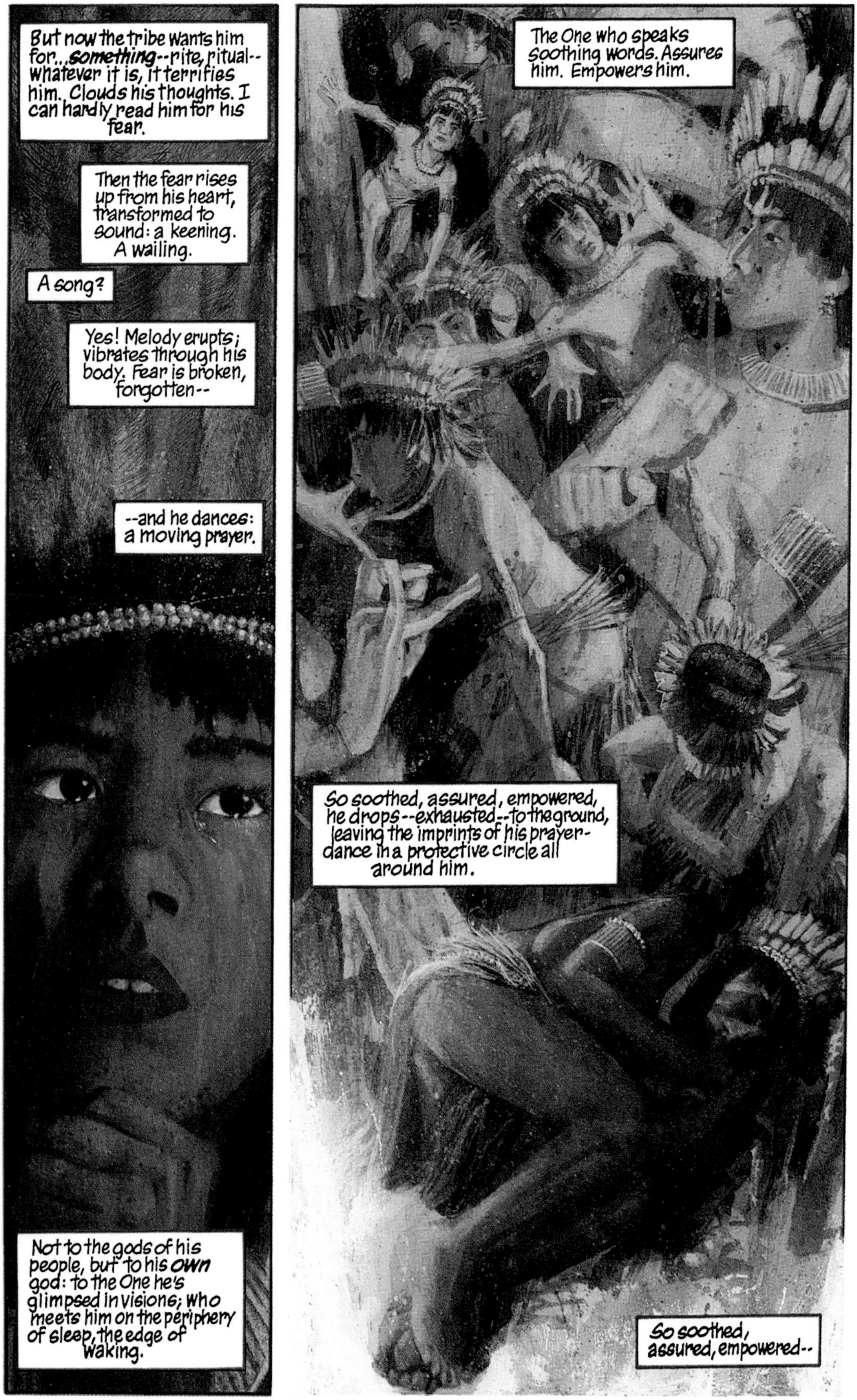
But now the tribe wants him for...something--rite, ritual--whatever it is, it terrifies him. Clouds his thoughts. I can hardly read him for his fear.
Then the fear rises up from his heart, transformed to sound: a keening. A wailing.
A song?
Yes! Melody erupts; vibrates through his body. Fear is broken, forgotten--
--and he dances: a moving prayer.
Not to the gods of his people, but to his own god: to the One he's glimpsed in visions; who meets him on the periphery of sleep, the edge of waking.
The One who speaks soothing words. Assures him. Empowers him.
So soothed, assured, empowered, he drops--exhausted--to the ground, leaving the imprints of his prayer-dance in a protective circle all around him.
So soothed, assured, empowered--

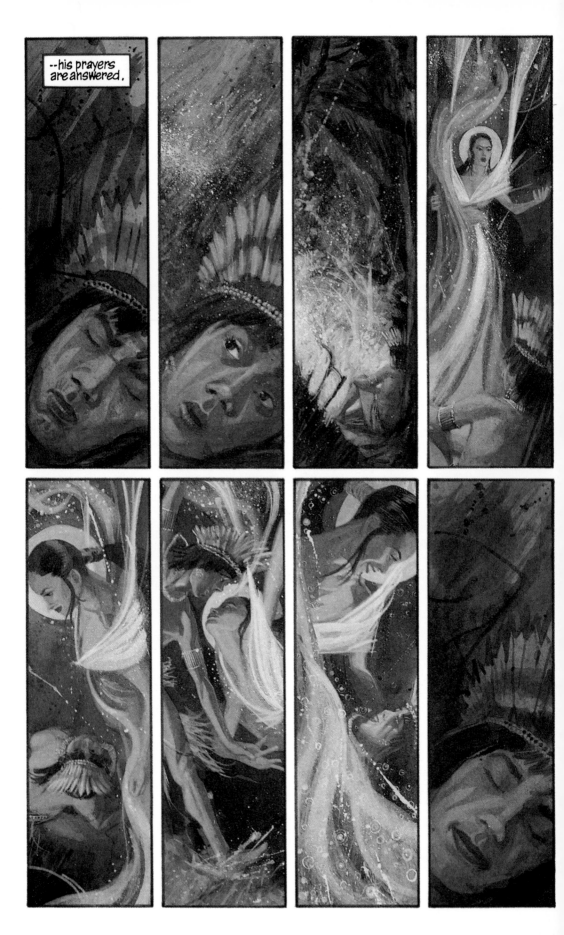

--his prayers are answered.

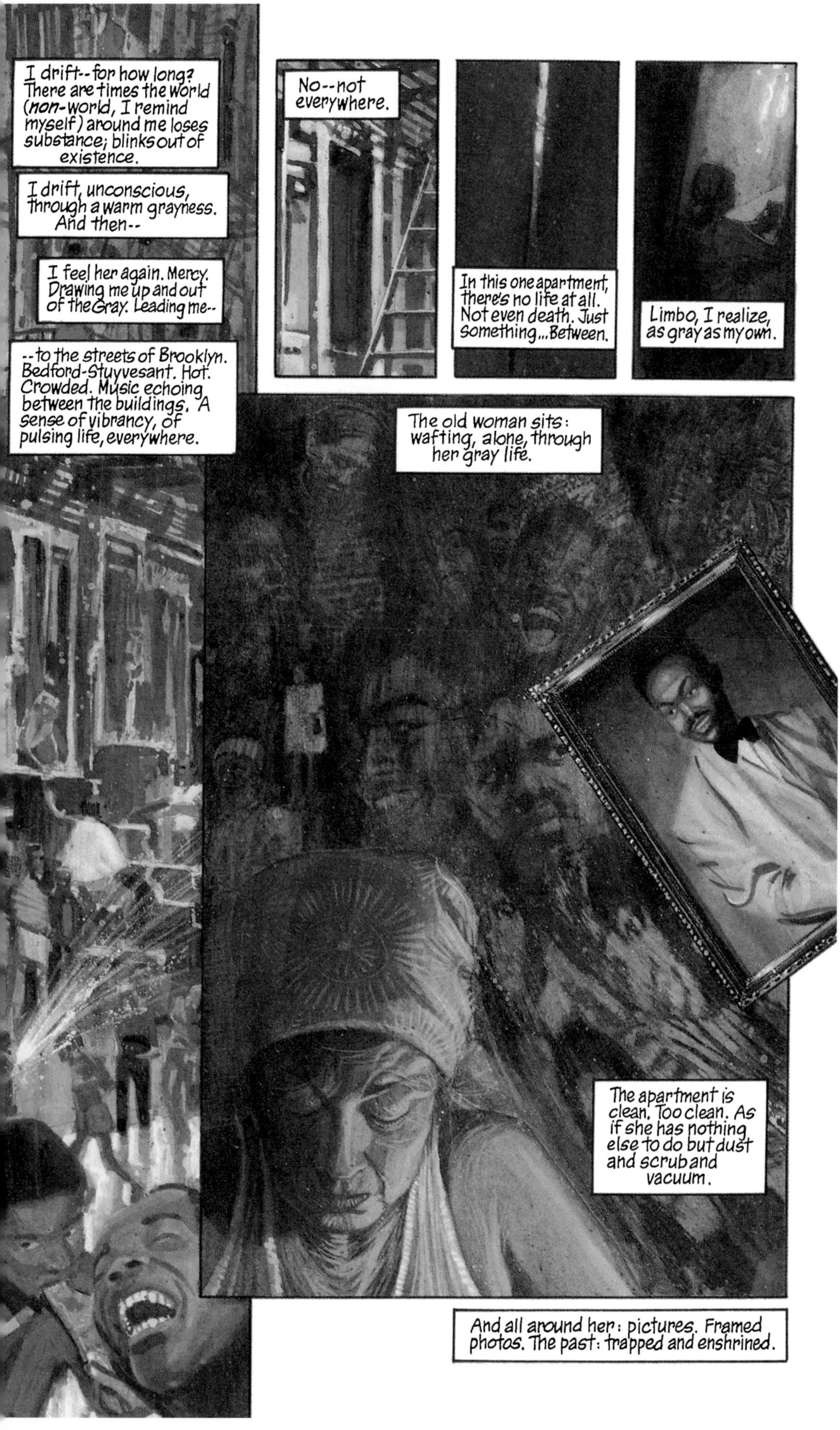

I drift--for how long? There are times the world (*non*-world, I remind myself) around me loses substance; blinks out of existence.
I drift, unconscious, through a warm grayness. And then--
I feel her again. Mercy. Drawing me up and out of the Gray. Leading me--
--to the streets of Brooklyn. Bedford-Stuyvesant. Hot. Crowded. Music echoing between the buildings. A sense of vibrancy, of pulsing life, everywhere.
No--not everywhere.
In this one apartment, there's no life at all. Not even death. Just something...Between.
Limbo, I realize, as gray as my own.
The old woman sits: wafting, alone, through her gray life.
The apartment is clean. Too clean. As if she has nothing else to do but dust and scrub and vacuum.
And all around her: pictures. Framed photos. The past: trapped and enshrined.

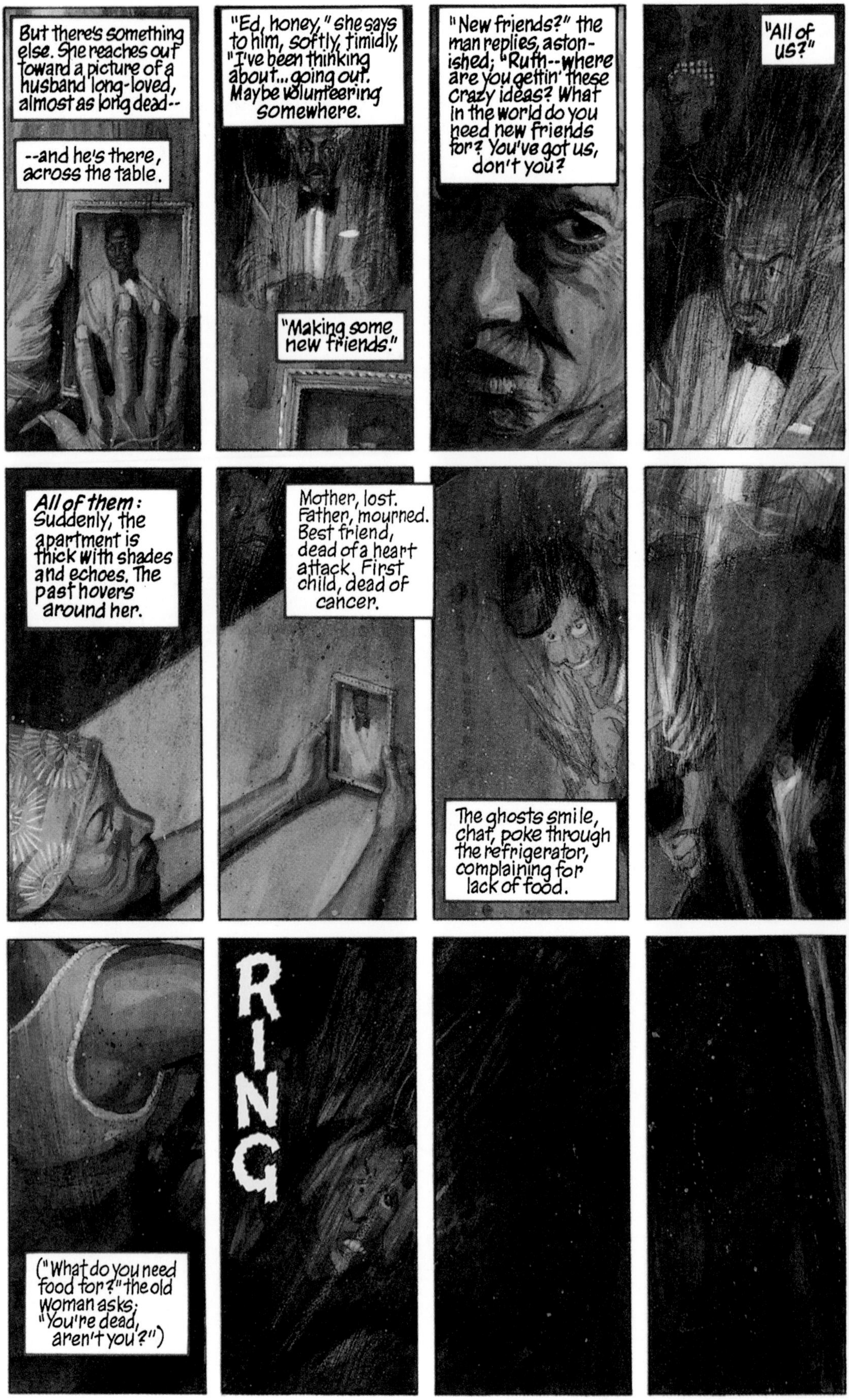

But there's something else. She reaches out toward a picture of a husband long-loved, almost as long dead--
--and he's there, across the table.
"Ed, honey," she says to him, softly, timidly, "I've been thinking about... going out. Maybe volunteering somewhere.
"Making some new friends."
"New friends?" the man replies, astonished; "Ruth--where are you gettin' these crazy ideas? What in the world do you need new friends for? You've got us, don't you?
"All of us?"
All of them: Suddenly, the apartment is thick with shades and echoes. The past hovers around her.
Mother, lost. Father, mourned. Best friend, dead of a heart attack. First child, dead of cancer.
The ghosts smile, chat, poke through the refrigerator, complaining for lack of food.
("What do you need food for?" the old woman asks; "You're dead, aren't you?")
RING

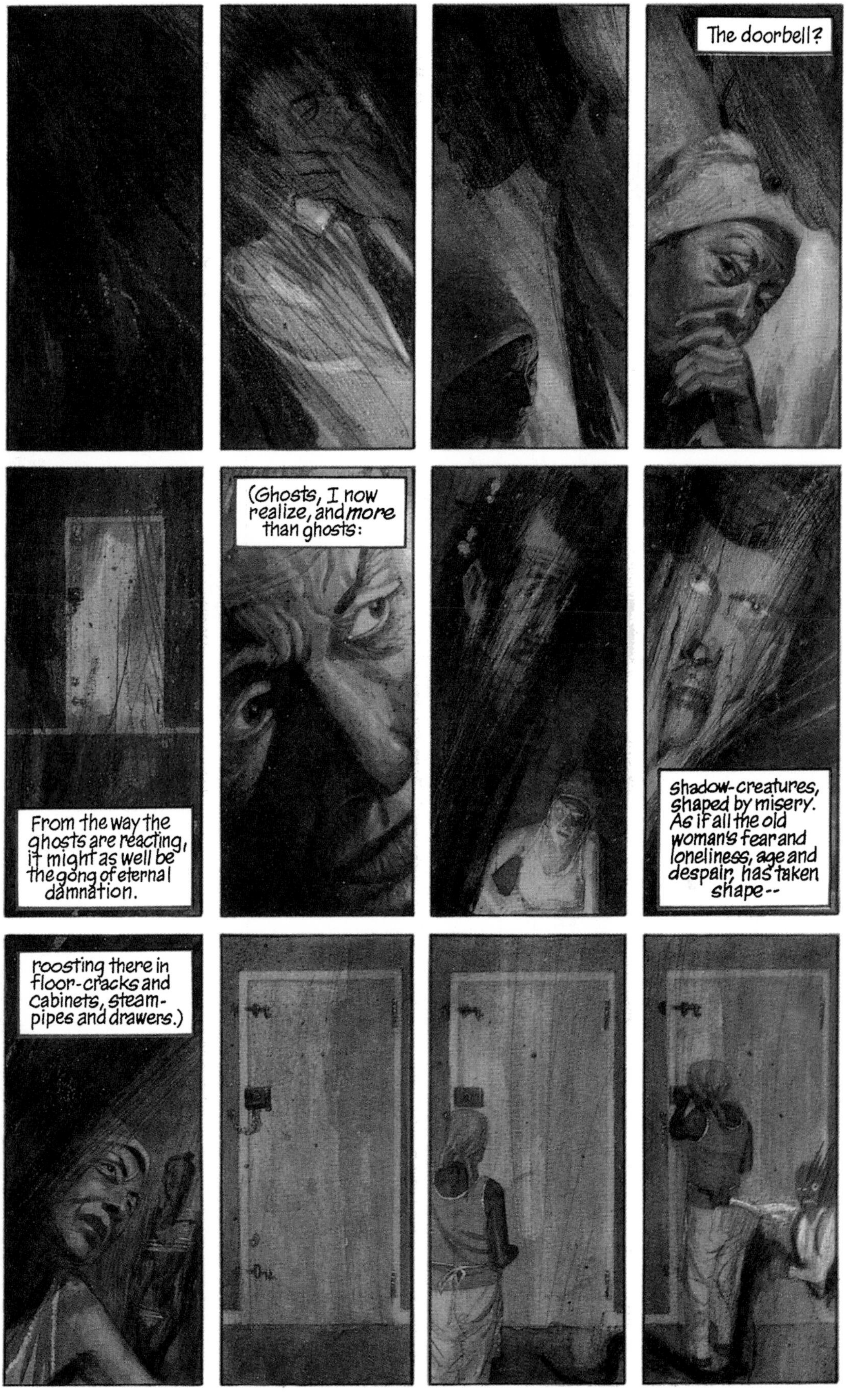
The doorbell?
From the way the ghosts are reacting, it might as well be the gong of eternal damnation.
(Ghosts, I now realize, and *more* than ghosts:
shadow-creatures, shaped by misery. As if all the old woman's fear and loneliness, age and despair, has taken shape --
roosting there in floor-cracks and cabinets, steam-pipes and drawers.)

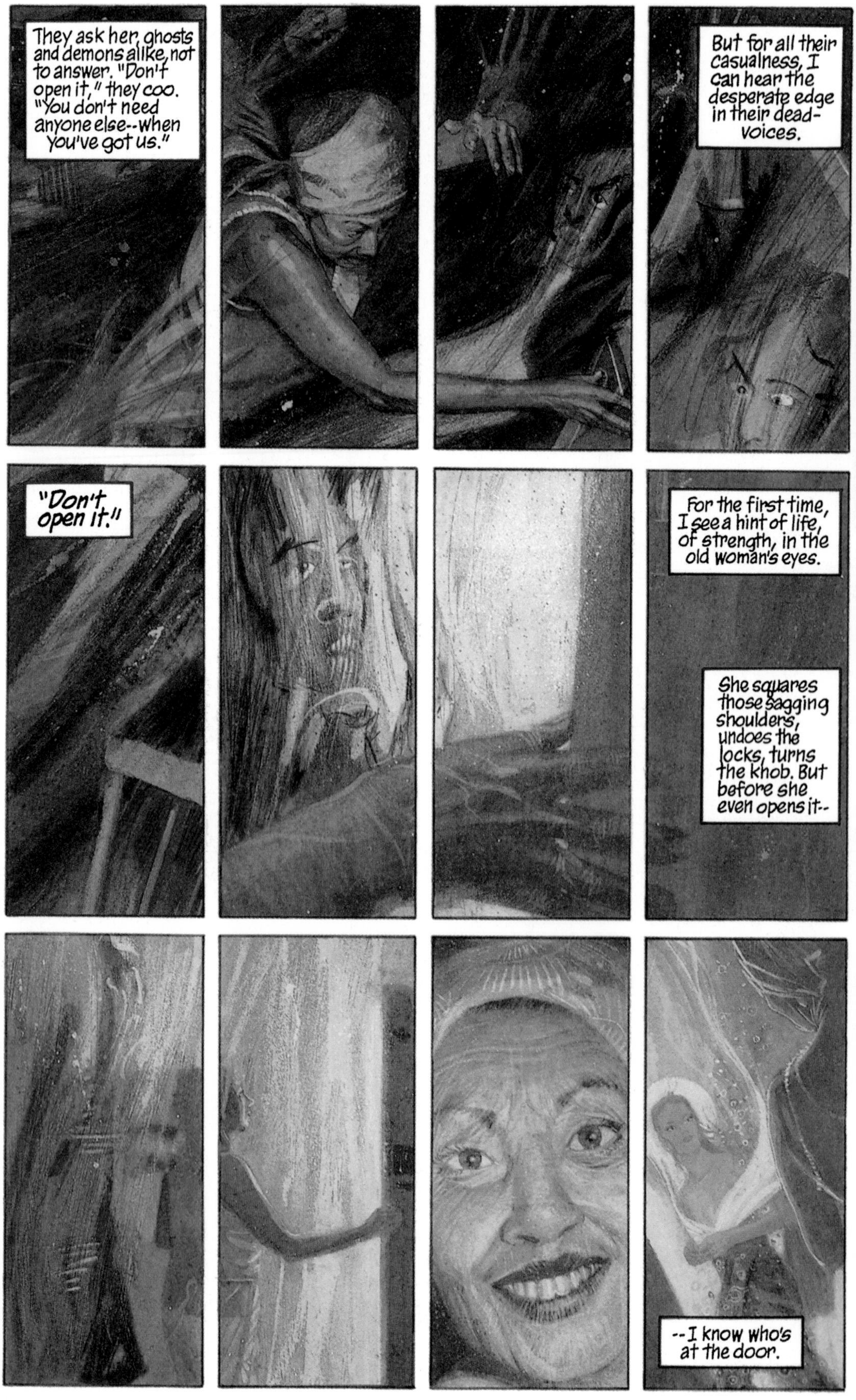
They ask her, ghosts and demons alike, not to answer. "Don't open it," they coo. "You don't need anyone else--when you've got us."
But for all their casualness, I can hear the desperate edge in their dead-voices.
"Don't open it."
For the first time, I see a hint of life, of strength, in the old woman's eyes.
She squares those sagging shoulders, undoes the locks, turns the knob. But before she even opens it--
--I know who's at the door.

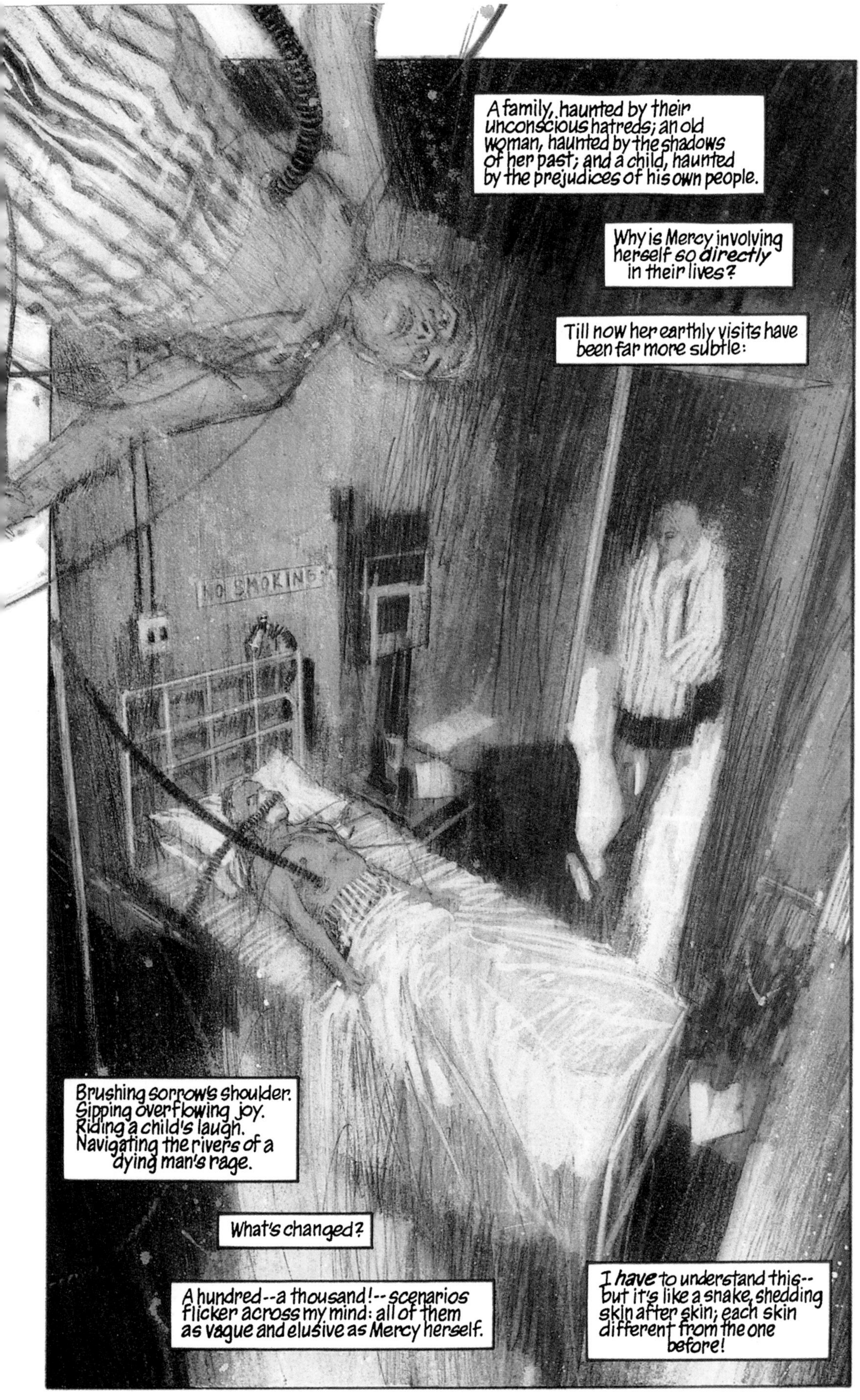

A family, haunted by their unconscious hatreds; an old woman, haunted by the shadows of her past; and a child, haunted by the prejudices of his own people.
Why is Mercy involving herself so *directly* in their lives?
Till now her earthly visits have been far more subtle:
NO SMOKING
Brushing sorrow's shoulder. Sipping overflowing joy. Riding a child's laugh. Navigating the rivers of a dying man's rage.
What's changed?
A hundred--a thousand!--scenarios flicker across my mind: all of them as vague and elusive as Mercy herself.
I *have* to understand this--but it's like a snake, shedding skin after skin; each skin different from the one before!

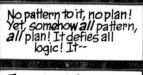

No pattern to it, no plan! Yet, *somehow* all pattern, *all* plan! It defies all logic! It--

Then I laugh (*un*laugh, I suppose. What else can an *un*man do?): "*Defies all logic*"? Maybe that's the point. Maybe that's the answer: *all* of this defies logic!

Doesn't it make more sense that this is just some...dream I'm dreaming, down there in my hospital bed?

Just my stroke-ravaged brain, shooting off random electrical impulses? A little mind-movie before I die?

A sobering thought. Sobering enough to banish all questions of Mercy, of plans and purposes without name or form, out of my mind.

I seek the comfort of my gray Limbo.

Of sweet gray sleep.

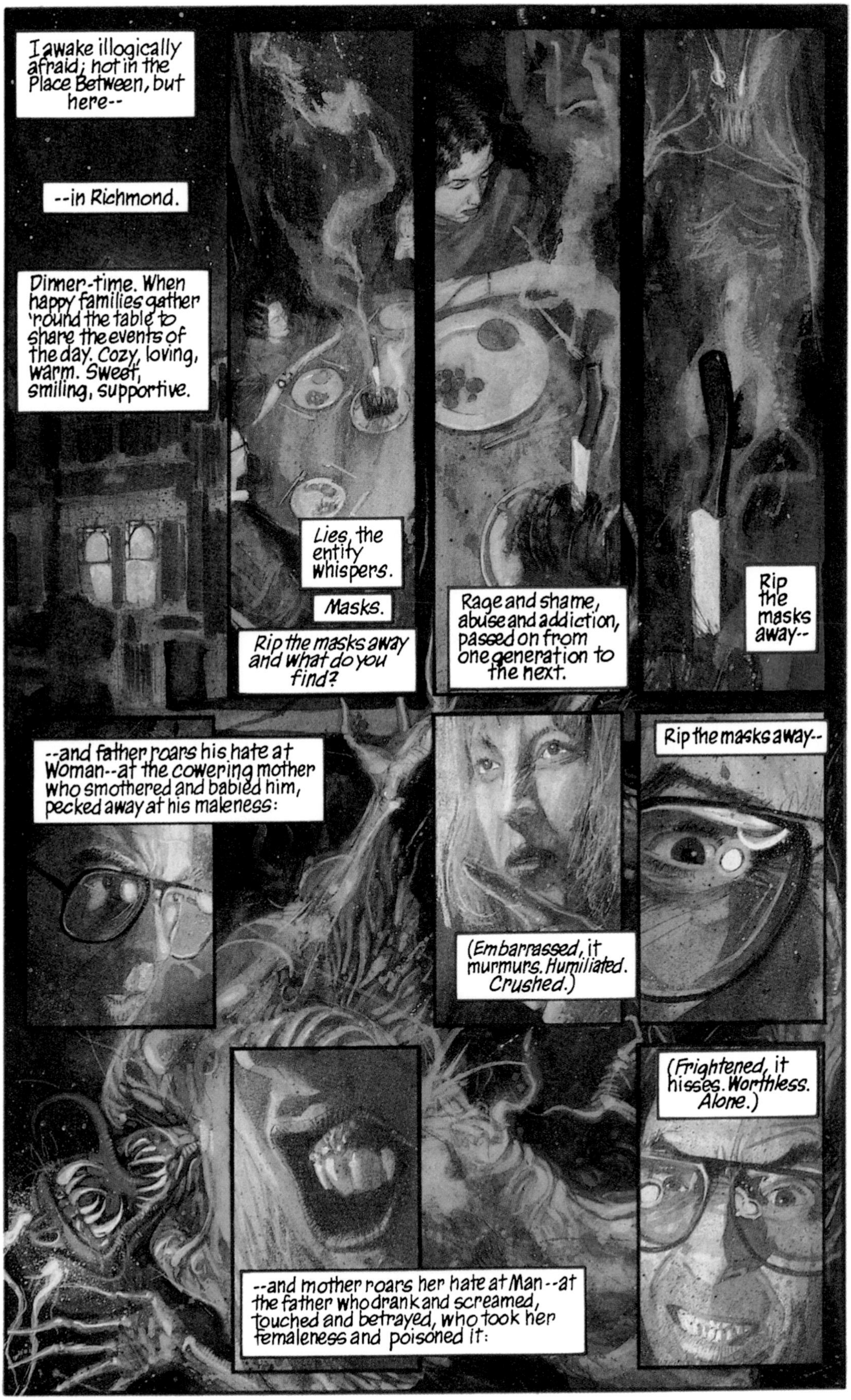
I awake illogically afraid; not in the Place Between, but here--
--in Richmond.
Dinner-time. When happy families gather 'round the table to share the events of the day. Cozy, loving, warm. Sweet, smiling, supportive.
Lies, the entity whispers.
Masks.
Rip the masks away and what do you find?
Rage and shame, abuse and addiction, passed on from one generation to the next.
Rip the masks away--
--and father roars his hate at Woman--at the cowering mother who smothered and babied him, pecked away at his maleness:
(Embarrassed, it murmurs. Humiliated. Crushed.)
Rip the masks away--
(Frightened, it hisses. Worthless. Alone.)
--and mother roars her hate at Man--at the father who drank and screamed, touched and betrayed, who took her femaleness and poisoned it:

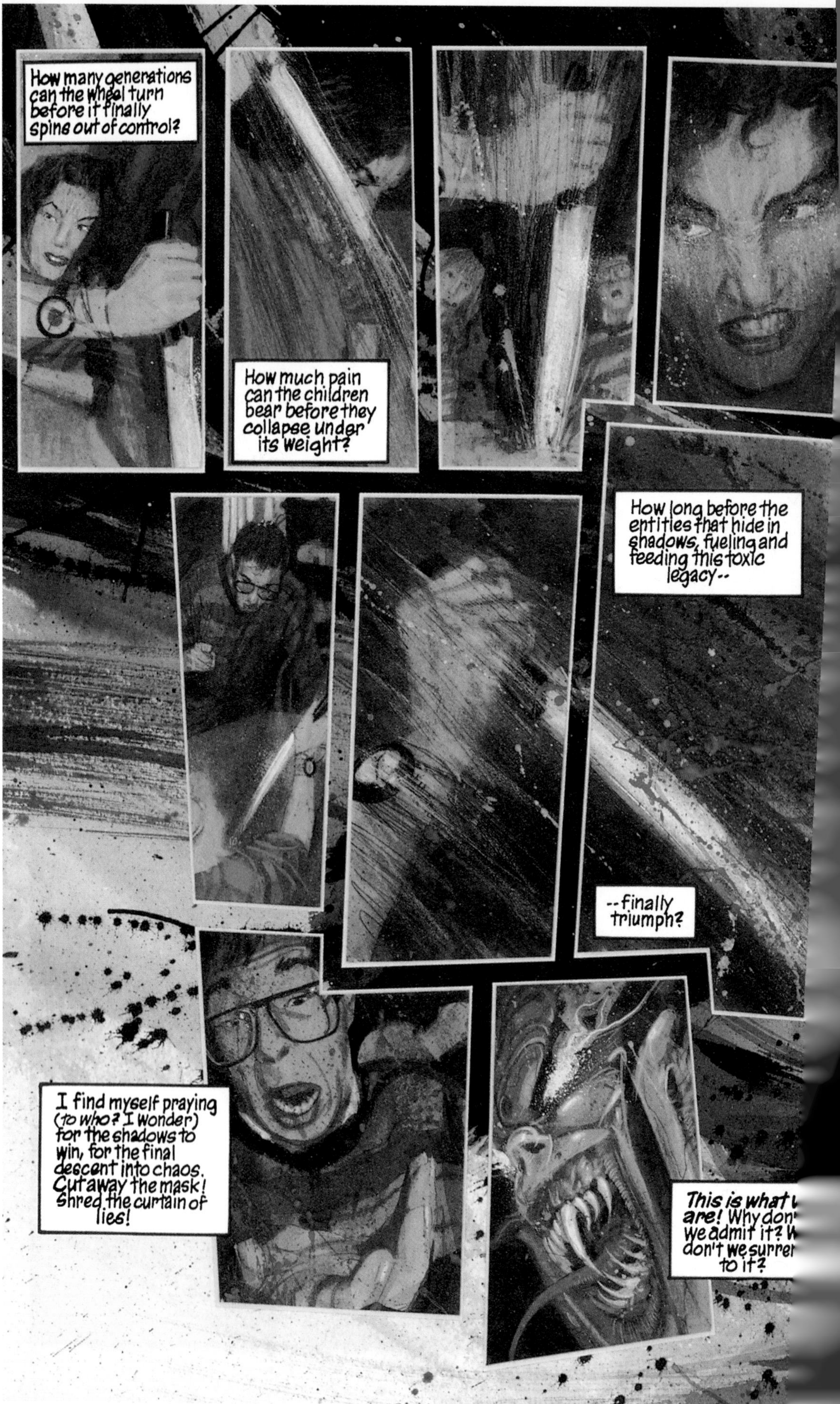
How many generations can the wheel turn before it finally spins out of control?
How much pain can the children bear before they collapse under its weight?
How long before the entities that hide in shadows, fueling and feeding this toxic legacy--
--finally triumph?
I find myself praying (to who? I wonder) for the shadows to win, for the final descent into chaos. Cut away the mask! Shred the curtain of lies!
This is what are! Why we admit it? don't we to it?

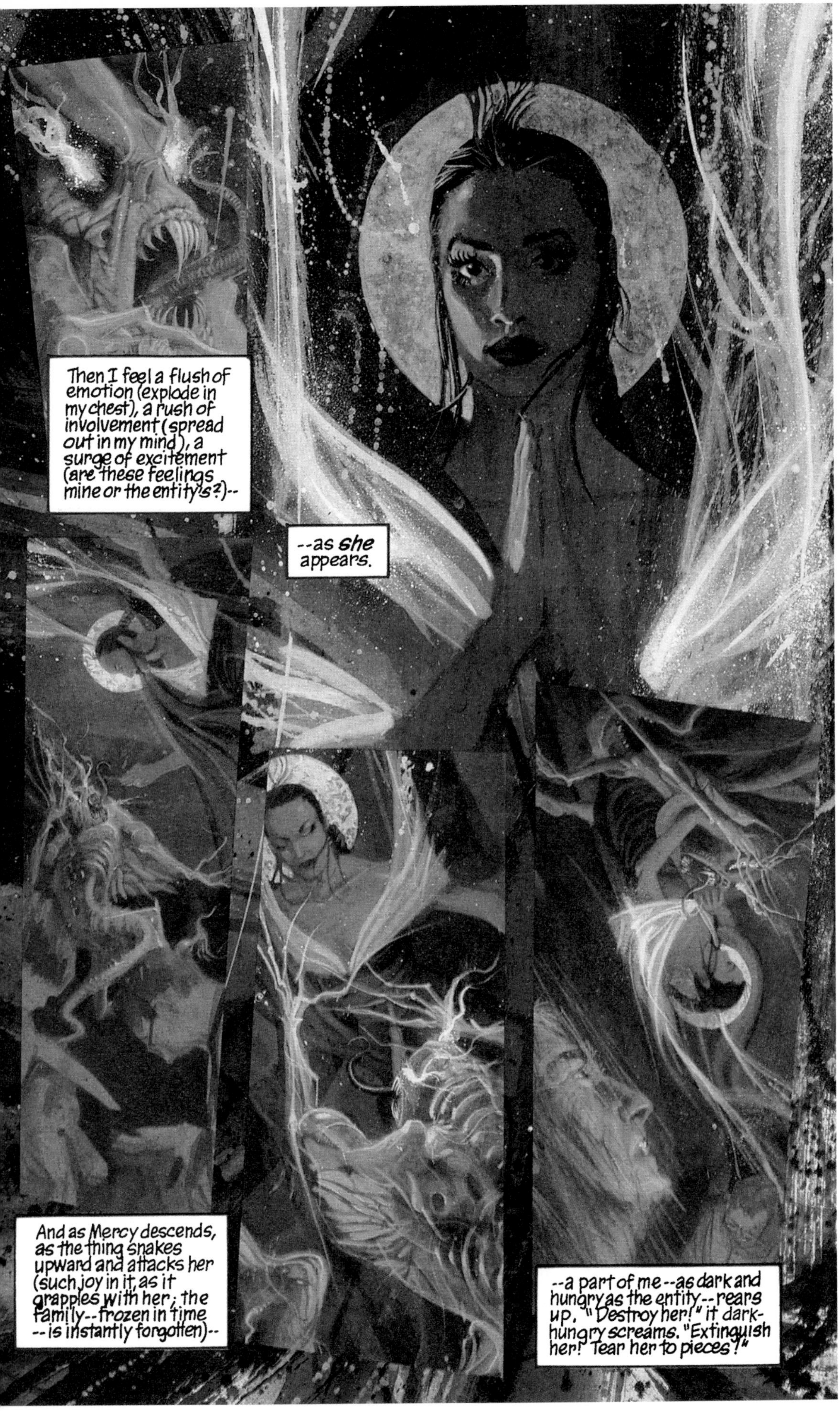
Then I feel a flush of emotion (explode in my chest), a rush of involvement (spread out in my mind), a surge of excitement (are these feelings mine or the entity's?)--
--as she appears.
And as Mercy descends, as the thing snakes upward and attacks her (such joy in it, as it grapples with her; the family--frozen in time --is instantly forgotten)--
--a part of me--as dark and hungry as the entity--rears up. "Destroy her!" it dark-hungry screams. "Extinguish her! Tear her to pieces!"

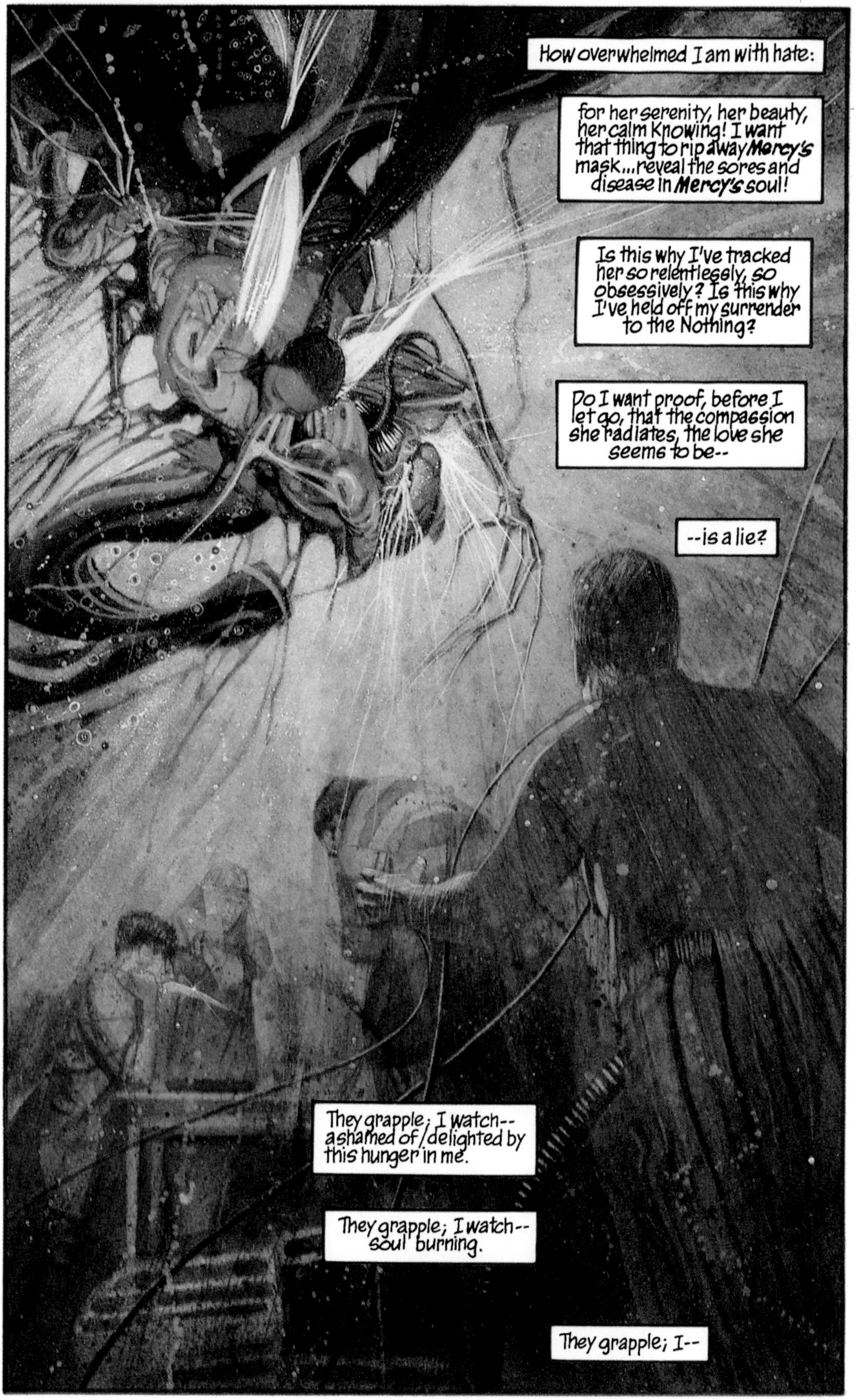
How overwhelmed I am with hate:
for her serenity, her beauty, her calm Knowing! I want that thing to rip away Mercy's mask...reveal the sores and disease in Mercy's soul!
Is this why I've tracked her so relentlessly, so obsessively? Is this why I've held off my surrender to the Nothing?
Do I want proof, before I let go, that the compassion she radiates, the love she seems to be--
--is a lie?
They grapple; I watch--ashamed of/delighted by this hunger in me.
They grapple; I watch--soul burning.
They grapple; I--

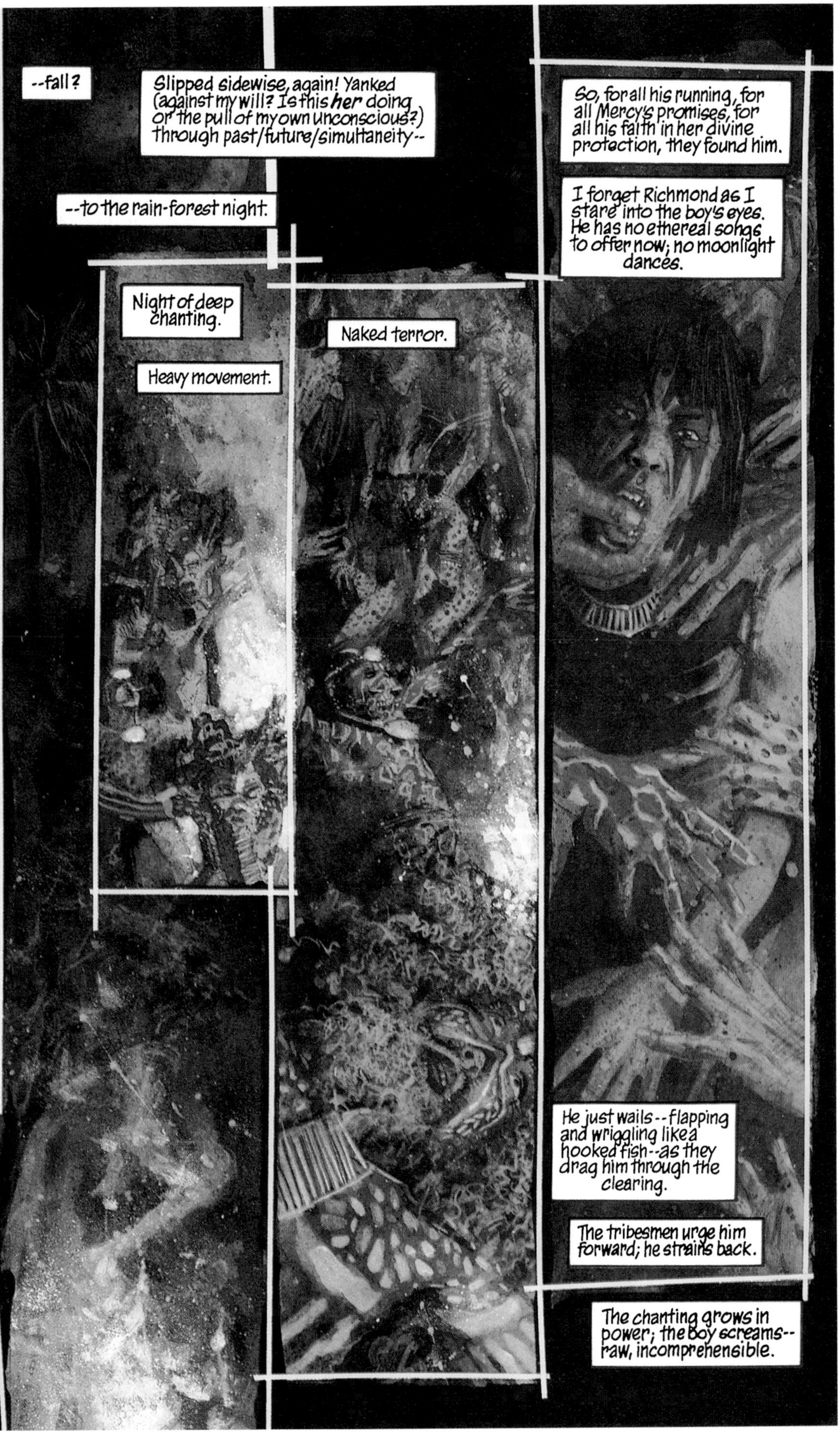
--fall?
Slipped sidewise, again! Yanked (against my will? Is this **her** doing or the pull of my own unconscious?) through past/future/simultaneity--
--to the rain-forest night.
Night of deep chanting.
Heavy movement.
Naked terror.
So, for all his running, for all Mercy's promises, for all his faith in her divine protection, they found him.
I forget Richmond as I stare into the boy's eyes. He has no ethereal songs to offer now; no moonlight dances.
He just wails--flapping and wriggling like a hooked fish--as they drag him through the clearing.
The tribesmen urge him forward; he strains back.
The chanting grows in power; the boy screams--raw, incomprehensible.

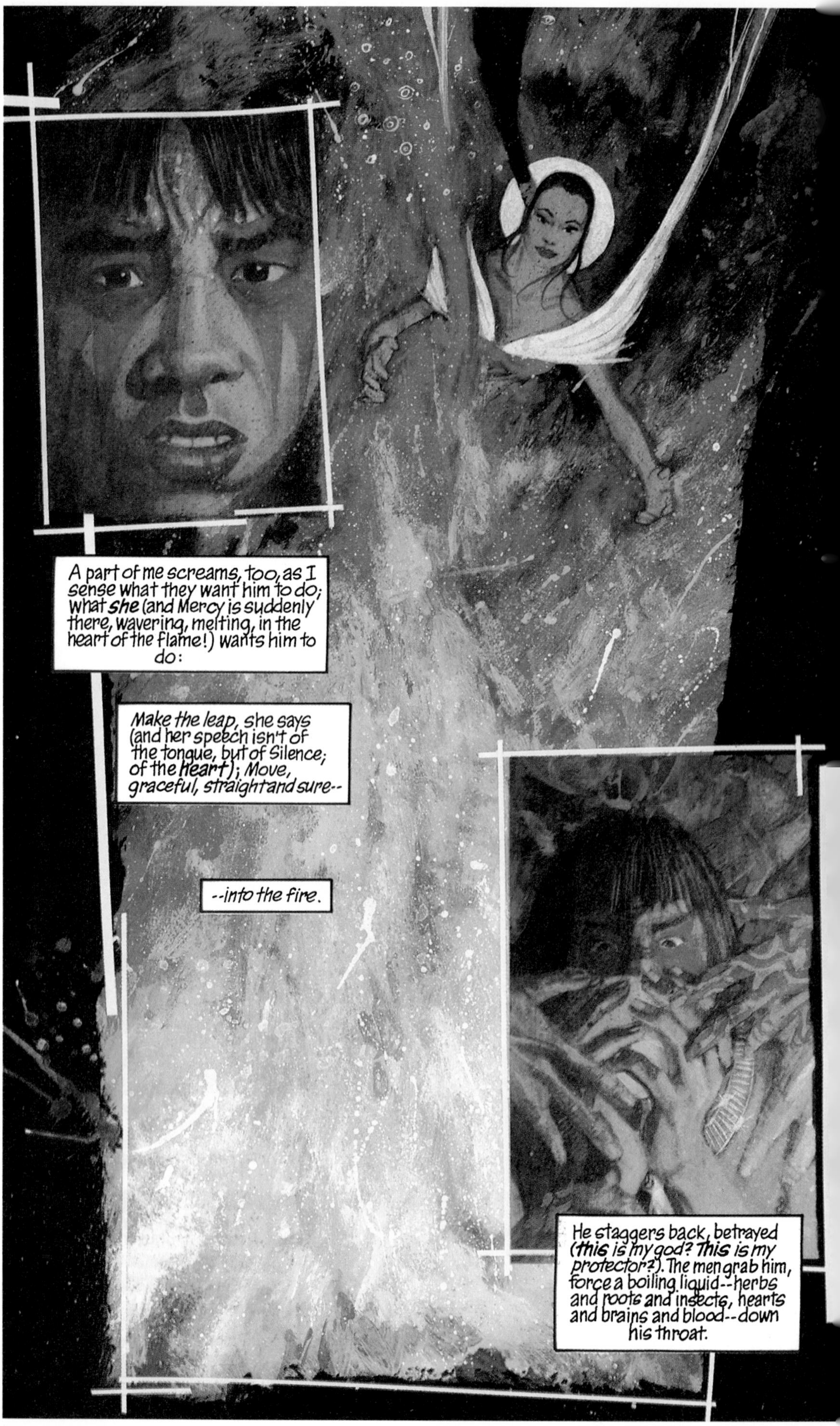
A part of me screams, too, as I sense what they want him to do; what *she* (and Mercy is suddenly there, wavering, melting, in the heart of the flame!) wants him to do:
Make the leap, she says (and her speech isn't of the tongue, but of Silence; of the ***heart****); Move, graceful, straight and sure--*
--into the fire.
He staggers back, betrayed (***this*** *is my god?* ***This*** *is my protector?*). The men grab him, force a boiling liquid--herbs and roots and insects, hearts and brains and blood--down his throat.

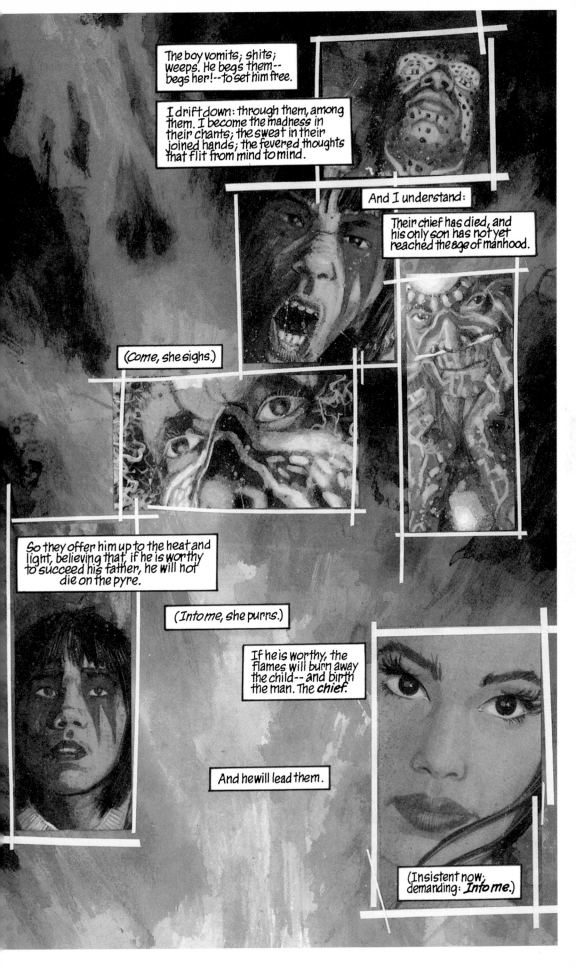

The boy vomits; shits; weeps. He begs them-- begs her!--to set him free.

I drift down: through them, among them. I become the madness in their chants; the sweat in their joined hands; the fevered thoughts that flit from mind to mind.

And I understand:

Their chief has died, and his only son has not yet reached the age of manhood.

(Come, she sighs.)

So they offer him up to the heat and light, believing that, if he is worthy to succeed his father, he will not die on the pyre.

(Into me, she purrs.)

If he is worthy, the flames will burn away the child-- and birth the man. The *chief*.

And he will lead them.

(Insistent now; demanding: *Into me*.)

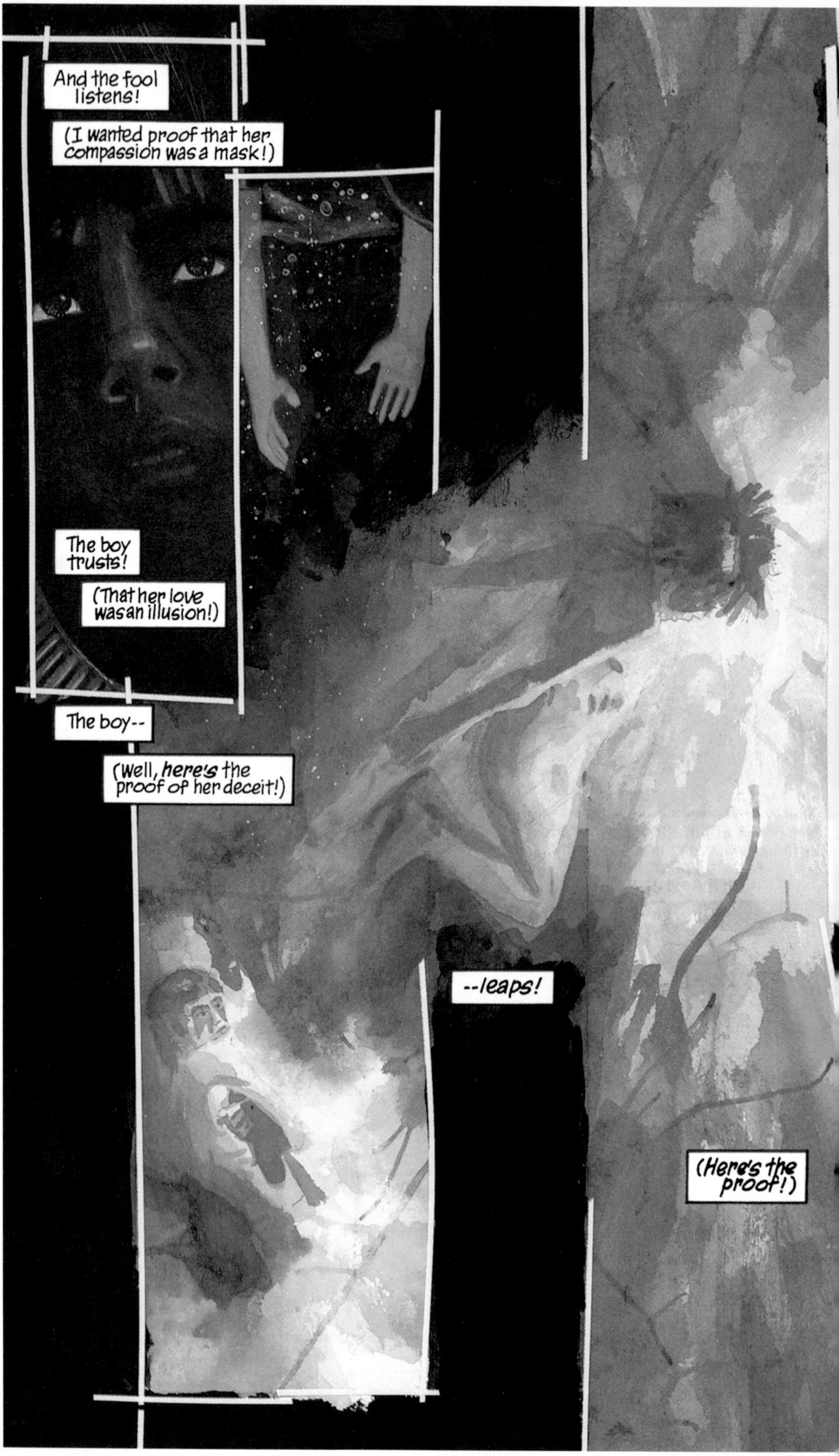
And the fool listens!
(I wanted proof that her compassion was a mask!)
The boy trusts!
(That her love was an illusion!)
The boy--
(Well, *here's* the proof of her deceit!)
--leaps!
(Here's the proof!)

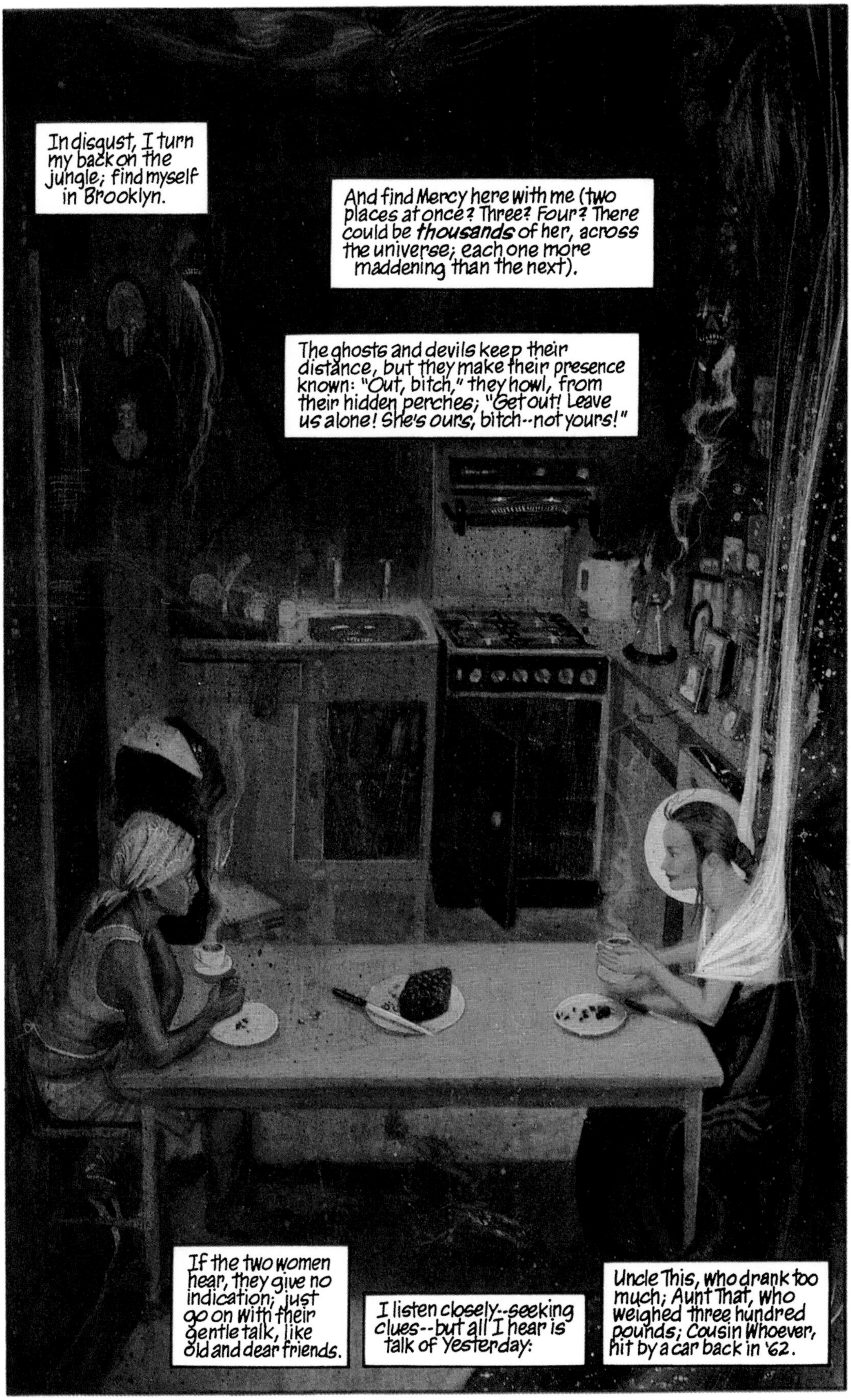
In disgust, I turn my back on the jungle; find myself in Brooklyn.
And find Mercy here with me (two places at once? Three? Four? There could be *thousands* of her, across the universe; each one more maddening than the next).
The ghosts and devils keep their distance, but they make their presence known: "Out, bitch," they howl, from their hidden perches; "Get out! Leave us alone! She's ours, bitch--not yours!"
If the two women hear, they give no indication; just go on with their gentle talk, like old and dear friends.
I listen closely--seeking clues--but all I hear is talk of Yesterday:
Uncle This, who drank too much; Aunt That, who weighed three hundred pounds; Cousin Whoever, hit by a car back in '62.

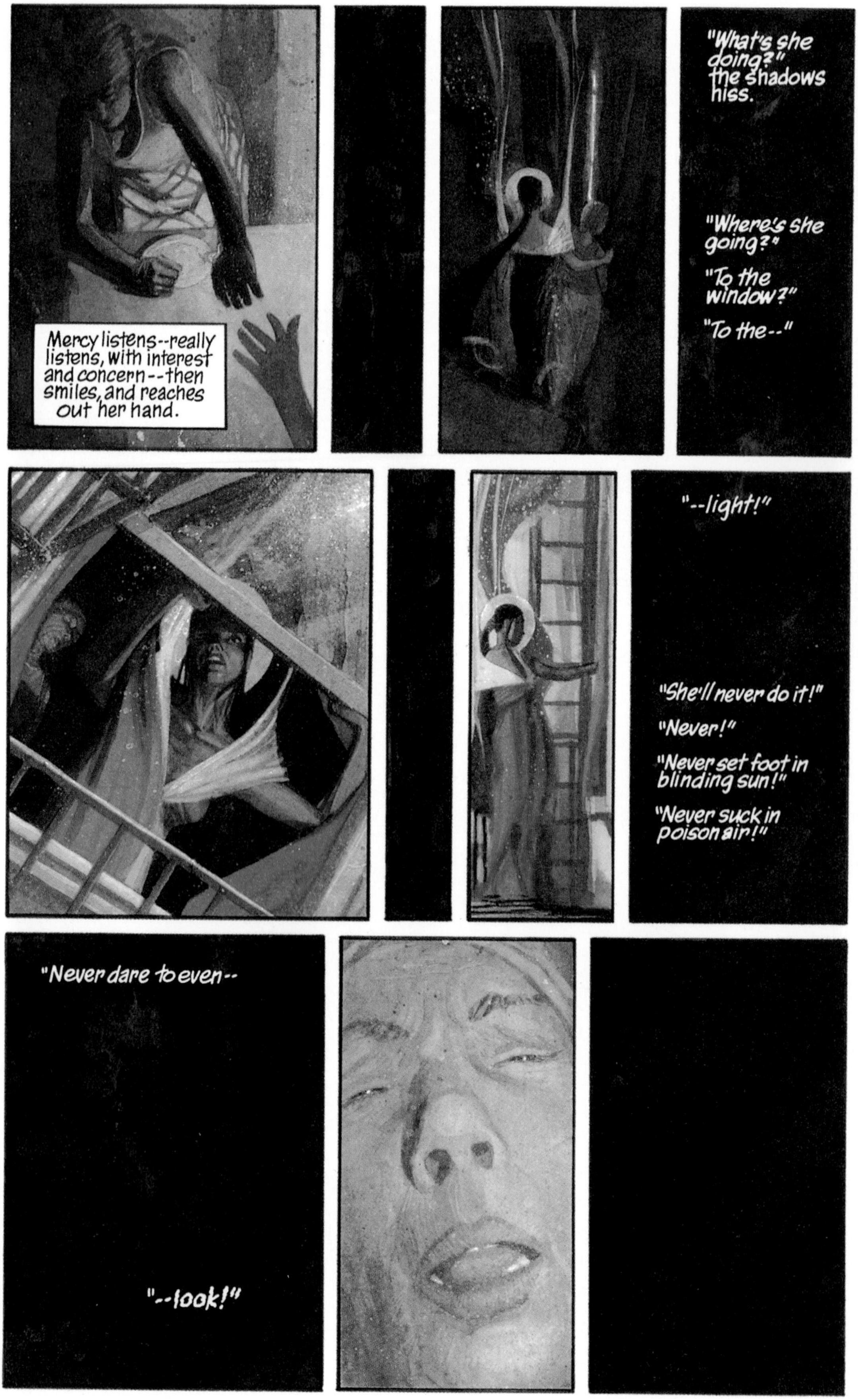

Mercy listens--really listens, with interest and concern--then smiles, and reaches out her hand.
"What's she doing?" the shadows hiss.
"Where's she going?"
"To the window?"
"To the--"
"--light!"
"She'll never do it!"
"Never!"
"Never set foot in blinding sun!"
"Never suck in poison air!"
"Never dare to even--
"--look!"

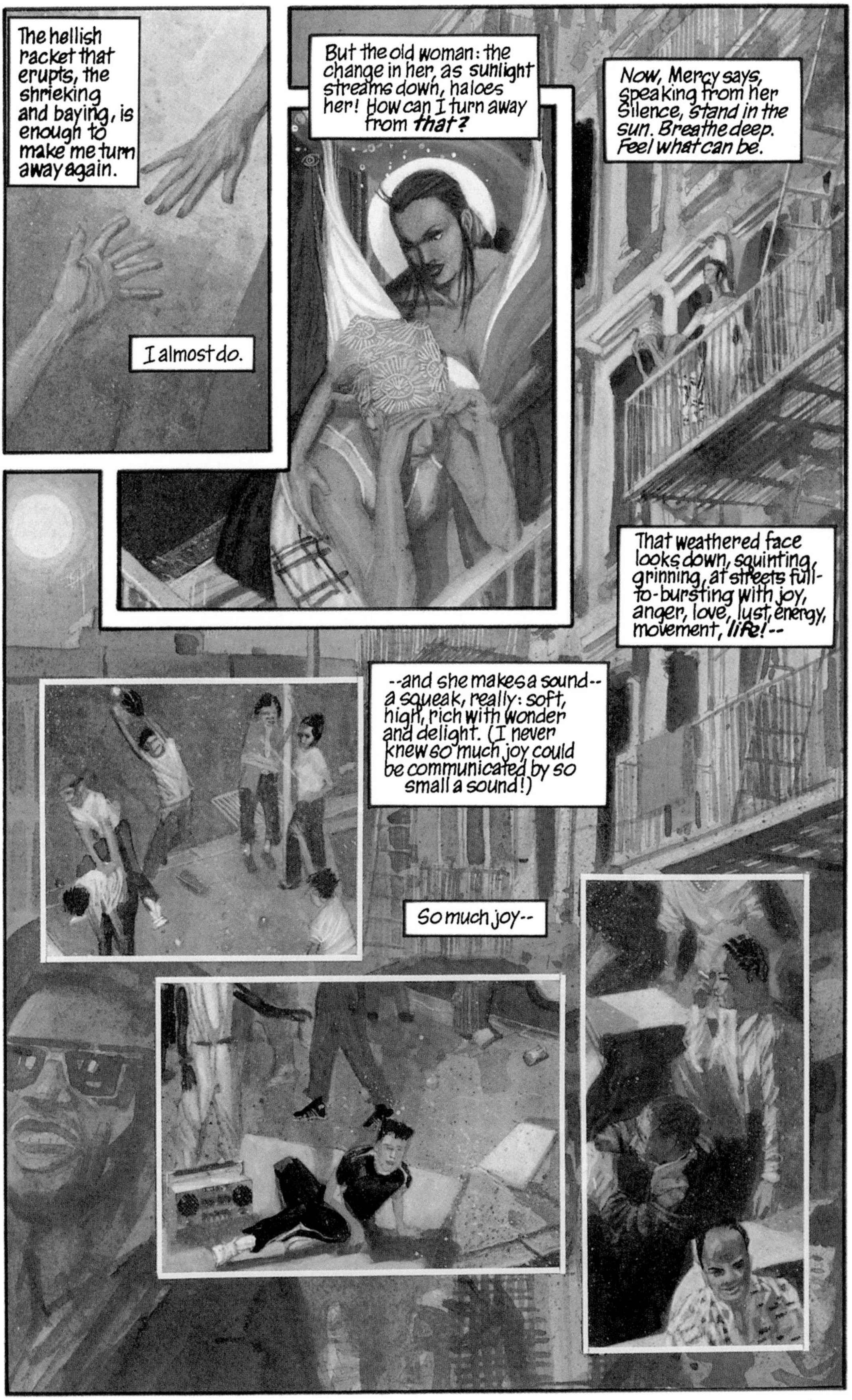
The hellish racket that erupts, the shrieking and baying, is enough to make me turn away again.
I almost do.
But the old woman: the change in her, as sunlight streams down, haloes her! How can I turn away from *that?*
Now, Mercy says, speaking from her Silence, stand in the sun. Breathe deep. Feel what can be.
That weathered face looks down, squinting, grinning, at streets full-to-bursting with joy, anger, love, lust, energy, movement, *life!*--
--and she makes a sound--a squeak, really: soft, high, rich with wonder and delight. (I never knew so much joy could be communicated by so small a sound!)
So much joy--

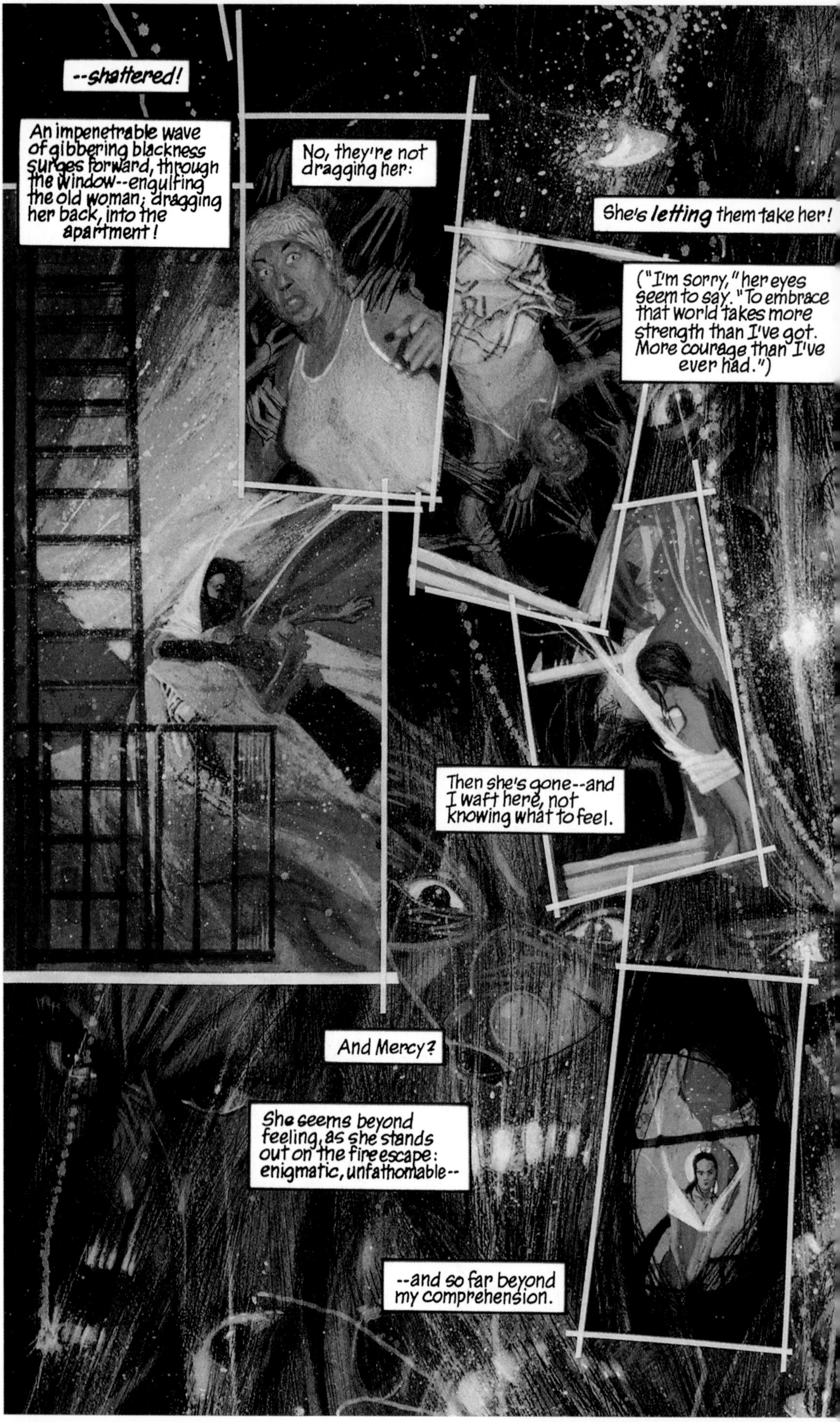
--shattered!
An impenetrable wave of gibbering blackness surges forward, through the window--engulfing the old woman; dragging her back, into the apartment!
No, they're not dragging her:
She's *letting* them take her!
("I'm sorry," her eyes seem to say. "To embrace that world takes more strength than I've got. More courage than I've ever had.")
Then she's gone--and I waft here, not knowing what to feel.
And Mercy?
She seems beyond feeling, as she stands out on the fire escape: enigmatic, unfathomable--
--and so far beyond my comprehension.

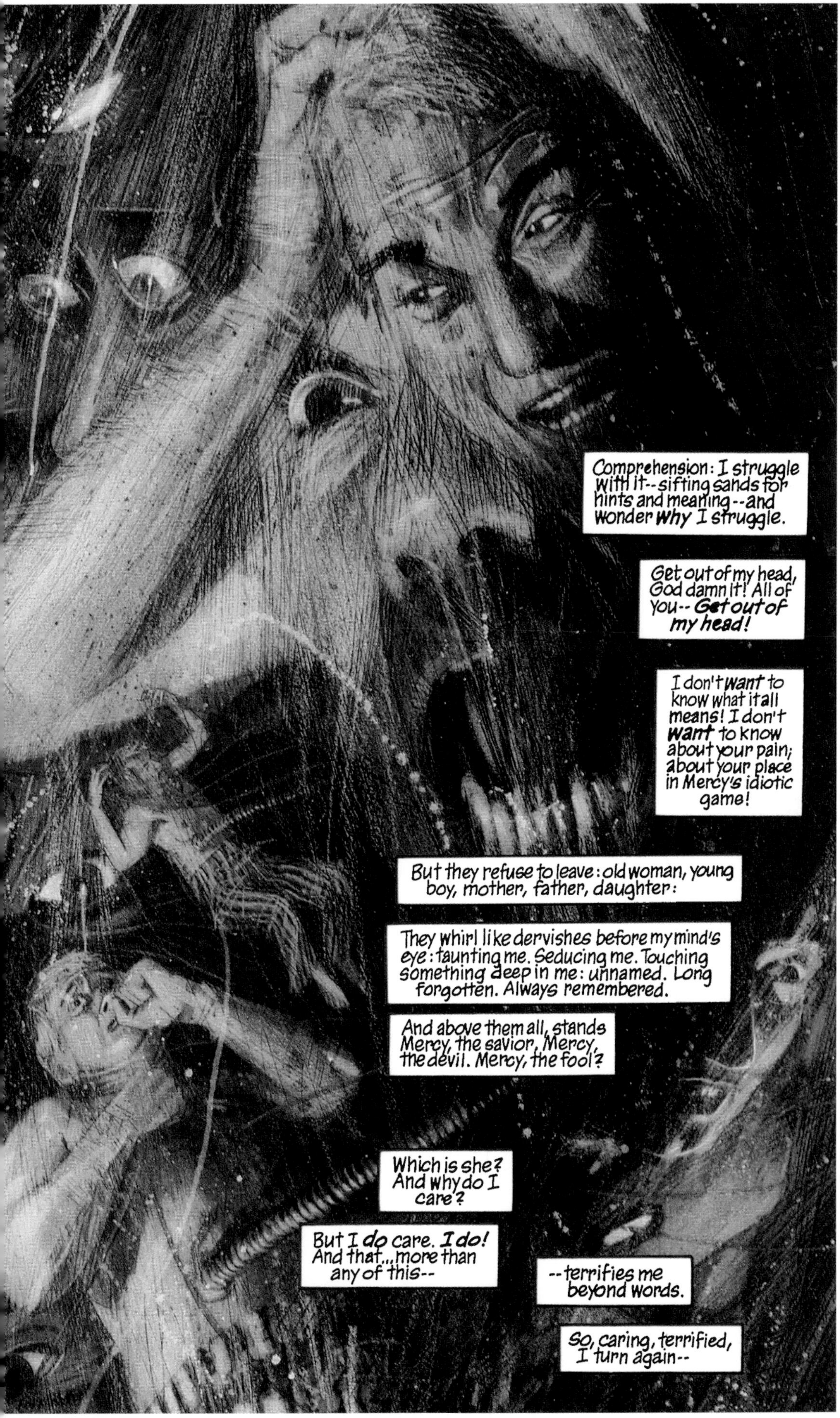
Comprehension: I struggle with it--sifting sands for hints and meaning--and wonder *why* I struggle.
Get out of my head, God damn it! All of you-- *Get out of my head!*
I don't *want* to know what it all means! I don't *want* to know about your pain; about your place in Mercy's idiotic game!
But they refuse to leave: old woman, young boy, mother, father, daughter:
They whirl like dervishes before my mind's eye: taunting me. Seducing me. Touching something deep in me: unnamed. Long forgotten. Always remembered.
And above them all, stands Mercy, the savior, Mercy, the devil. Mercy, the fool?
Which is she? And why do I care?
But I *do* care. *I do!* And that...more than any of this--
--terrifies me beyond words.
So, caring, terrified, I turn again--

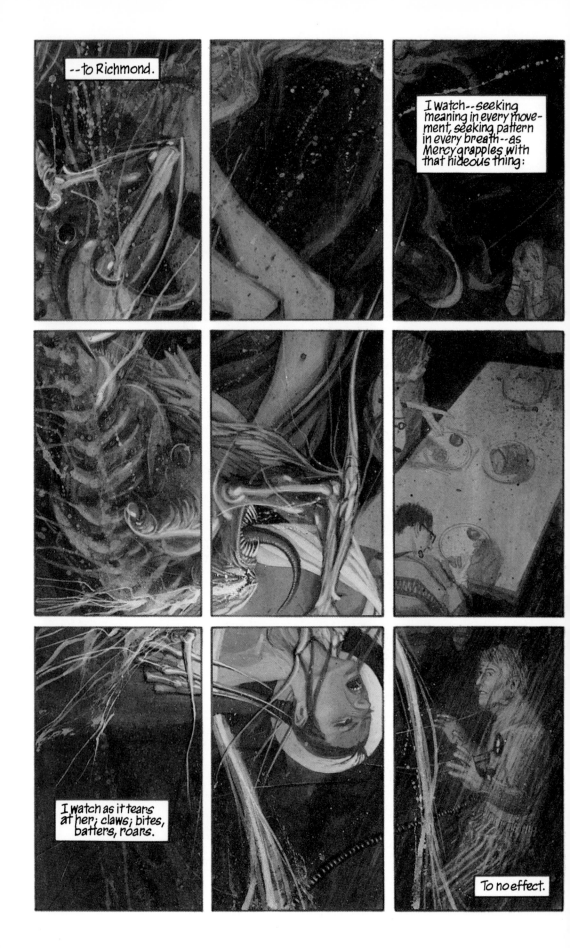

--to Richmond.

I watch--seeking meaning in every movement, seeking pattern in every breath--as Mercy grapples with that hideous thing:

I watch as it tears at her; claws; bites, batters, roars.

To no effect.

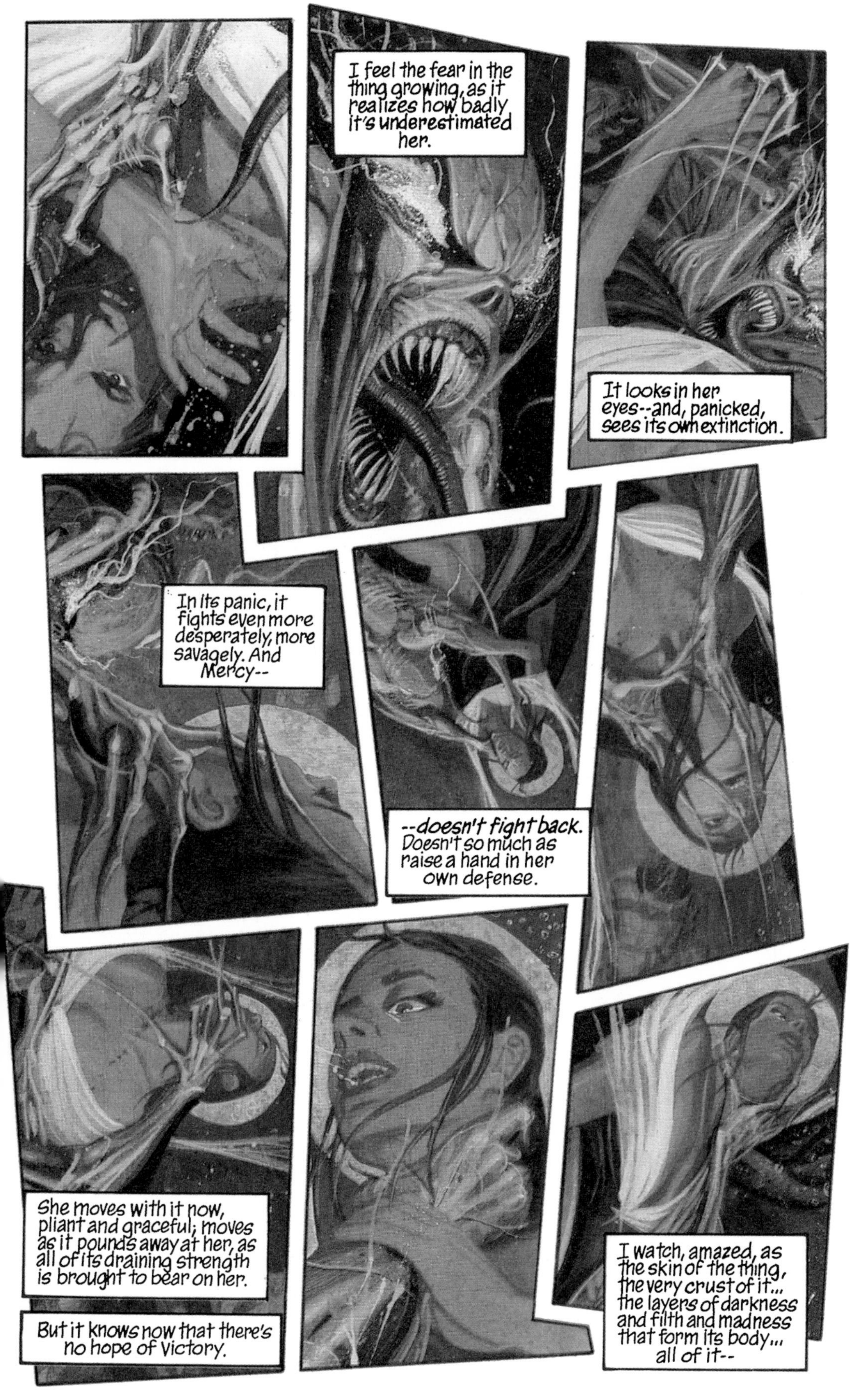
I feel the fear in the thing growing, as it realizes how badly it's underestimated her.
It looks in her eyes--and, panicked, sees its own extinction.
In its panic, it fights even more desperately, more savagely. And Mercy--
--doesn't fight back. Doesn't so much as raise a hand in her own defense.
She moves with it now, pliant and graceful; moves as it pounds away at her, as all of its draining strength is brought to bear on her.
But it knows now that there's no hope of victory.
I watch, amazed, as the skin of the thing, the very crust of it... the layers of darkness and filth and madness that form its body... all of it--

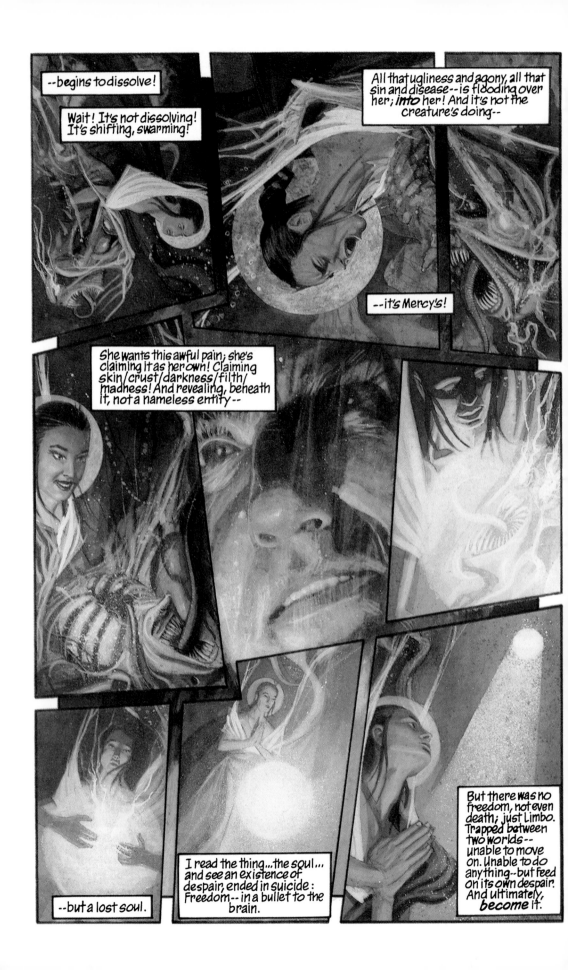

--begins to dissolve!

Wait! It's not dissolving! It's shifting, swarming!

All that ugliness and agony, all that sin and disease--is flooding over her; *into* her! And it's not the creature's doing--

--it's Mercy's!

She wants this awful pain; she's claiming it as her own! Claiming skin/crust/darkness/filth/madness! And revealing, beneath it, not a nameless entity--

--but a lost soul.

I read the thing...the soul...and see an existence of despair, ended in suicide: Freedom--in a bullet to the brain.

But there was no freedom, not even death; just Limbo. Trapped between two worlds--unable to move on. Unable to do anything--but feed on its own despair. And ultimately, *become* it.

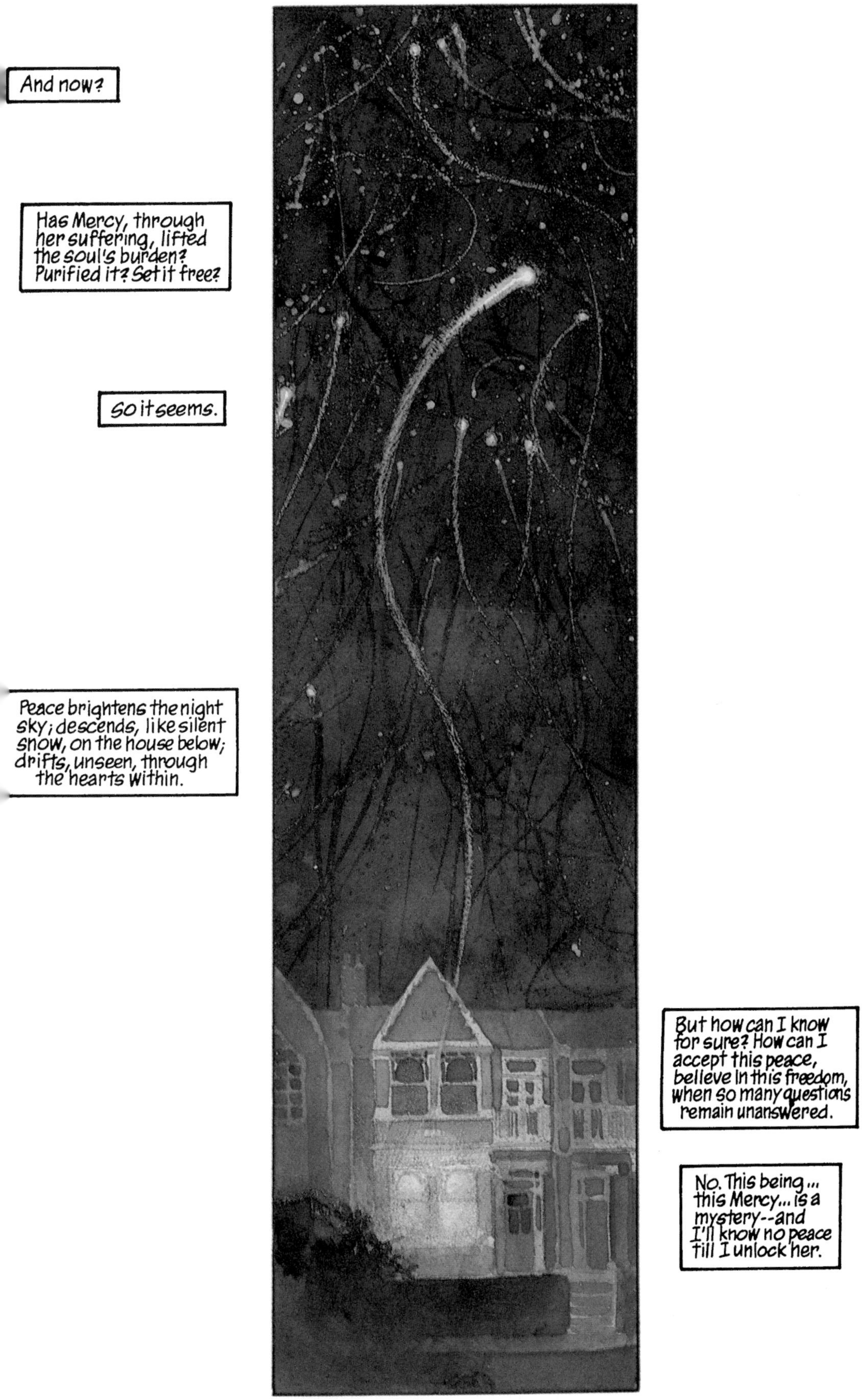
And now?
Has Mercy, through her suffering, lifted the soul's burden? Purified it? Set it free?
So it seems.
Peace brightens the night sky; descends, like silent snow, on the house below; drifts, unseen, through the hearts within.
But how can I know for sure? How can I accept this peace, believe in this freedom, when so many questions remain unanswered.
No. This being... this Mercy... is a mystery--and I'll know no peace till I unlock her.

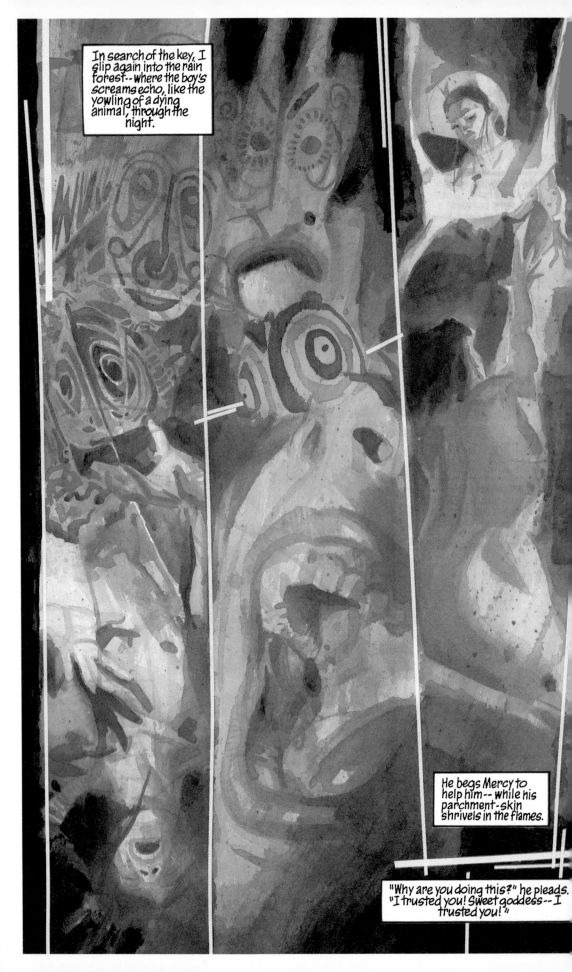

In search of the key, I slip again into the rain forest--where the boy's screams echo, like the yowling of a dying animal, through the night.

He begs Mercy to help him--while his parchment-skin shrivels in the flames.

"Why are you doing this?" he pleads. "I trusted you! Sweet goddess--I trusted you!"

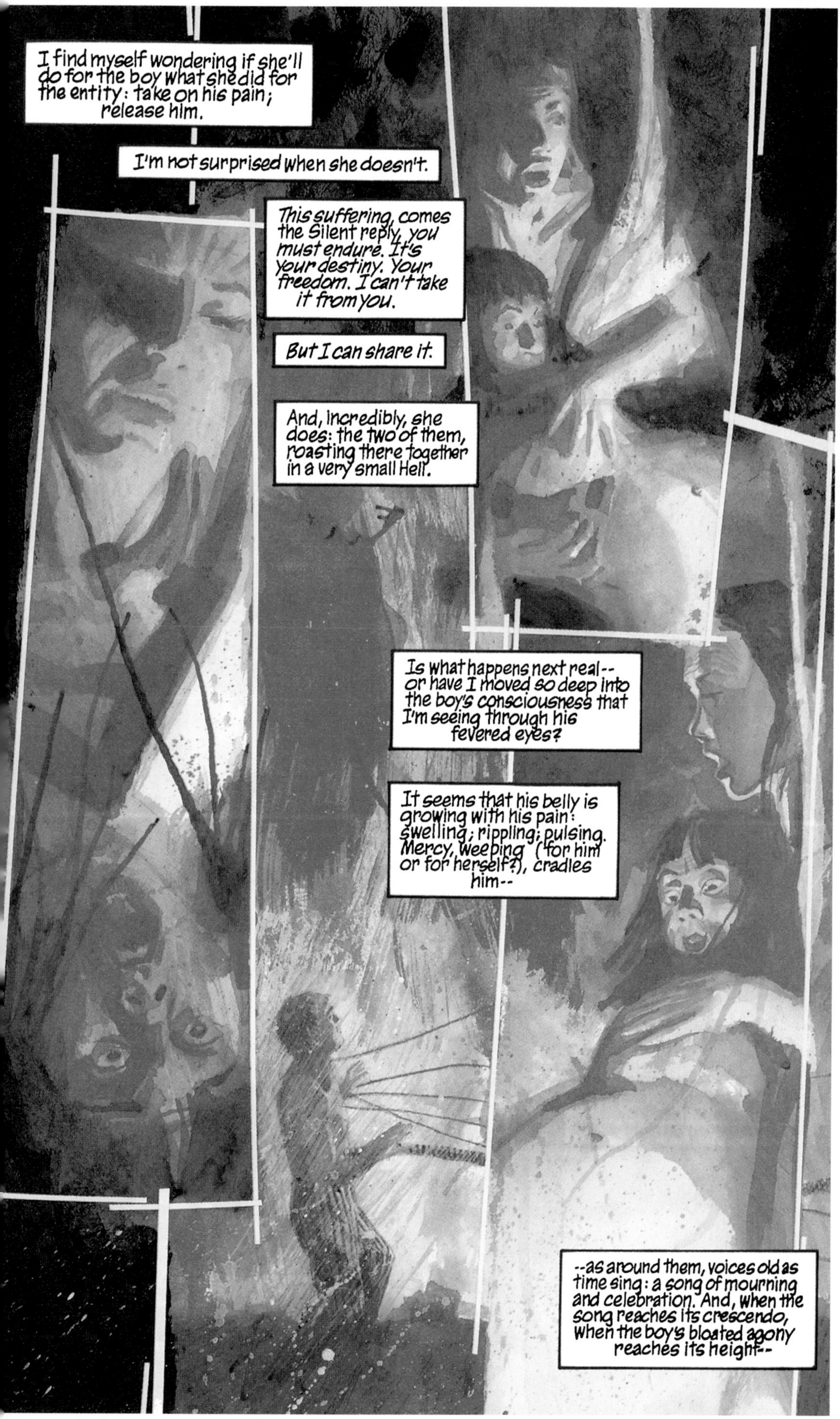
I find myself wondering if she'll do for the boy what she did for the entity: take on his pain; release him.
I'm not surprised when she doesn't.
This suffering, comes the Silent reply, you must endure. It's your destiny. Your freedom. I can't take it from you.
But I can share it.
And, incredibly, she does: the two of them, roasting there together in a very small Hell.
Is what happens next real--or have I moved so deep into the boy's consciousness that I'm seeing through his fevered eyes?
It seems that his belly is growing with his pain: swelling; rippling; pulsing. Mercy, weeping (for him or for herself?), cradles him--
--as around them, voices old as time sing: a song of mourning and celebration. And, when the song reaches its crescendo, when the boy's bloated agony reaches its height--

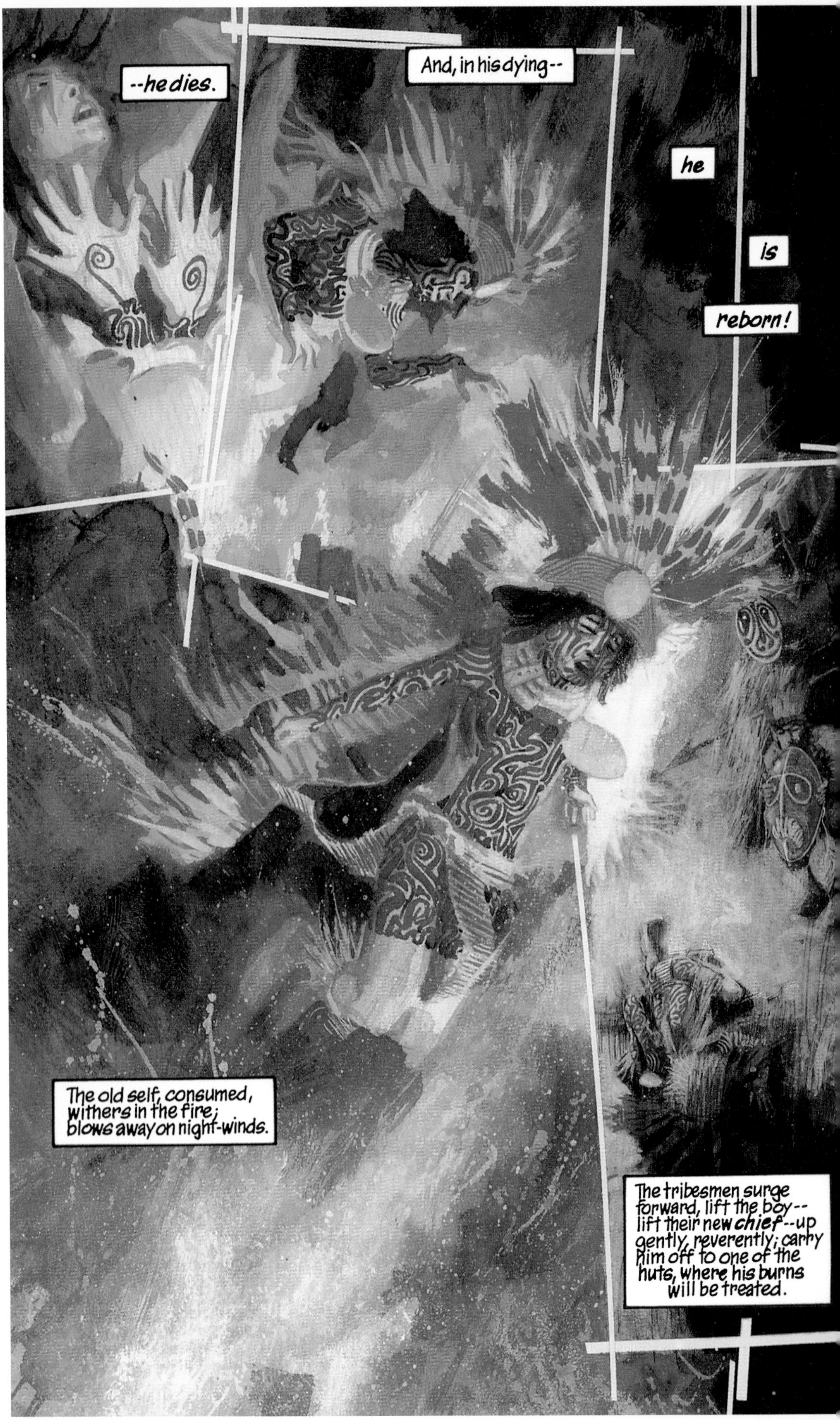
--he dies.
And, in his dying--
he
is
reborn!
The old self, consumed, withers in the fire; blows away on night-winds.
The tribesmen surge forward, lift the boy-- lift their new chief--up gently, reverently; carry him off to one of the huts, where his burns will be treated.

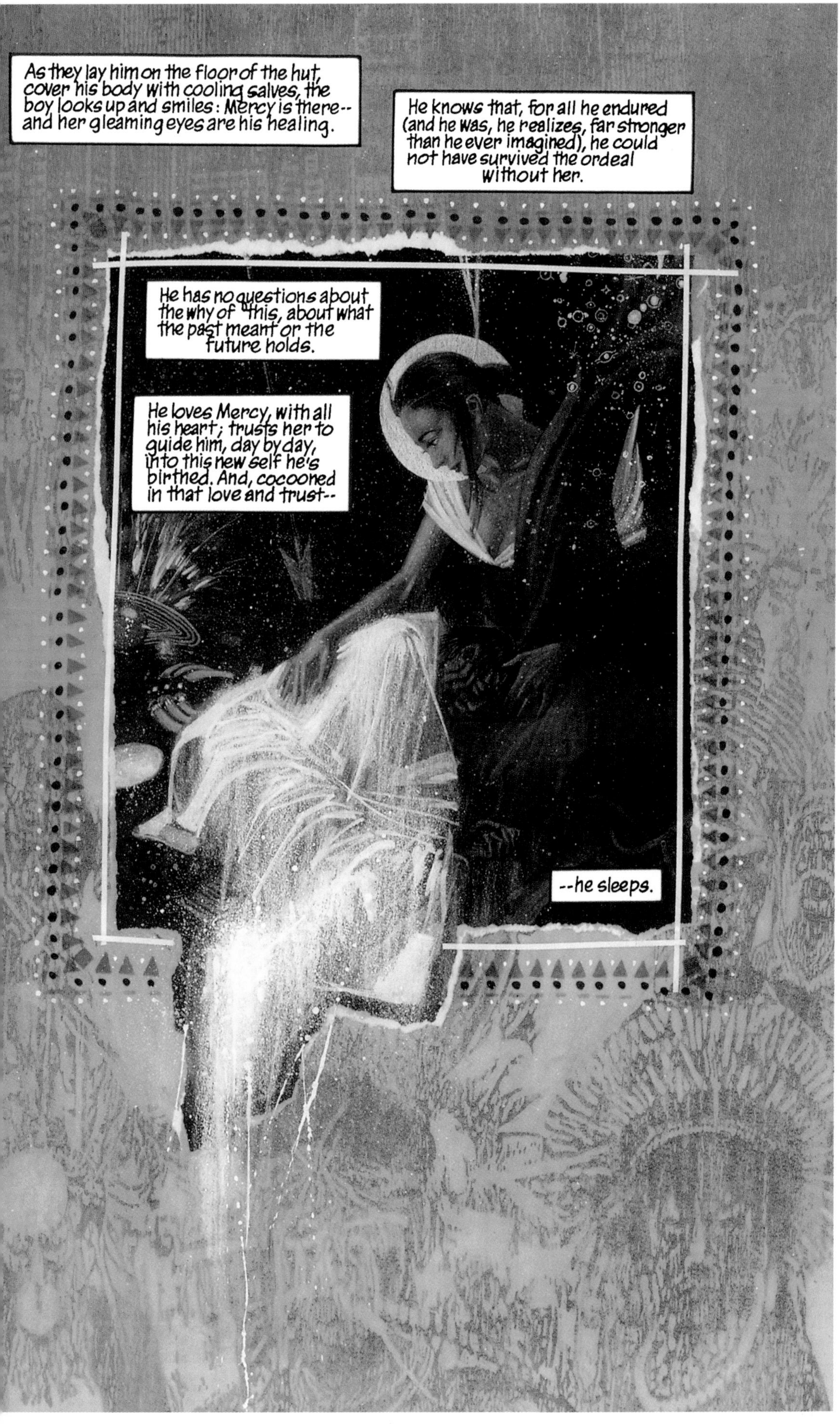
As they lay him on the floor of the hut, cover his body with cooling salves, the boy looks up and smiles: Mercy is there--and her gleaming eyes are his healing.
He knows that, for all he endured (and he was, he realizes, far stronger than he ever imagined), he could not have survived the ordeal without her.
He has no questions about the why of this, about what the past meant or the future holds.
He loves Mercy, with all his heart; trusts her to guide him, day by day, into this new self he's birthed. And, cocooned in that love and trust--
--he sleeps.

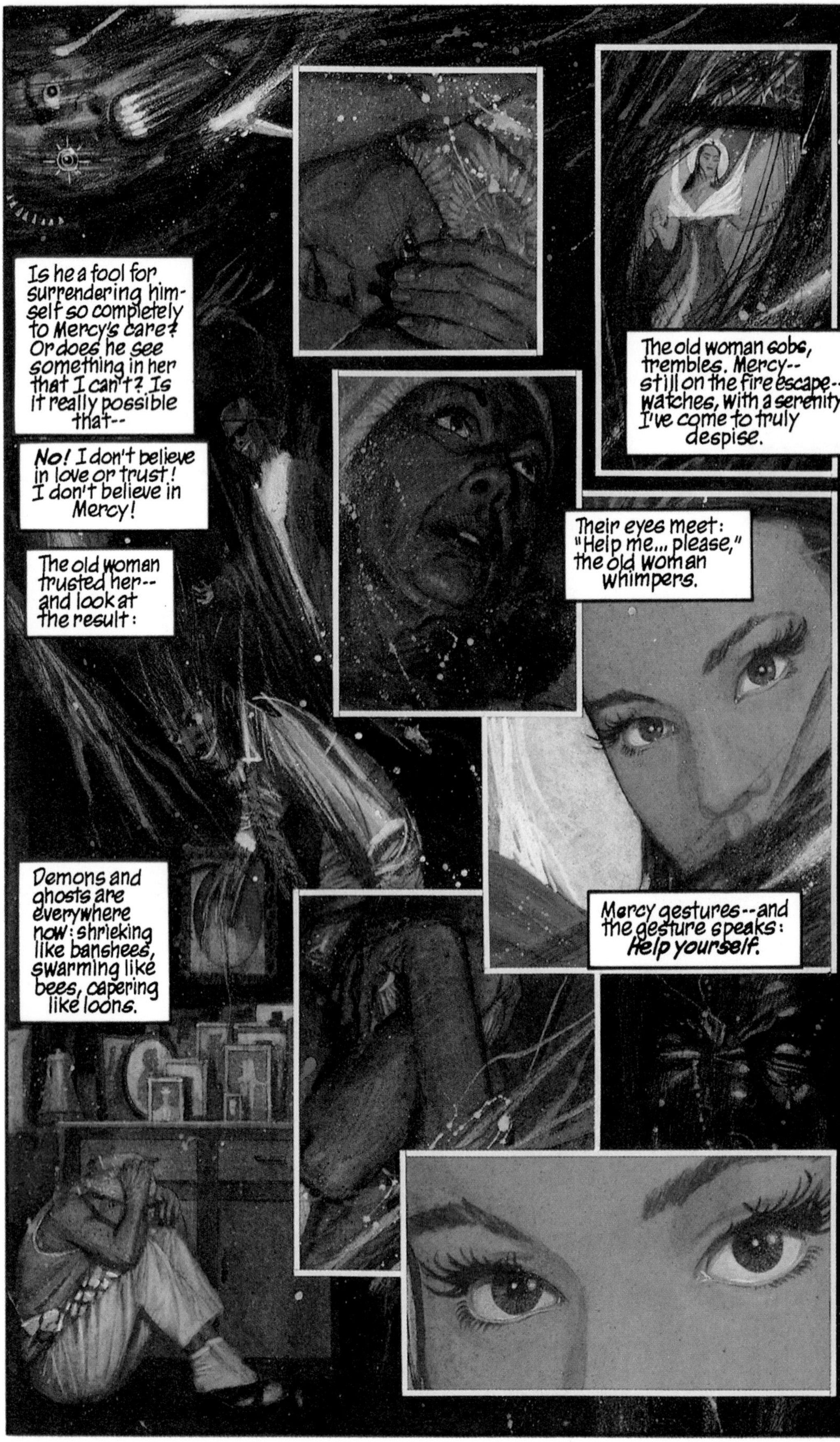
Is he a fool for surrendering himself so completely to Mercy's care? Or does he see something in her that I can't? Is it really possible that--
No! I don't believe in love or trust! I don't believe in Mercy!
The old woman trusted her--and look at the result:
The old woman sobs, trembles. Mercy--still on the fire escape--watches, with a serenity I've come to truly despise.
Their eyes meet: "Help me... please," the old woman whimpers.
Demons and ghosts are everywhere now: shrieking like banshees, swarming like bees, capering like loons.
Mercy gestures--and the gesture speaks: *Help yourself.*

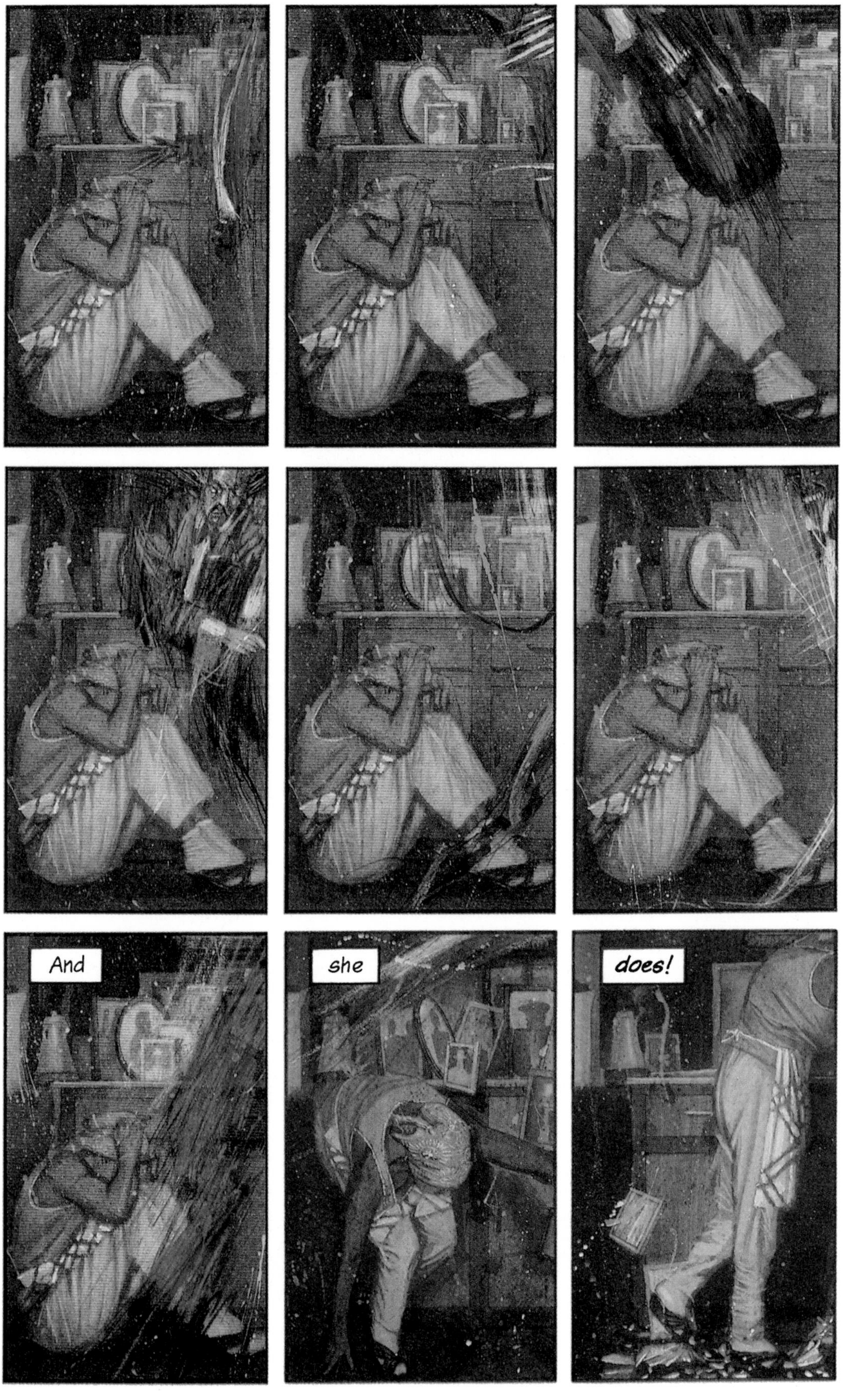
And
she
does!

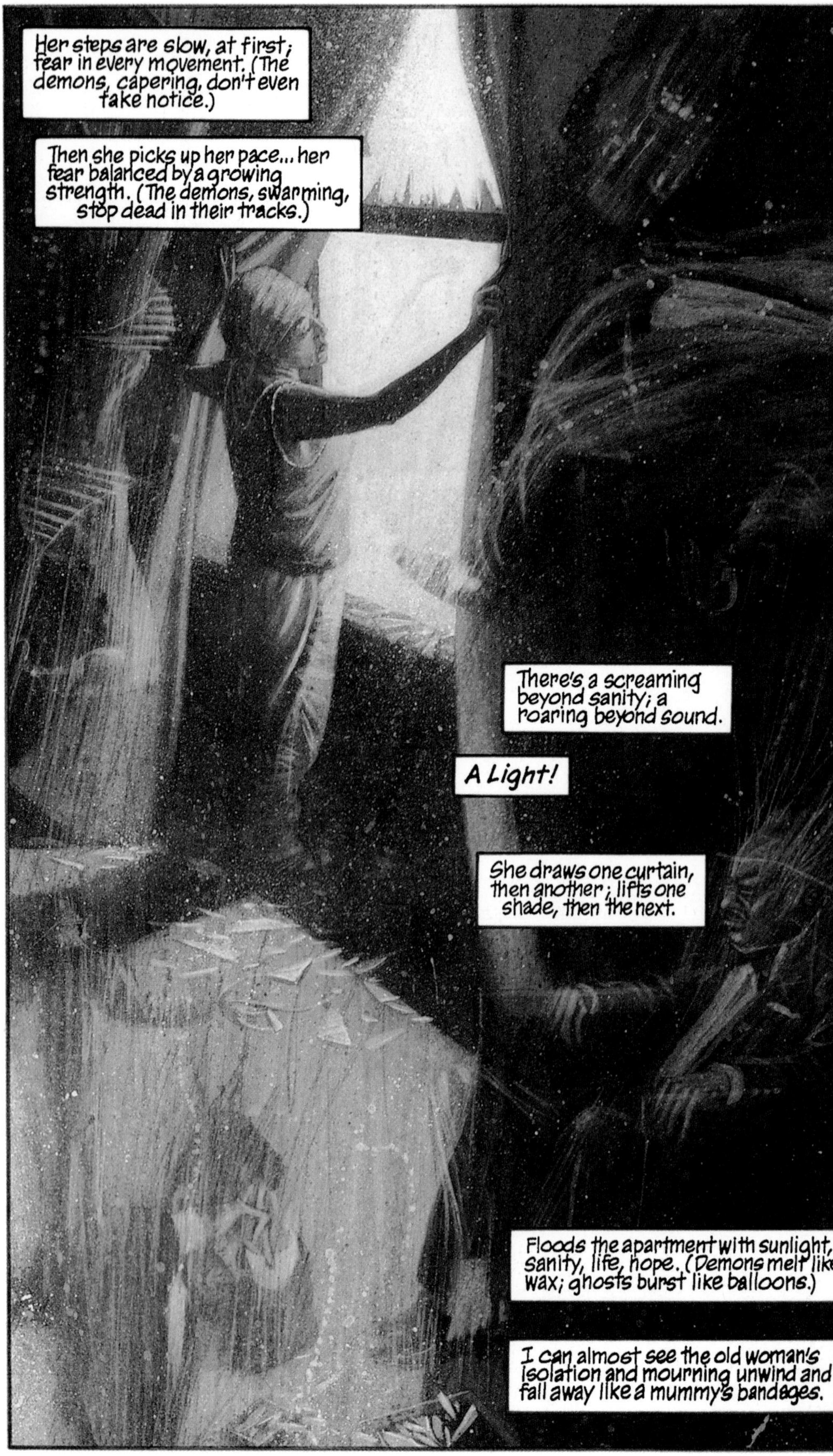
Her steps are slow, at first; fear in every movement. (The demons, capering, don't even take notice.)
Then she picks up her pace... her fear balanced by a growing strength. (The demons, swarming, stop dead in their tracks.)
There's a screaming beyond sanity; a roaring beyond sound.
A Light!
She draws one curtain, then another; lifts one shade, then the next.
Floods the apartment with sunlight, sanity, life, hope. (Demons melt like wax; ghosts burst like balloons.)
I can almost see the old woman's isolation and mourning unwind and fall away like a mummy's bandages.

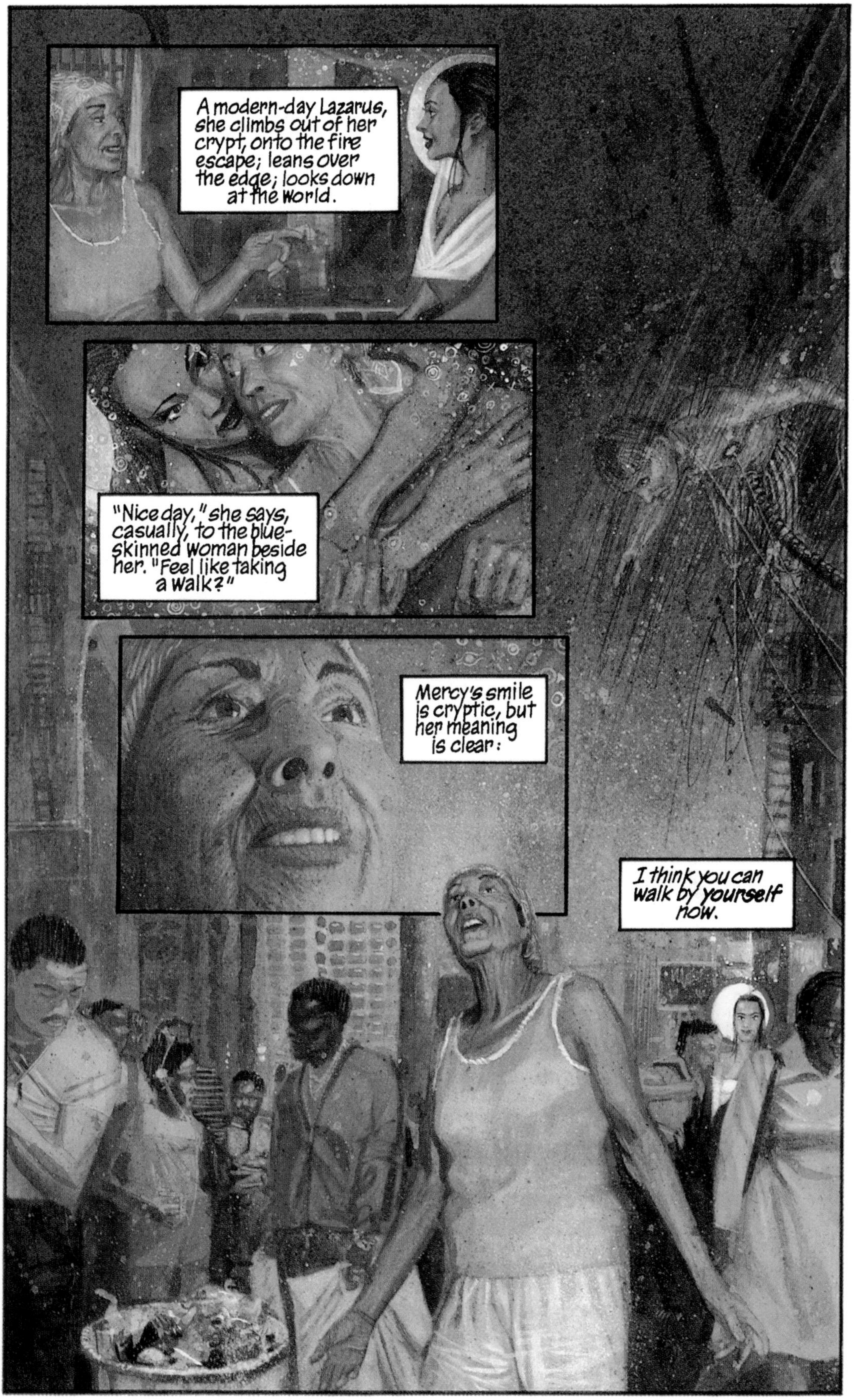
A modern-day Lazarus, she climbs out of her crypt, onto the fire escape; leans over the edge; looks down at the world.
"Nice day," she says, casually, to the blue-skinned woman beside her. "Feel like taking a walk?"
Mercy's smile is cryptic, but her meaning is clear:
I think you can walk by yourself now.

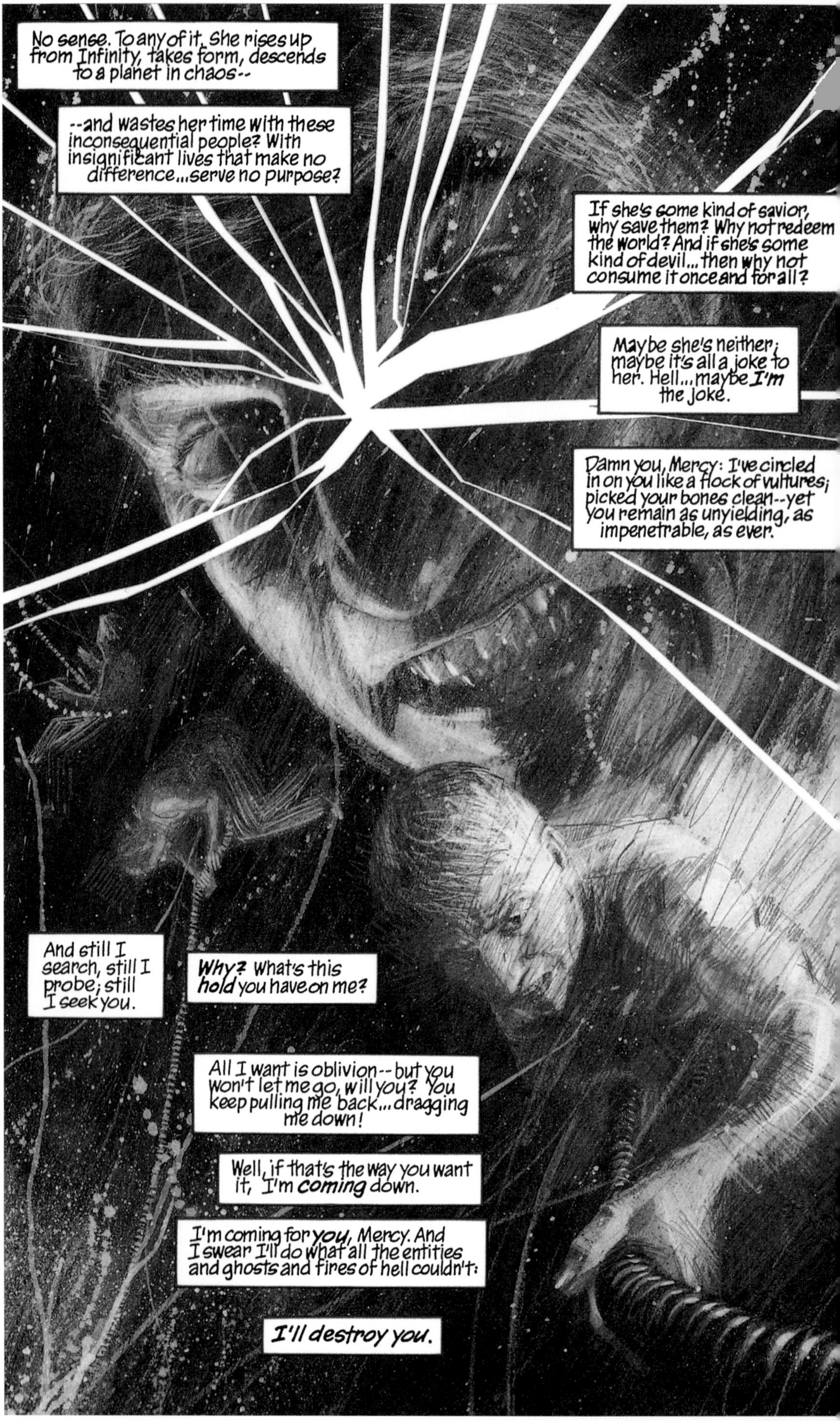
No sense. To any of it. She rises up from Infinity, takes form, descends to a planet in chaos--
--and wastes her time with these inconsequential people? With insignificant lives that make no difference...serve no purpose?
If she's some kind of savior, why save them? Why not redeem the world? And if she's some kind of devil... then why not consume it once and for all?
Maybe she's neither; maybe it's all a joke to her. Hell...maybe I'm the joke.
Damn you, Mercy: I've circled in on you like a flock of vultures; picked your bones clean--yet you remain as unyielding, as impenetrable, as ever.
And still I search, still I probe; still I seek you.
Why? What's this hold you have on me?
All I want is oblivion--but you won't let me go, will you? You keep pulling me back...dragging me down!
Well, if that's the way you want it, I'm coming down.
I'm coming for you, Mercy. And I swear I'll do what all the entities and ghosts and fires of hell couldn't:
I'll destroy you.

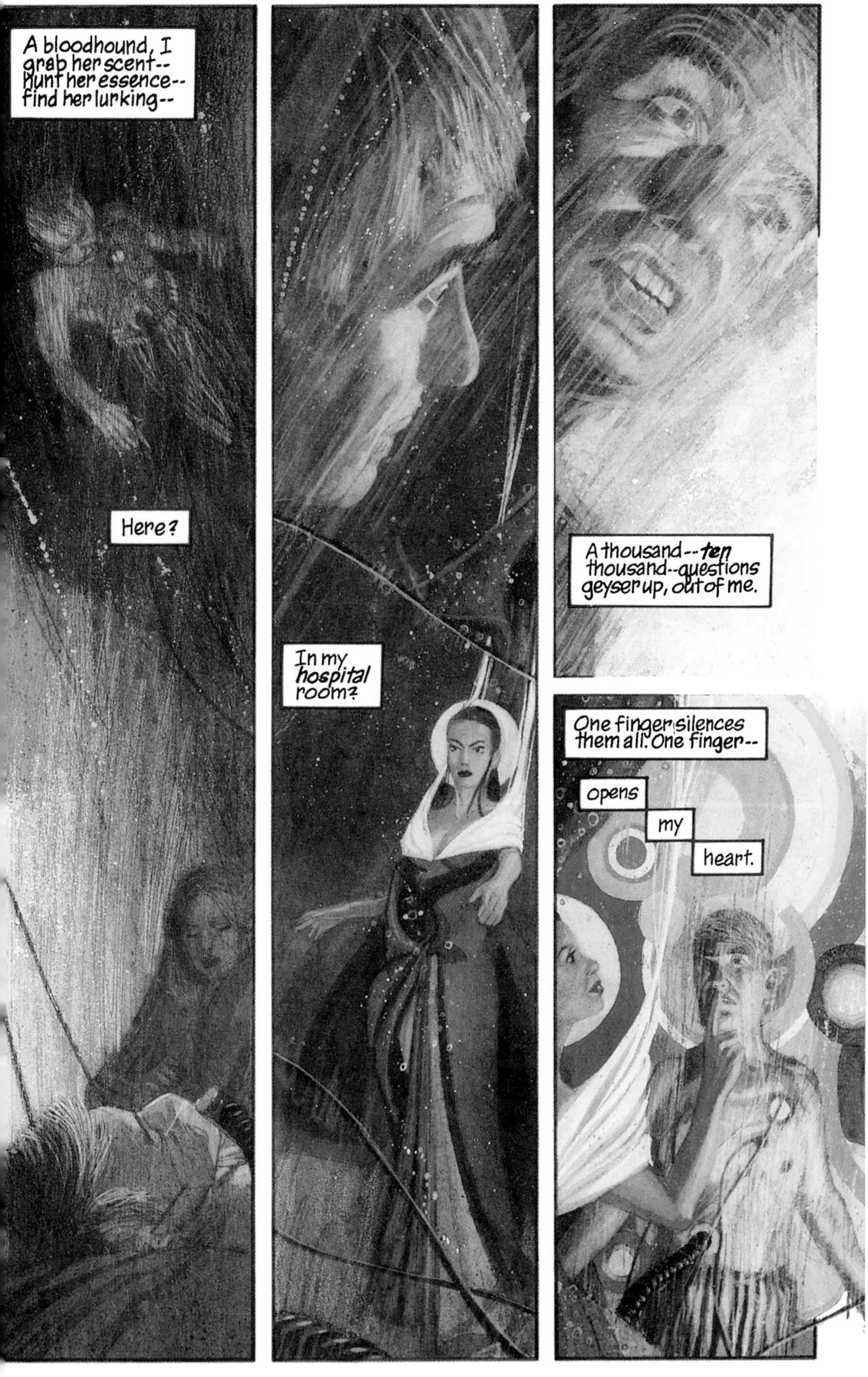
A bloodhound, I grab her scent--hunt her essence--find her lurking--
Here?
In my hospital room?
A thousand--ten thousand--questions geyser up, out of me.
One finger silences them all. One finger--
opens
my
heart.

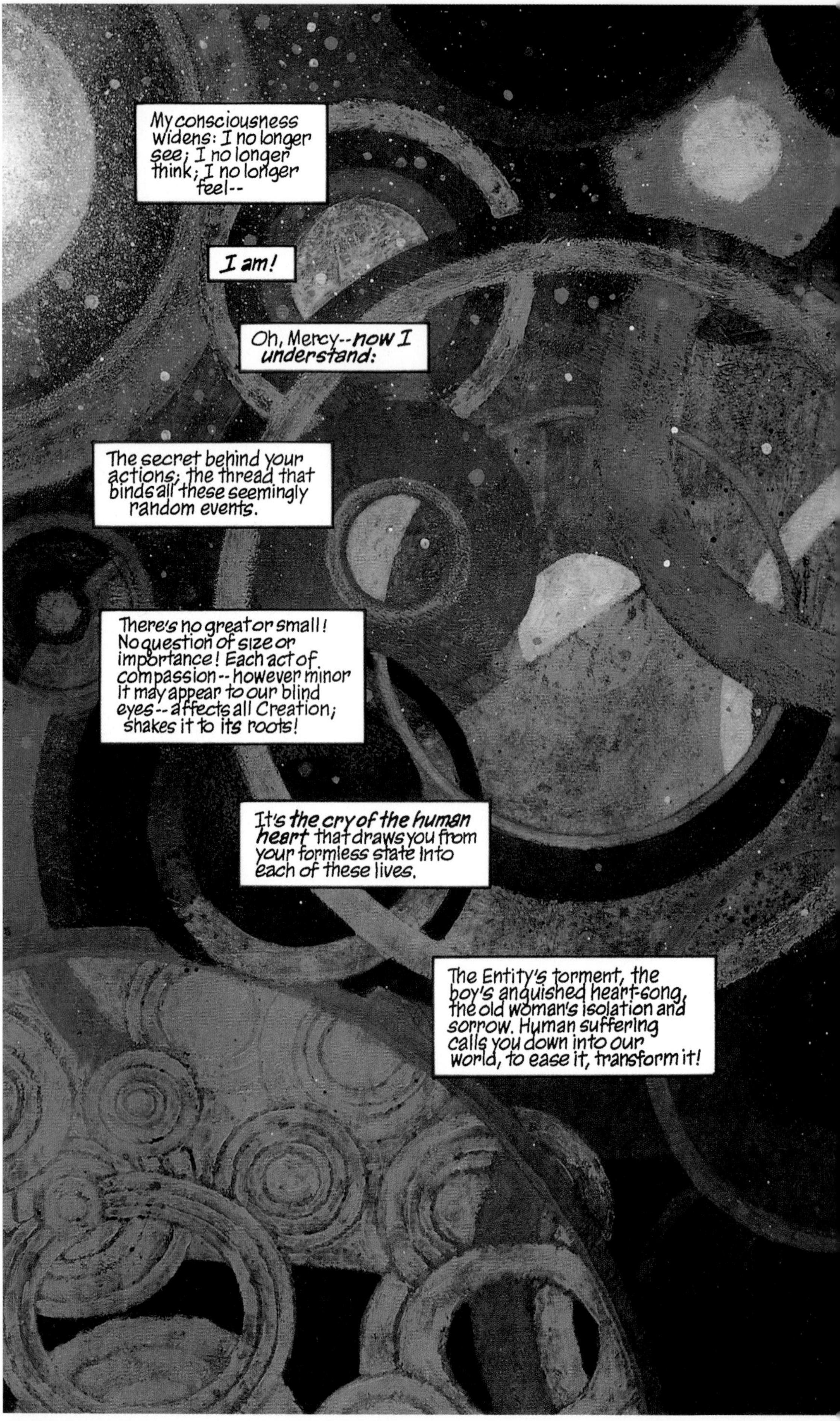

My consciousness widens: I no longer see; I no longer think; I no longer feel--
I am!
Oh, Mercy--now I understand:
The secret behind your actions; the thread that binds all these seemingly random events.
There's no great or small! No question of size or importance! Each act of compassion--however minor it may appear to our blind eyes--affects all Creation; shakes it to its roots!
It's the cry of the human heart that draws you from your formless state into each of these lives.
The Entity's torment, the boy's anguished heart-song, the old woman's isolation and sorrow. Human suffering calls you down into our world, to ease it, transform it!

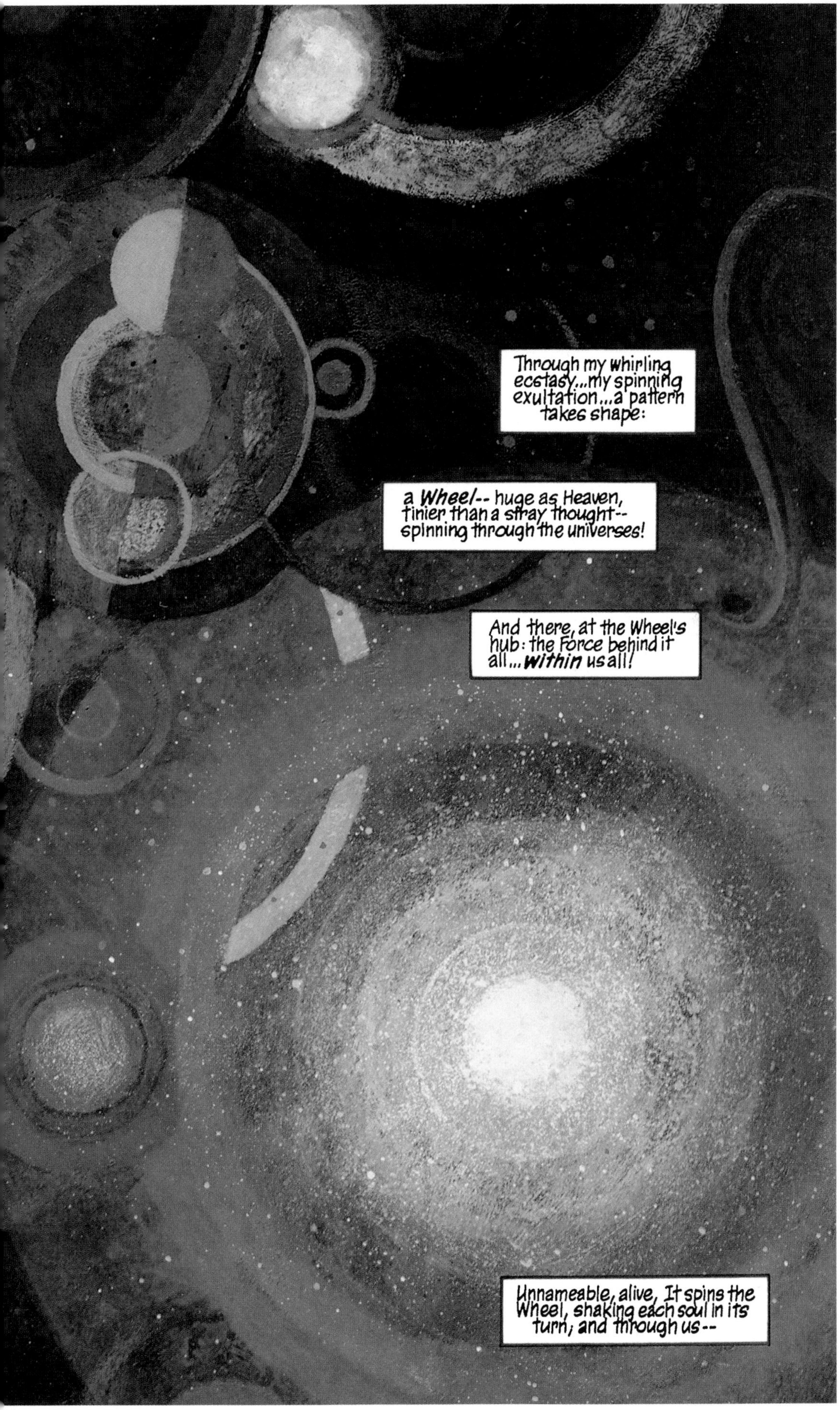
Through my whirling ecstasy...my spinning exultation...a pattern takes shape:
a *Wheel*-- huge as Heaven, tinier than a stray thought-- spinning through the universes!
And there, at the Wheel's hub: the Force behind it all...*within* us all!
Unnameable, alive, It spins the Wheel, shaking each soul in its turn; and through us--

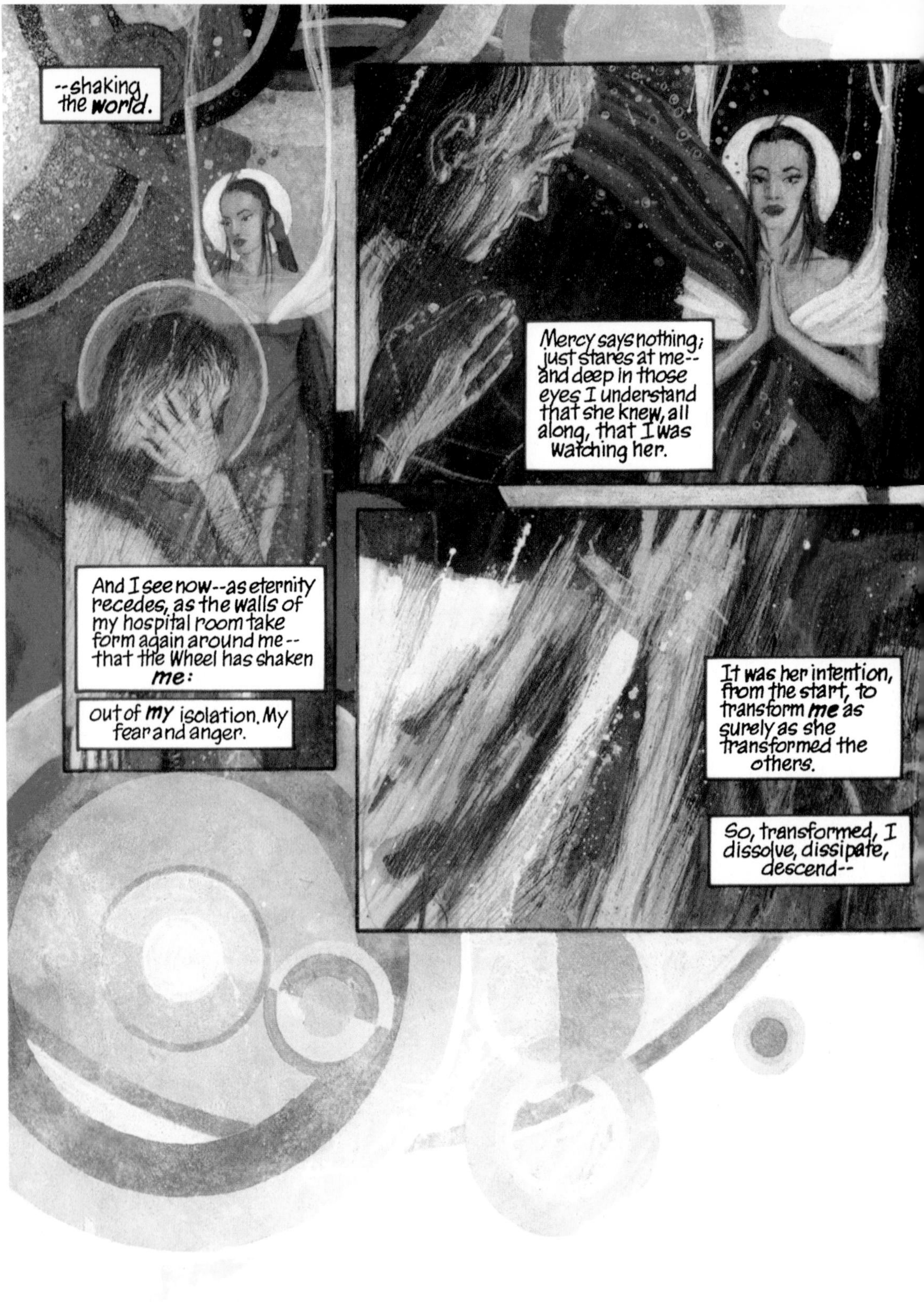
--shaking the world.
Mercy says nothing; just stares at me-- and deep in those eyes I understand that she knew, all along, that I was watching her.
And I see now--as eternity recedes, as the walls of my hospital room take form again around me-- that the Wheel has shaken me:
out of my isolation. My fear and anger.
It was her intention, from the start, to transform me as surely as she transformed the others.
So, transformed, I dissolve, dissipate, descend--

--back into my body.

Into a world that seems suddenly charged with Divinity, with Secrets and Truths of greatest profundity--

--and greatest simplicity.

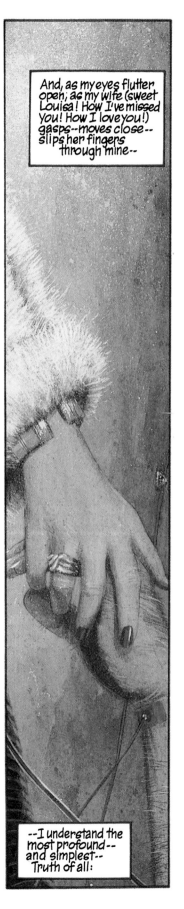

And, as my eyes flutter open; as my wife (sweet Louisa! How I've missed you! How I love you!) gasps--moves close-- slips her fingers through mine--

--I understand the most profound-- and simplest-- Truth of all:

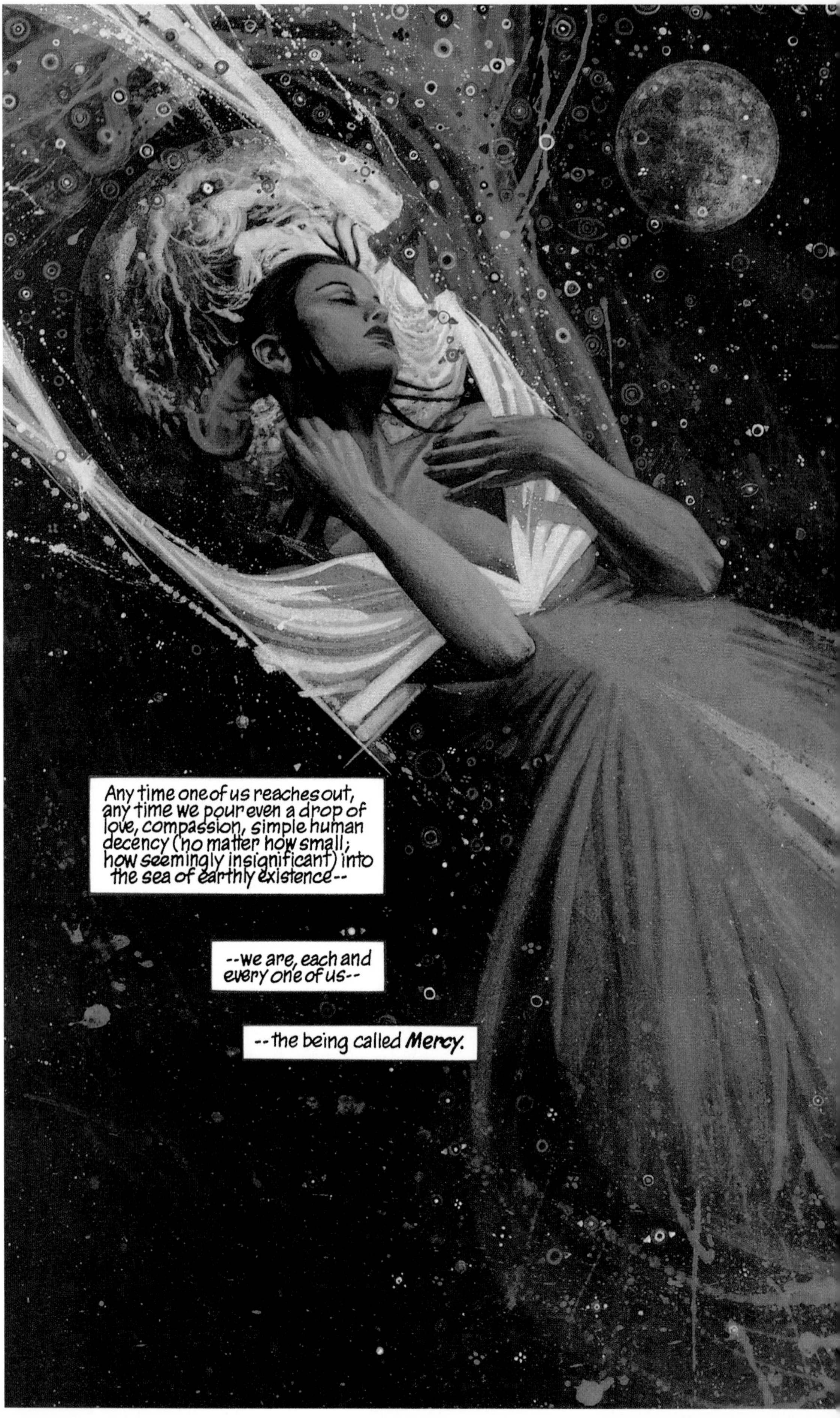
Any time one of us reaches out, any time we pour even a drop of love, compassion, simple human decency (no matter how small; how seemingly insignificant) into the sea of earthly existence--
--we are, each and every one of us--
--the being called *Mercy*.

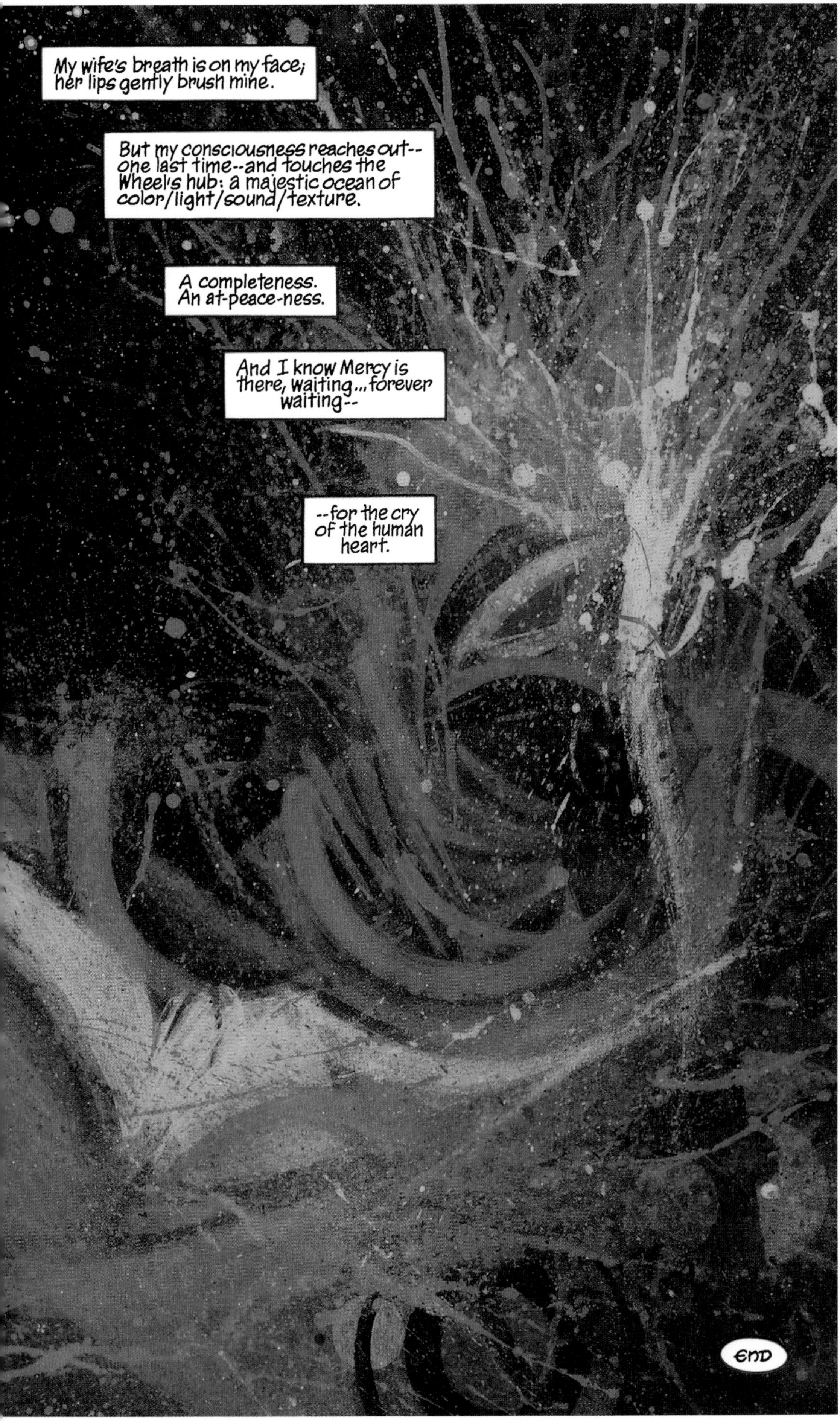
My wife's breath is on my face; her lips gently brush mine.
But my consciousness reaches out--one last time--and touches the Wheel's hub: a majestic ocean of color/light/sound/texture.
A completeness. An at-peace-ness.
And I know Mercy is there, waiting...forever waiting--
--for the cry of the human heart.
END

For Baba, Mehera, and Diane: *eye to eye, breath to breath, heart to heart. Avatar Meher Baba Ki Jai!*

—J.M. DeMatteis

My thanks go out to those people *who made this project possible: to Phil Gascoine, Chris Bell and Ed Hillyer, Ellie de Ville, Pat and Harry Johnson, Steve and Linda Johnson, Charlotte Rogers, and Phil Bevan (as ever) for holding all those difficult poses; to Art Young for making sure this project didn't disappear after the Touchmark line was cancelled; but most of all to Marc DeMatteis for writing a story that displays a message of hope— something often missing from comics today.*

—Paul Johnson

EXCERPTS FROM THE OUTLINE

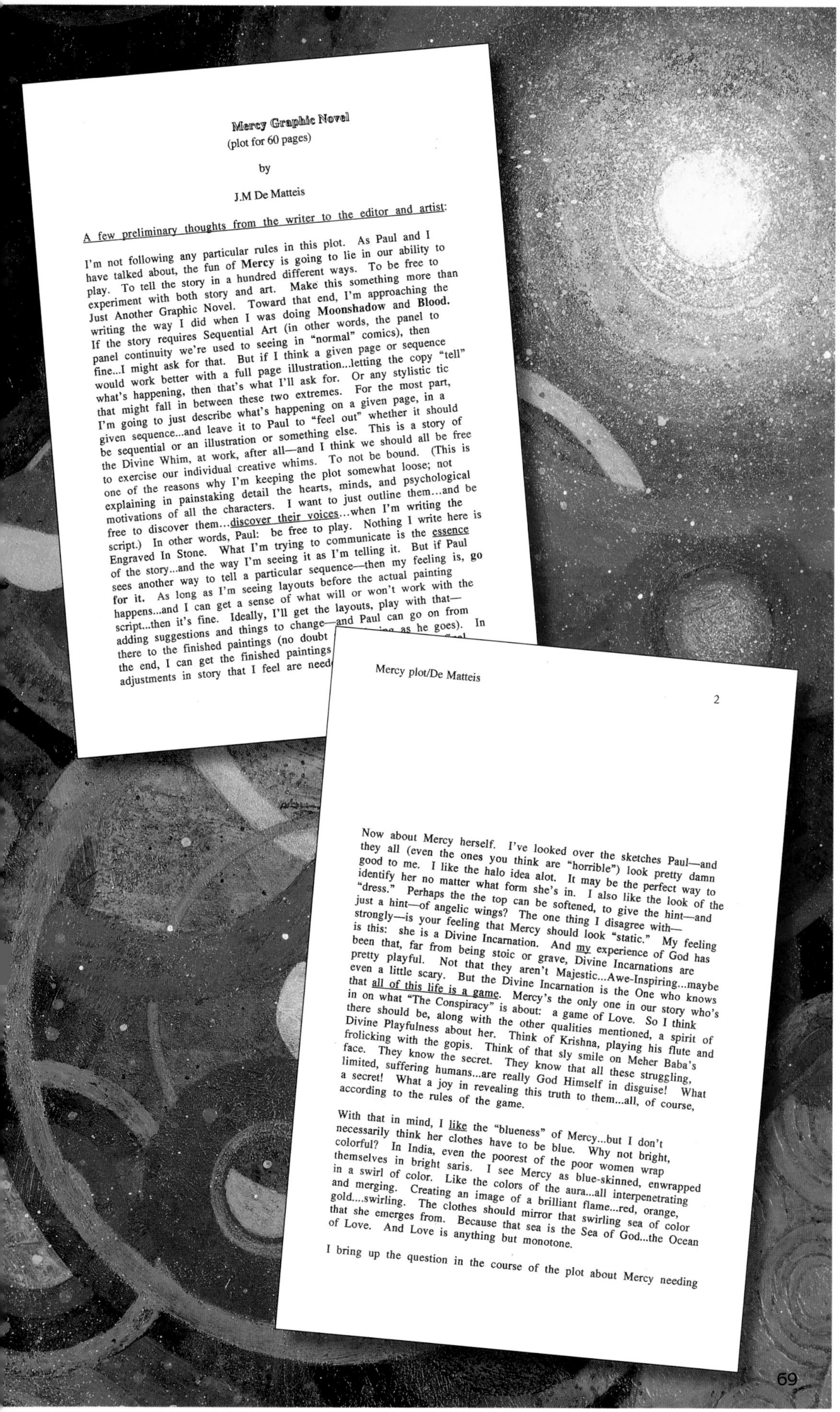

Mercy Graphic Novel
(plot for 60 pages)

by

J.M De Matteis

A few preliminary thoughts from the writer to the editor and artist:

I'm not following any particular rules in this plot. As Paul and I have talked about, the fun of **Mercy** is going to lie in our ability to play. To tell the story in a hundred different ways. To be free to experiment with both story and art. Make this something more than Just Another Graphic Novel. Toward that end, I'm approaching the writing the way I did when I was doing **Moonshadow** and **Blood.** If the story requires Sequential Art (in other words, the panel to panel continuity we're used to seeing in "normal" comics), then fine...I might ask for that. But if I think a given page or sequence would work better with a full page illustration...letting the copy "tell" what's happening, then that's what I'll ask for. Or any stylistic tic that might fall in between these two extremes. For the most part, I'm going to just describe what's happening on a given page, in a given sequence...and leave it to Paul to "feel out" whether it should be sequential or an illustration or something else. This is a story of the Divine Whim, at work, after all—and I think we should all be free to exercise our individual creative whims. To not be bound. (This is one of the reasons why I'm keeping the plot somewhat loose; not explaining in painstaking detail the hearts, minds, and psychological motivations of all the characters. I want to just outline them...and be free to discover them...<u>discover their voices</u>...when I'm writing the script.) In other words, Paul: be free to play. Nothing I write here is Engraved In Stone. What I'm trying to communicate is the <u>essence</u> of the story...and the way I'm seeing it as I'm telling it. But if Paul sees another way to tell a particular sequence—then my feeling is, go for it. As long as I'm seeing layouts before the actual painting happens...and I can get a sense of what will or won't work with the script...then it's fine. Ideally, I'll get the layouts, play with that— adding suggestions and things to change—and Paul can go on from there to the finished paintings (no doubt [   ] as he goes). In the end, I can get the finished paintings [   ] adjustments in story that I feel are need[   ]

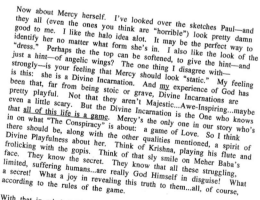

Mercy plot/De Matteis

2

Now about Mercy herself. I've looked over the sketches Paul—and they all (even the ones you think are "horrible") look pretty damn good to me. I like the halo idea alot. It may be the perfect way to identify her no matter what form she's in. I also like the look of the "dress." Perhaps the the top can be softened, to give the hint—and just a hint—of angelic wings? The one thing I disagree with— strongly—is your feeling that Mercy should look "static." My feeling is this: she is a Divine Incarnation. And <u>my</u> experience of God has been that, far from being stoic or grave, Divine Incarnations are pretty playful. Not that they aren't Majestic...Awe-Inspiring...maybe even a little scary. But the Divine Incarnation is the One who knows that <u>all of this life is a game</u>. Mercy's the only one in our story who's in on what "The Conspiracy" is about: a game of Love. So I think there should be, along with the other qualities mentioned, a spirit of Divine Playfulness about her. Think of Krishna, playing his flute and frolicking with the gopis. Think of that sly smile on Meher Baba's face. They know the secret. They know that all these struggling, limited, suffering humans...are really God Himself in disguise! What a secret! What a joy in revealing this truth to them...all, of course, according to the rules of the game.

With that in mind, I <u>like</u> the "blueness" of Mercy...but I don't necessarily think her clothes have to be blue. Why not bright, colorful? In India, even the poorest of the poor women wrap themselves in bright saris. I see Mercy as blue-skinned, enwrapped in a swirl of color. Like the colors of the aura...all interpenetrating and merging. Creating an image of a brilliant flame...red, orange, gold....swirling. The clothes should mirror that swirling sea of color that she emerges from. Because that sea is the Sea of God...the Ocean of Love. And Love is anything but monotone.

I bring up the question in the course of the plot about Mercy needing

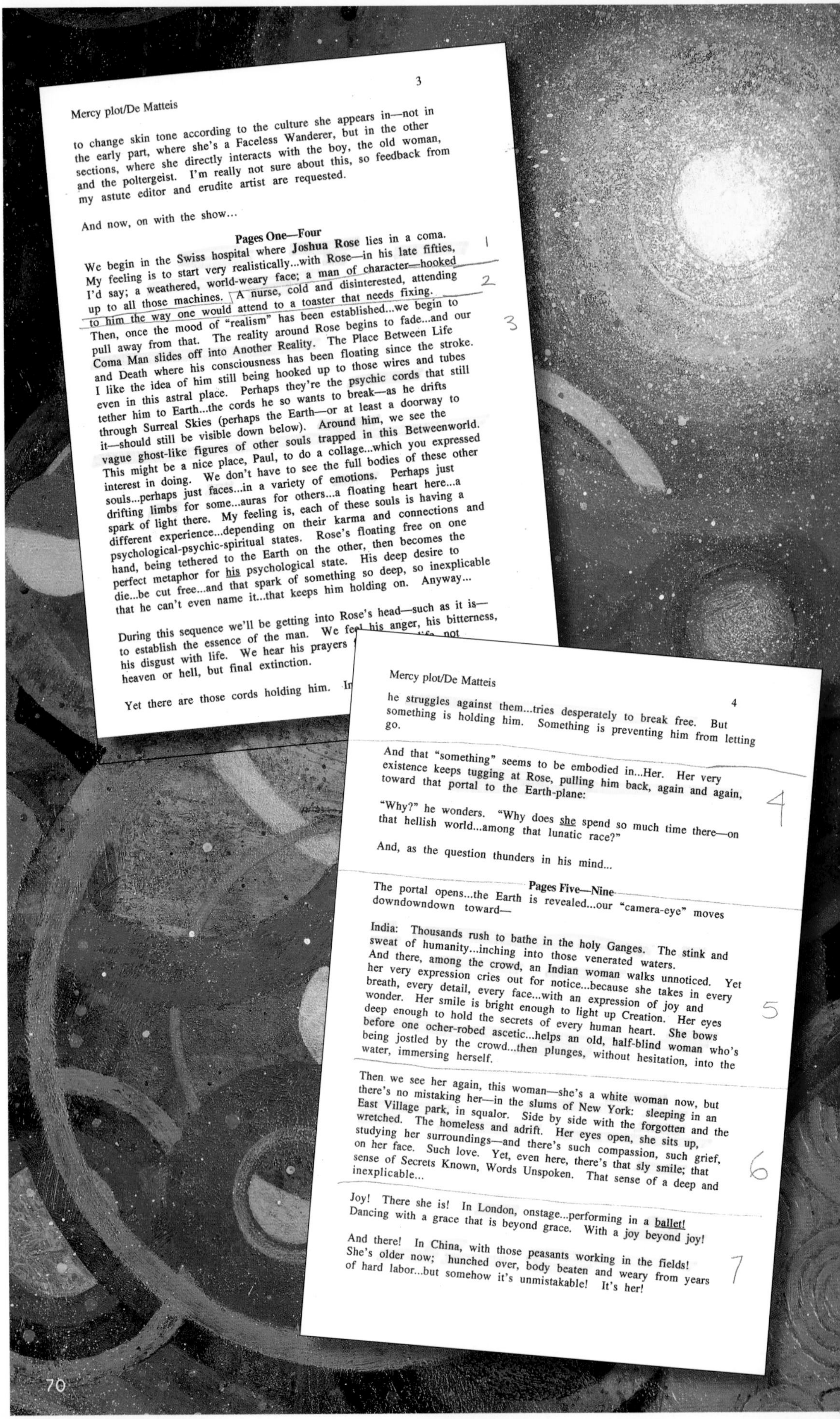

Mercy plot/De Matteis 3

to change skin tone according to the culture she appears in—not in the early part, where she's a Faceless Wanderer, but in the other sections, where she directly interacts with the boy, the old woman, and the poltergeist. I'm really not sure about this, so feedback from my astute editor and erudite artist are requested.

And now, on with the show...

Pages One—Four

We begin in the Swiss hospital where **Joshua Rose** lies in a coma. 1
My feeling is to start very realistically...with Rose—in his late fifties, I'd say; a weathered, world-weary face; a man of character—hooked up to all those machines. 2
A nurse, cold and disinterested, attending to him the way one would attend to a toaster that needs fixing.
Then, once the mood of "realism" has been established...we begin to pull away from that. The reality around Rose begins to fade...and our Coma Man slides off into Another Reality. The Place Between Life and Death where his consciousness has been floating since the stroke. 3
I like the idea of him still being hooked up to those wires and tubes even in this astral place. Perhaps they're the psychic cords that still tether him to Earth...the cords he so wants to break—as he drifts through Surreal Skies (perhaps the Earth—or at least a doorway to it—should still be visible down below). Around him, we see the vague ghost-like figures of other souls trapped in this Betweenworld. This might be a nice place, Paul, to do a collage...which you expressed interest in doing. We don't have to see the full bodies of these other souls...perhaps just faces...in a variety of emotions. Perhaps just drifting limbs for some...auras for others...a floating heart here...a spark of light there. My feeling is, each of these souls is having a different experience...depending on their karma and connections and psychological-psychic-spiritual states. Rose's floating free on one hand, being tethered to the Earth on the other, then becomes the perfect metaphor for his psychological state. His deep desire to die...be cut free...and that spark of something so deep, so inexplicable that he can't even name it...that keeps him holding on. Anyway...

During this sequence we'll be getting into Rose's head—such as it is—to establish the essence of the man. We feel his anger, his bitterness, his disgust with life. We hear his prayers ... life, not heaven or hell, but final extinction.

Yet there are those cords holding him. In...

Mercy plot/De Matteis 4

he struggles against them...tries desperately to break free. But something is holding him. Something is preventing him from letting go.

And that "something" seems to be embodied in...Her. Her very existence keeps tugging at Rose, pulling him back, again and again, toward that portal to the Earth-plane: 4

"Why?" he wonders. "Why does she spend so much time there—on that hellish world...among that lunatic race?"

And, as the question thunders in his mind...

Pages Five—Nine

The portal opens...the Earth is revealed...our "camera-eye" moves downdowndown toward—

India: Thousands rush to bathe in the holy Ganges. The stink and sweat of humanity...inching into those venerated waters. And there, among the crowd, an Indian woman walks unnoticed. Yet her very expression cries out for notice...because she takes in every breath, every detail, every face...with an expression of joy and wonder. Her smile is bright enough to light up Creation. Her eyes deep enough to hold the secrets of every human heart. She bows before one ocher-robed ascetic...helps an old, half-blind woman who's being jostled by the crowd...then plunges, without hesitation, into the water, immersing herself. 5

Then we see her again, this woman—she's a white woman now, but there's no mistaking her—in the slums of New York: sleeping in an East Village park, in squalor. Side by side with the forgotten and the wretched. The homeless and adrift. Her eyes open, she sits up, studying her surroundings—and there's such compassion, such grief, on her face. Such love. Yet, even here, there's that sly smile; that sense of Secrets Known, Words Unspoken. That sense of a deep and inexplicable... 6

Joy! There she is! In London, onstage...performing in a ballet! Dancing with a grace that is beyond grace. With a joy beyond joy!

And there! In China, with those peasants working in the fields! She's older now; hunched over, body beaten and weary from years of hard labor...but somehow it's unmistakable! It's her! 7

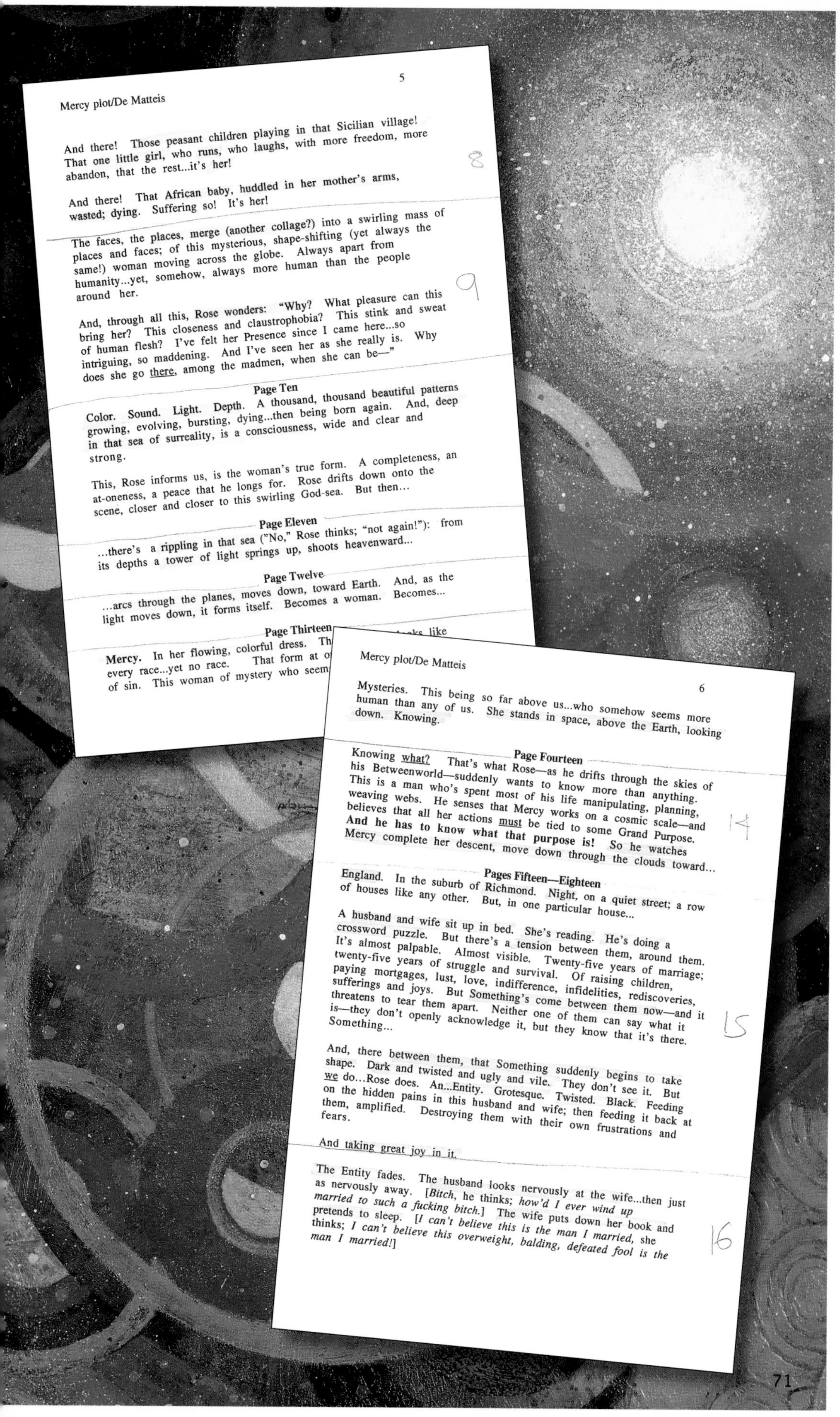

Mercy plot/De Matteis 5

And there! Those peasant children playing in that Sicilian village! That one little girl, who runs, who laughs, with more freedom, more abandon, that the rest...it's her! 8

And there! That African baby, huddled in her mother's arms, wasted; dying. Suffering so! It's her!

The faces, the places, merge (another collage?) into a swirling mass of places and faces; of this mysterious, shape-shifting (yet always the same!) woman moving across the globe. Always apart from humanity...yet, somehow, always more human than the people around her. 9

And, through all this, Rose wonders: "Why? What pleasure can this bring her? This closeness and claustrophobia? This stink and sweat of human flesh? I've felt her Presence since I came here...so intriguing, so maddening. And I've seen her as she really is. Why does she go <u>there</u>, among the madmen, when she can be—"

Page Ten

Color. Sound. Light. Depth. A thousand, thousand beautiful patterns growing, evolving, bursting, dying...then being born again. And, deep in that sea of surreality, is a consciousness, wide and clear and strong.

This, Rose informs us, is the woman's true form. A completeness, an at-oneness, a peace that he longs for. Rose drifts down onto the scene, closer and closer to this swirling God-sea. But then...

Page Eleven

...there's a rippling in that sea ("No," Rose thinks; "not again!"): from its depths a tower of light springs up, shoots heavenward...

Page Twelve

...arcs through the planes, moves down, toward Earth. And, as the light moves down, it forms itself. Becomes a woman. Becomes...

Page Thirteen

Mercy. In her flowing, colorful dress. Th... looks like every race...yet no race. That form at o... of sin. This woman of mystery who seem...

Mercy plot/De Matteis 6

Mysteries. This being so far above us...who somehow seems more human than any of us. She stands in space, above the Earth, looking down. Knowing.

Page Fourteen

Knowing <u>what?</u> That's what Rose—as he drifts through the skies of his Betweenworld—suddenly wants to know more than anything. This is a man who's spent most of his life manipulating, planning, weaving webs. He senses that Mercy works on a cosmic scale—and believes that all her actions <u>must</u> be tied to some Grand Purpose. **And he has to know what that purpose is!** So he watches Mercy complete her descent, move down through the clouds toward... 14

Pages Fifteen—Eighteen

England. In the suburb of Richmond. Night, on a quiet street; a row of houses like any other. But, in one particular house...

A husband and wife sit up in bed. She's reading. He's doing a crossword puzzle. But there's a tension between them, around them. It's almost palpable. Almost visible. Twenty-five years of marriage; twenty-five years of struggle and survival. Of raising children, paying mortgages, lust, love, indifference, infidelities, rediscoveries, sufferings and joys. But Something's come between them now—and it threatens to tear them apart. Neither one of them can say what it is—they don't openly acknowledge it, but they know that it's there. Something... 15

And, there between them, that Something suddenly begins to take shape. Dark and twisted and ugly and vile. They don't see it. But <u>we</u> do...Rose does. An...Entity. Grotesque. Twisted. Black. Feeding on the hidden pains in this husband and wife; then feeding it back at them, amplified. Destroying them with their own frustrations and fears.

And taking great joy in it.

The Entity fades. The husband looks nervously at the wife...then just as nervously away. [*Bitch*, he thinks; *how'd I ever wind up married to such a fucking bitch.*] The wife puts down her book and pretends to sleep. [*I can't believe this is the man I married,* she thinks; *I can't believe this overweight, balding, defeated fool is the man I married!*] 16

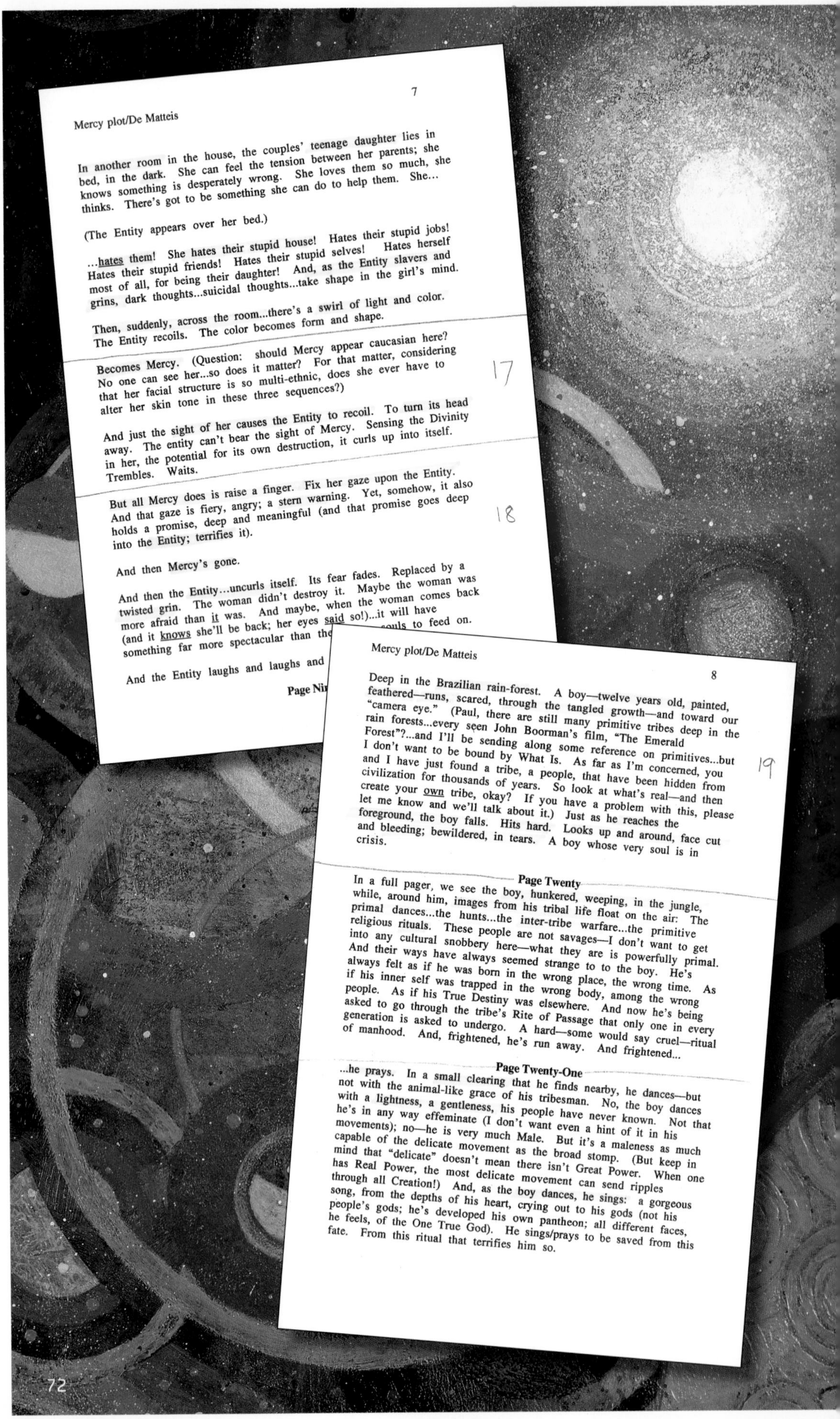

7

Mercy plot/De Matteis

In another room in the house, the couples' teenage daughter lies in bed, in the dark. She can feel the tension between her parents; she knows something is desperately wrong. She loves them so much, she thinks. There's got to be something she can do to help them. She...

(The Entity appears over her bed.)

...<u>hates</u> them! She hates their stupid house! Hates their stupid jobs! Hates their stupid friends! Hates their stupid selves! Hates herself most of all, for being their daughter! And, as the Entity slavers and grins, dark thoughts...suicidal thoughts...take shape in the girl's mind.

Then, suddenly, across the room...there's a swirl of light and color. The Entity recoils. The color becomes form and shape.

Becomes Mercy. (Question: should Mercy appear caucasian here? No one can see her...so does it matter? For that matter, considering that her facial structure is so multi-ethnic, does she ever have to alter her skin tone in these three sequences?) 17

And just the sight of her causes the Entity to recoil. To turn its head away. The entity can't bear the sight of Mercy. Sensing the Divinity in her, the potential for its own destruction, it curls up into itself. Trembles. Waits.

But all Mercy does is raise a finger. Fix her gaze upon the Entity. And that gaze is fiery, angry; a stern warning. Yet, somehow, it also holds a promise, deep and meaningful (and that promise goes deep into the Entity; terrifies it). 18

And then Mercy's gone.

And then the Entity...uncurls itself. Its fear fades. Replaced by a twisted grin. The woman didn't destroy it. Maybe the woman was more afraid than <u>it</u> was. And maybe, when the woman comes back (and it <u>knows</u> she'll be back; her eyes <u>said</u> so!)...it will have something far more spectacular than the [...] souls to feed on.

And the Entity laughs and laughs and [...]

Page Ni[...]

Mercy plot/De Matteis

8

Deep in the Brazilian rain-forest. A boy—twelve years old, painted, feathered—runs, scared, through the tangled growth—and toward our "camera eye." (Paul, there are still many primitive tribes deep in the rain forests...every sęen John Boorman's film, "The Emerald Forest"?...and I'll be sending along some reference on primitives...but I don't want to be bound by What Is. As far as I'm concerned, you and I have just found a tribe, a people, that have been hidden from civilization for thousands of years. So look at what's real—and then create your <u>own</u> tribe, okay? If you have a problem with this, please let me know and we'll talk about it.) Just as he reaches the foreground, the boy falls. Hits hard. Looks up and around, face cut and bleeding; bewildered, in tears. A boy whose very soul is in crisis. 19

Page Twenty

In a full pager, we see the boy, hunkered, weeping, in the jungle, while, around him, images from his tribal life float on the air: The primal dances...the hunts...the inter-tribe warfare...the primitive religious rituals. These people are not savages—I don't want to get into any cultural snobbery here—what they are is powerfully primal. And their ways have always seemed strange to to the boy. He's always felt as if he was born in the wrong place, the wrong time. As if his inner self was trapped in the wrong body, among the wrong people. As if his True Destiny was elsewhere. And now he's being asked to go through the tribe's Rite of Passage that only one in every generation is asked to undergo. A hard—some would say cruel—ritual of manhood. And, frightened, he's run away. And frightened...

Page Twenty-One

...he prays. In a small clearing that he finds nearby, he dances—but not with the animal-like grace of his tribesman. No, the boy dances with a lightness, a gentleness, his people have never known. Not that he's in any way effeminate (I don't want even a hint of it in his movements); no—he is very much Male. But it's a maleness as much capable of the delicate movement as the broad stomp. (But keep in mind that "delicate" doesn't mean there isn't Great Power. When one has Real Power, the most delicate movement can send ripples through all Creation!) And, as the boy dances, he sings: a gorgeous song, from the depths of his heart, crying out to his gods (not his people's gods; he's developed his own pantheon; all different faces, he feels, of the One True God). He sings/prays to be saved from this fate. From this ritual that terrifies him so.

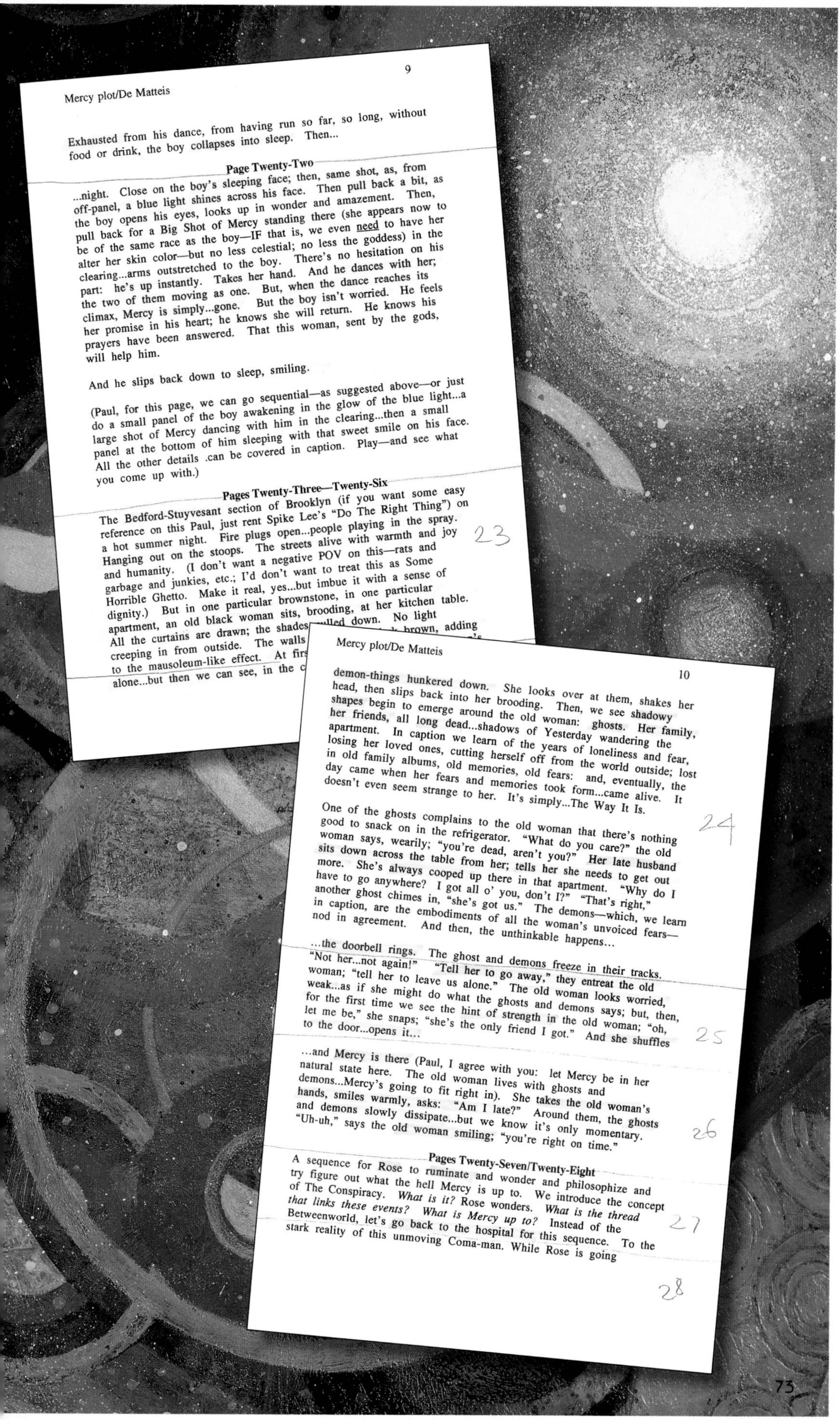

Mercy plot/De Matteis 9

Exhausted from his dance, from having run so far, so long, without food or drink, the boy collapses into sleep. Then...

Page Twenty-Two

...night. Close on the boy's sleeping face; then, same shot, as, from off-panel, a blue light shines across his face. Then pull back a bit, as the boy opens his eyes, looks up in wonder and amazement. Then, pull back for a Big Shot of Mercy standing there (she appears now to be of the same race as the boy—IF that is, we even <u>need</u> to have her alter her skin color—but no less celestial; no less the goddess) in the clearing...arms outstretched to the boy. There's no hesitation on his part: he's up instantly. Takes her hand. And he dances with her; the two of them moving as one. But, when the dance reaches its climax, Mercy is simply...gone. But the boy isn't worried. He feels her promise in his heart; he knows she will return. He knows his prayers have been answered. That this woman, sent by the gods, will help him.

And he slips back down to sleep, smiling.

(Paul, for this page, we can go sequential—as suggested above—or just do a small panel of the boy awakening in the glow of the blue light...a large shot of Mercy dancing with him in the clearing...then a small panel at the bottom of him sleeping with that sweet smile on his face. All the other details .can be covered in caption. Play—and see what you come up with.)

Pages Twenty-Three—Twenty-Six

The Bedford-Stuyvesant section of Brooklyn (if you want some easy reference on this Paul, just rent Spike Lee's "Do The Right Thing") on a hot summer night. Fire plugs open...people playing in the spray. 23
Hanging out on the stoops. The streets alive with warmth and joy and humanity. (I don't want a negative POV on this—rats and garbage and junkies, etc.; I'd don't want to treat this as Some Horrible Ghetto. Make it real, yes...but imbue it with a sense of dignity.) But in one particular brownstone, in one particular apartment, an old black woman sits, brooding, at her kitchen table. All the curtains are drawn; the shades pulled down. No light creeping in from outside. The walls ... brown, adding to the mausoleum-like effect. At firs... alone...but then we can see, in the c...

Mercy plot/De Matteis

10

demon-things hunkered down. She looks over at them, shakes her head, then slips back into her brooding. Then, we see shadowy shapes begin to emerge around the old woman: ghosts. Her family, her friends, all long dead...shadows of Yesterday wandering the apartment. In caption we learn of the years of loneliness and fear, losing her loved ones, cutting herself off from the world outside; lost in old family albums, old memories, old fears: and, eventually, the day came when her fears and memories took form...came alive. It doesn't even seem strange to her. It's simply...The Way It Is.

One of the ghosts complains to the old woman that there's nothing good to snack on in the refrigerator. "What do you care?" the old woman says, wearily; "you're dead, aren't you?" Her late husband sits down across the table from her; tells her she needs to get out more. She's always cooped up there in that apartment. "Why do I have to go anywhere? I got all o' you, don't I?" "That's right," another ghost chimes in, "she's got us." The demons—which, we learn in caption, are the embodiments of all the woman's unvoiced fears—nod in agreement. And then, the unthinkable happens... 24

...the doorbell rings. The ghost and demons freeze in their tracks. "Not her...not again!" "Tell her to go away," they entreat the old woman; "tell her to leave us alone." The old woman looks worried, weak...as if she might do what the ghosts and demons says; but, then, for the first time we see the hint of strength in the old woman; "oh, let me be," she snaps; "she's the only friend I got." And she shuffles to the door...opens it... 25

...and Mercy is there (Paul, I agree with you: let Mercy be in her natural state here. The old woman lives with ghosts and demons...Mercy's going to fit right in). She takes the old woman's hands, smiles warmly, asks: "Am I late?" Around them, the ghosts and demons slowly dissipate...but we know it's only momentary. "Uh-uh," says the old woman smiling; "you're right on time." 26

Pages Twenty-Seven/Twenty-Eight

A sequence for Rose to ruminate and wonder and philosophize and try figure out what the hell Mercy is up to. We introduce the concept of The Conspiracy. *What is it?* Rose wonders. *What is the thread that links these events? What is Mercy up to?* Instead of the Betweenworld, let's go back to the hospital for this sequence. To the stark reality of this unmoving Coma-man. While Rose is going 27

28

PAGE LAYOUTS

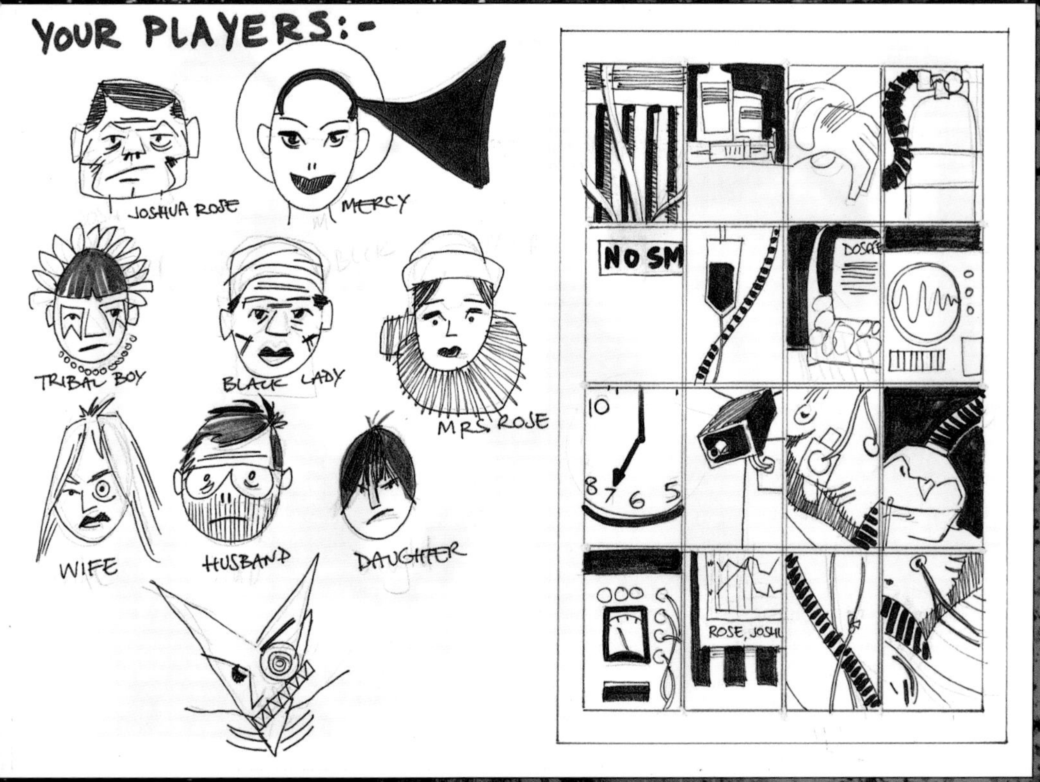
YOUR PLAYERS:-
JOSHUA ROSE
MERCY
TRIBAL BOY
BLACK LADY
MRS. ROSE
WIFE
HUSBAND
DAUGHTER

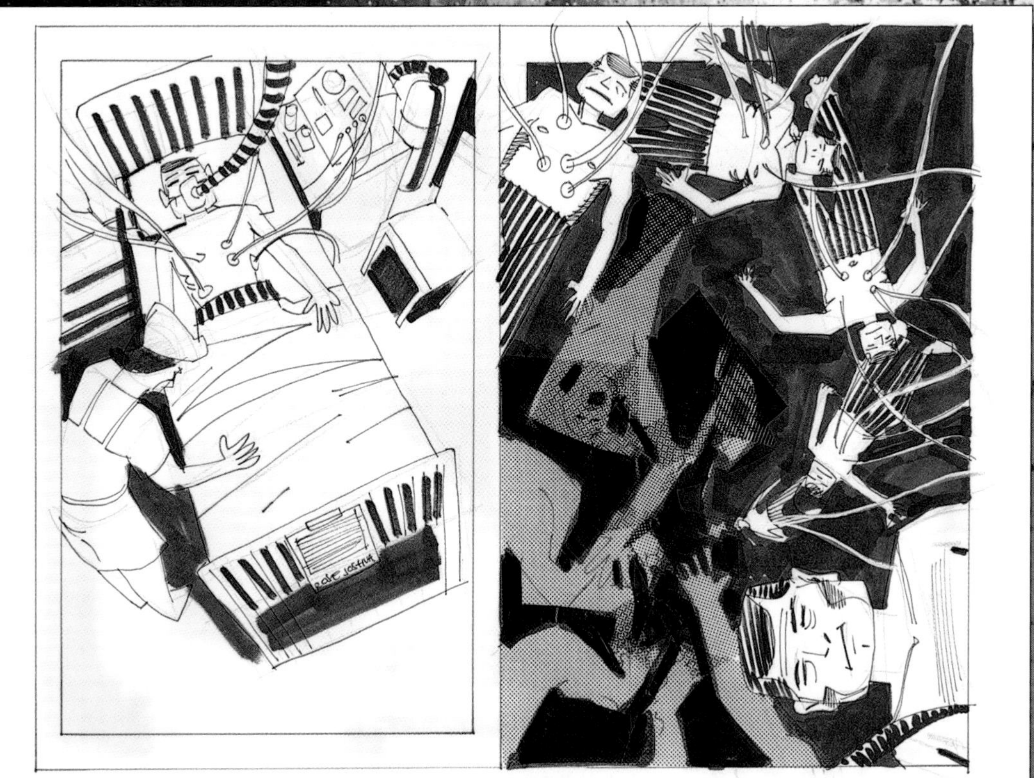

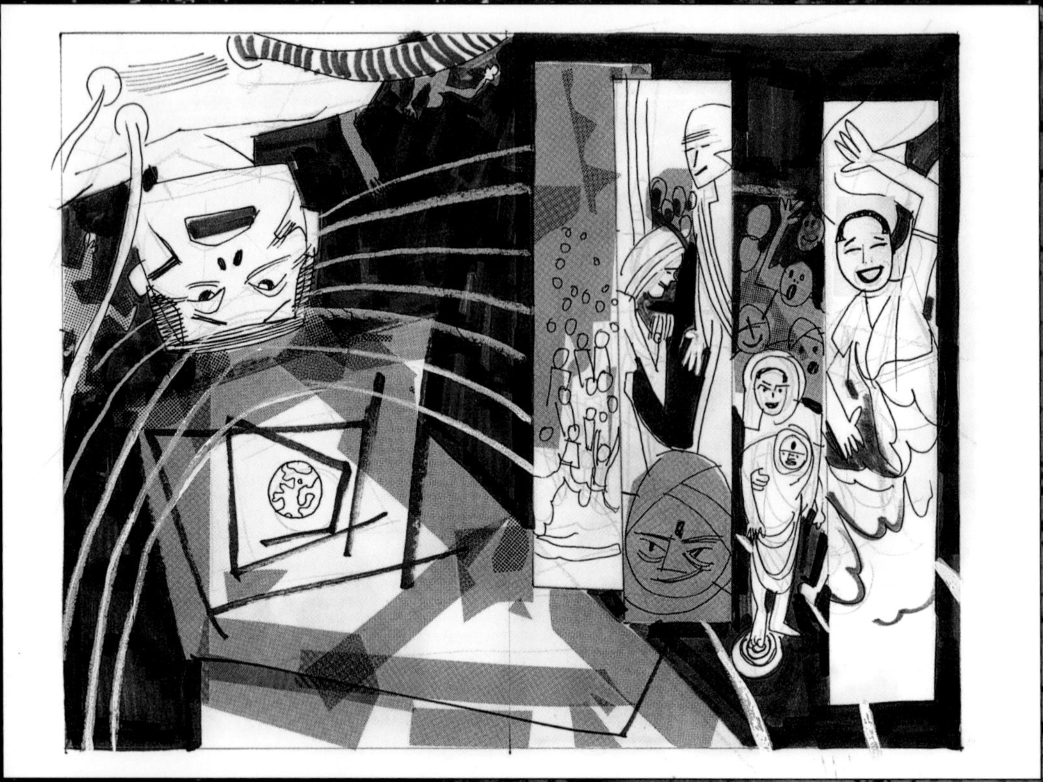

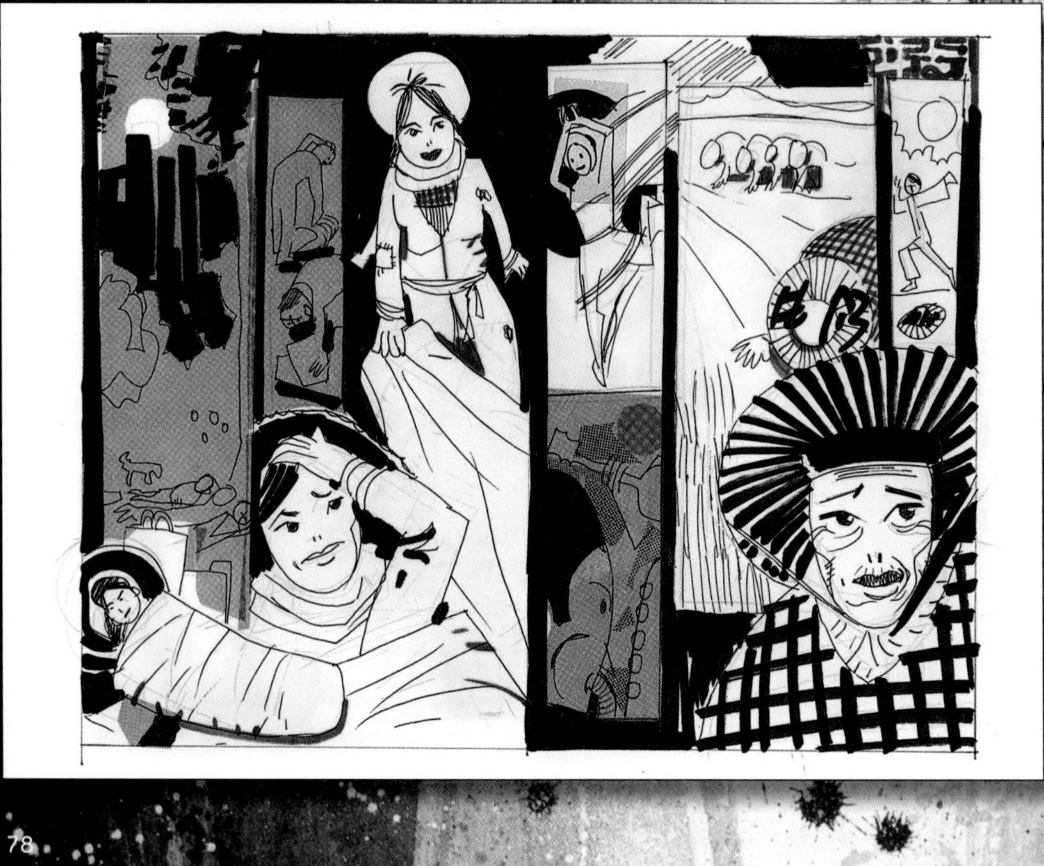

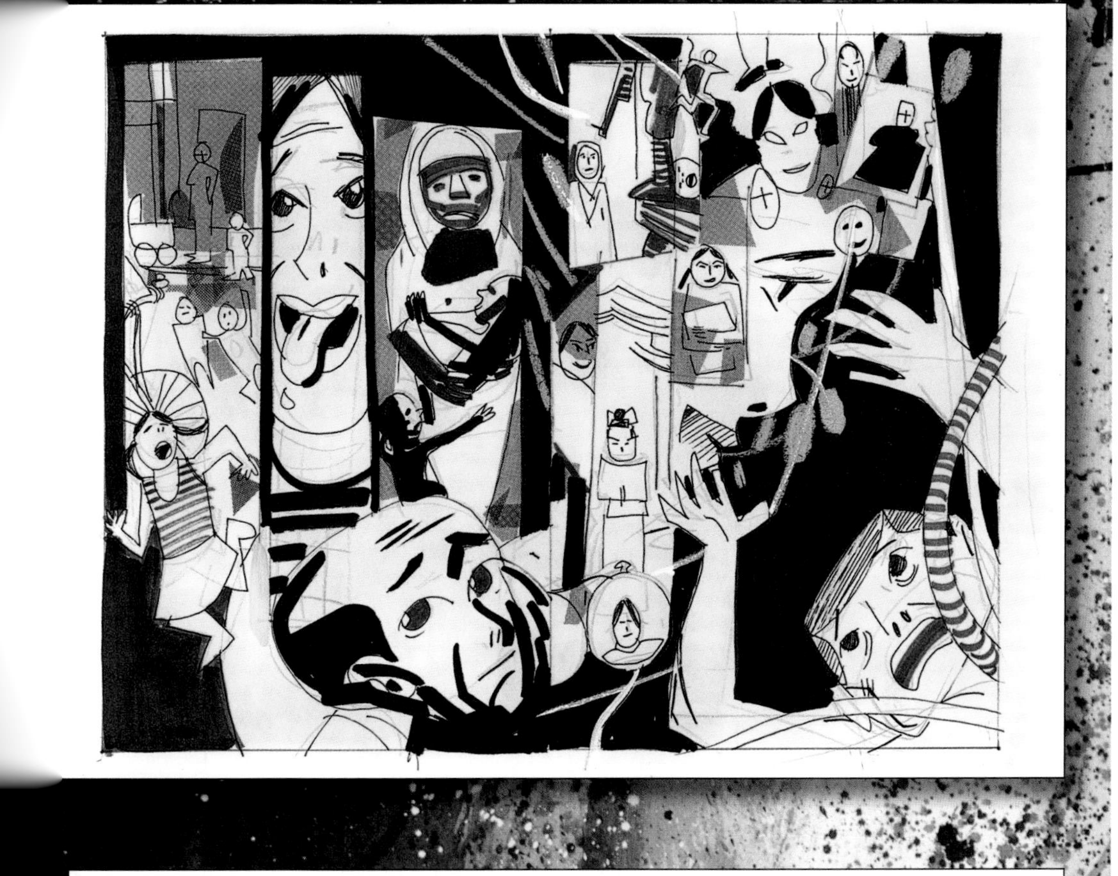

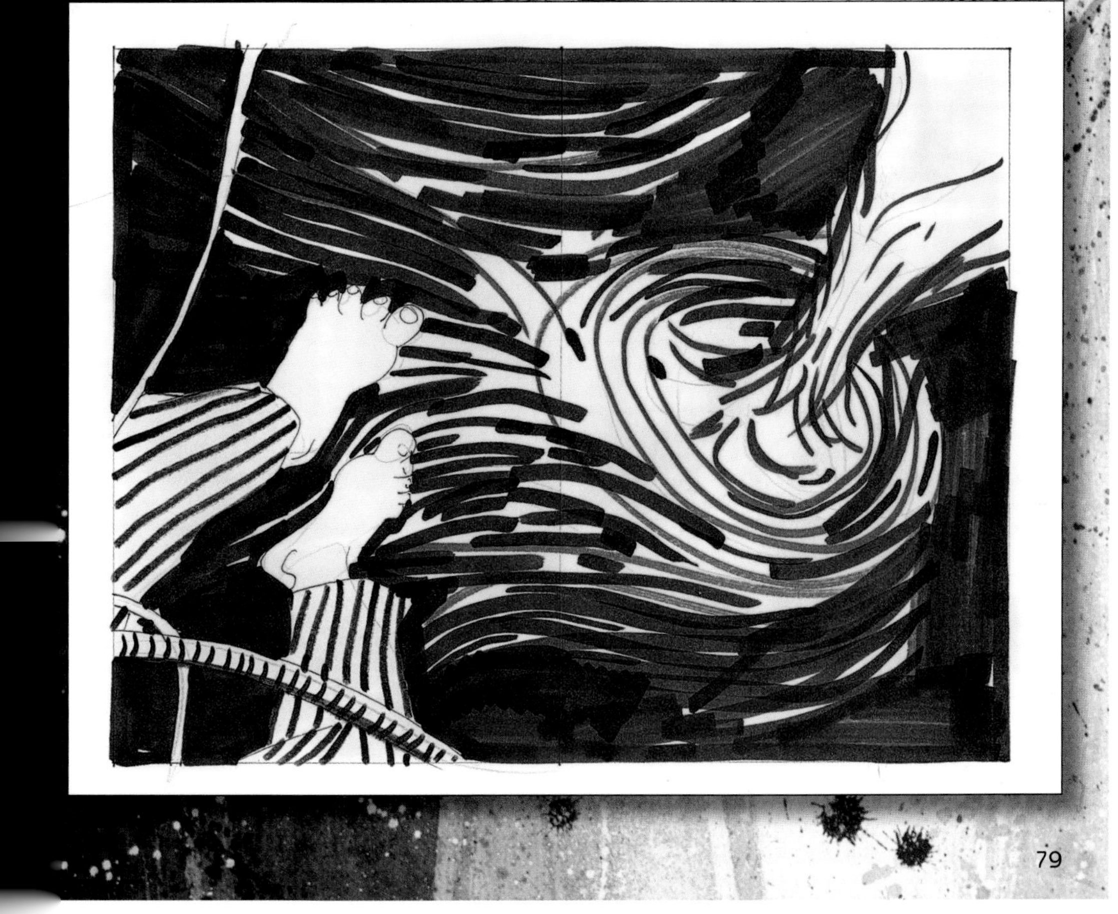

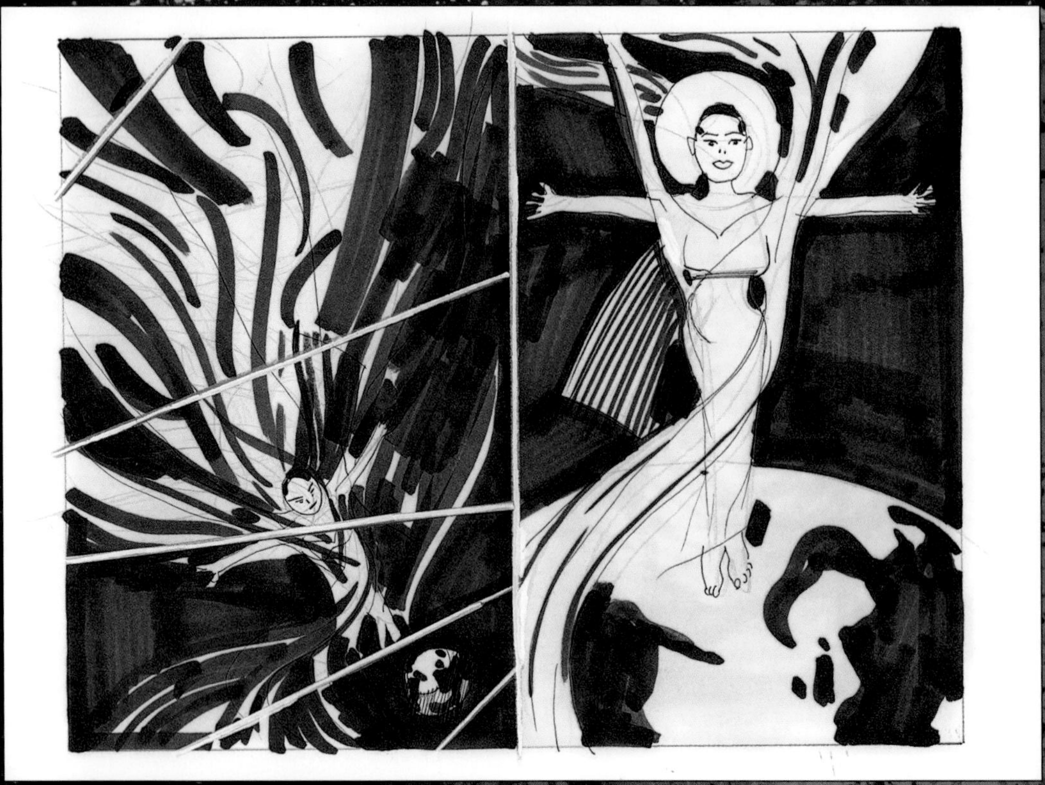

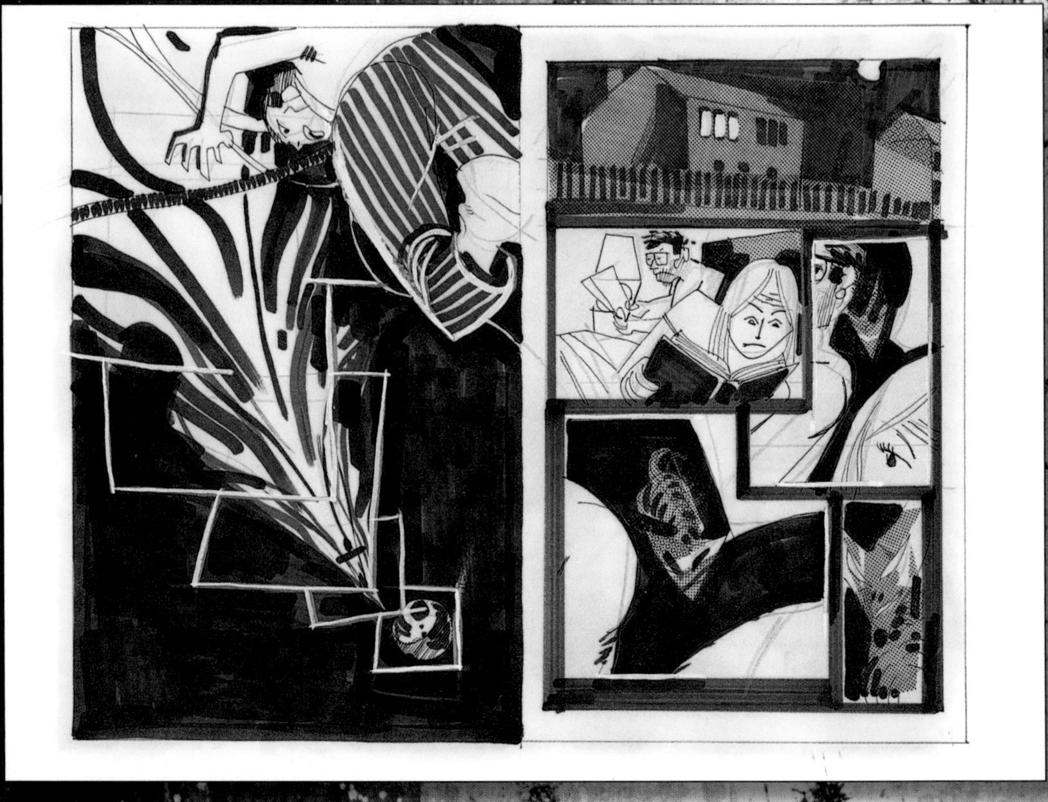

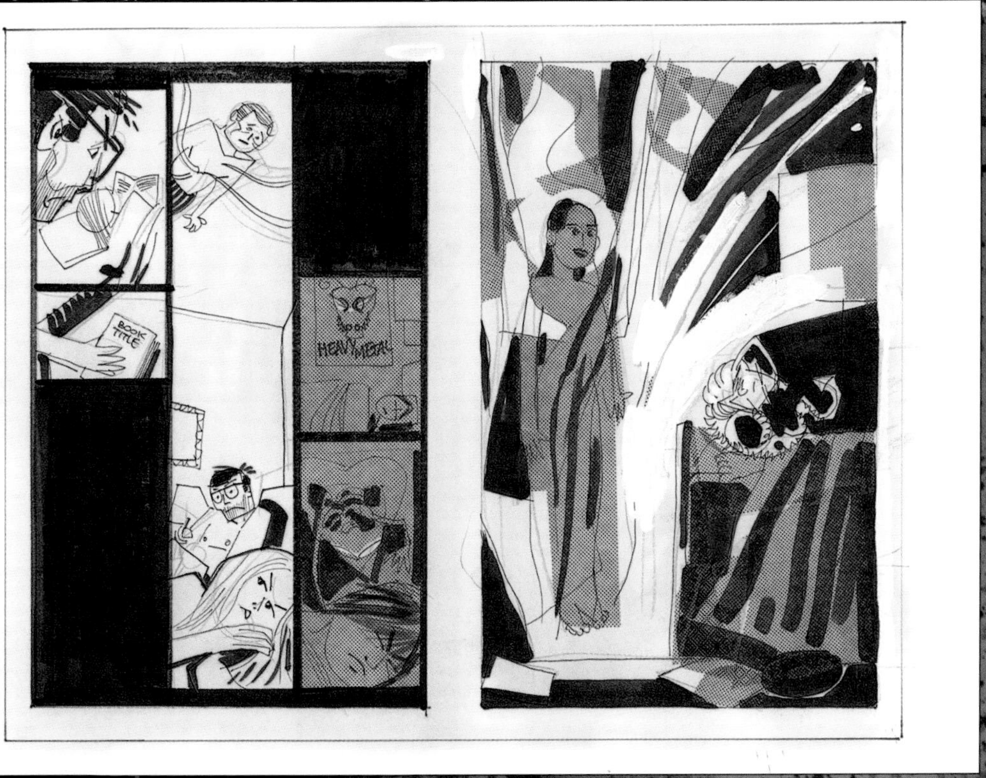
BOOK TITLE
HEAVY METAL

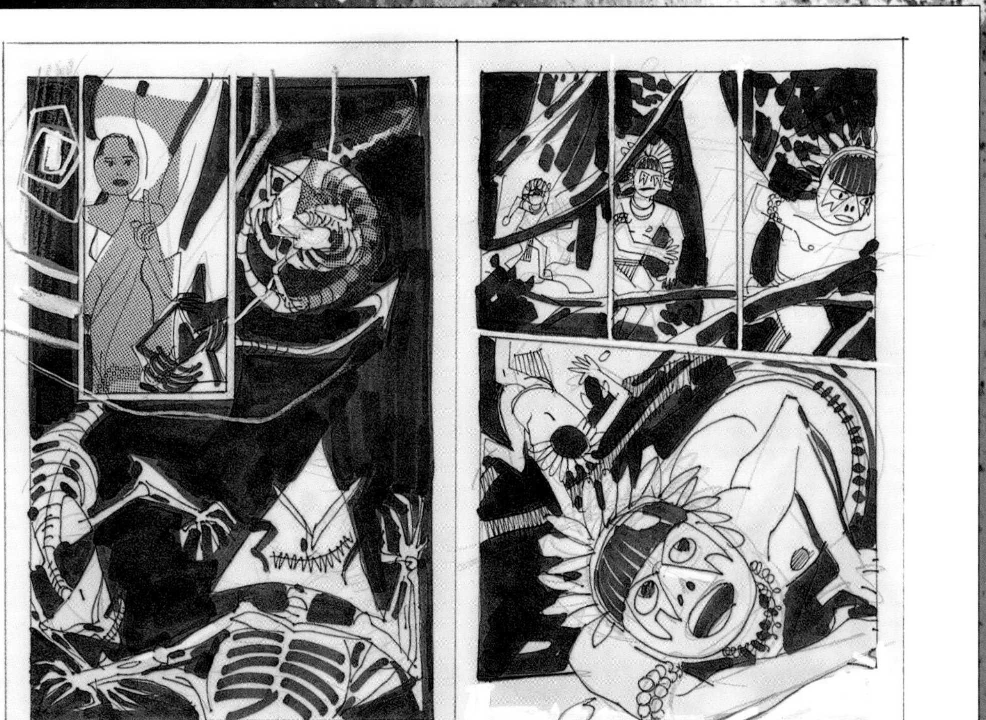

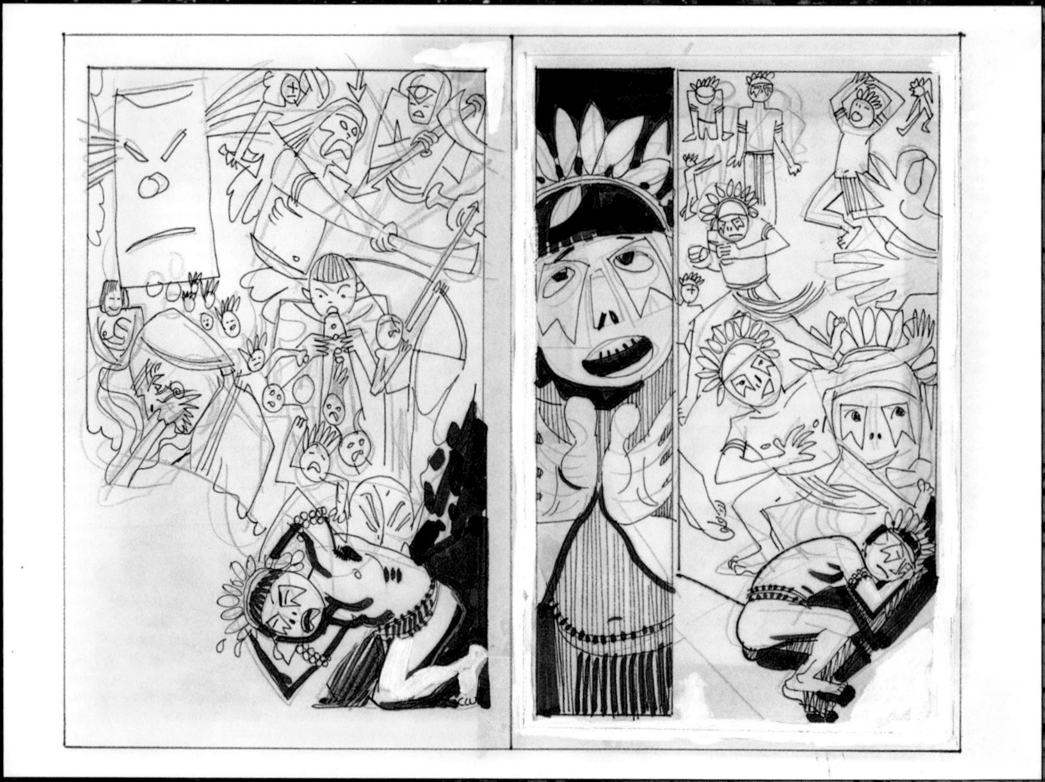

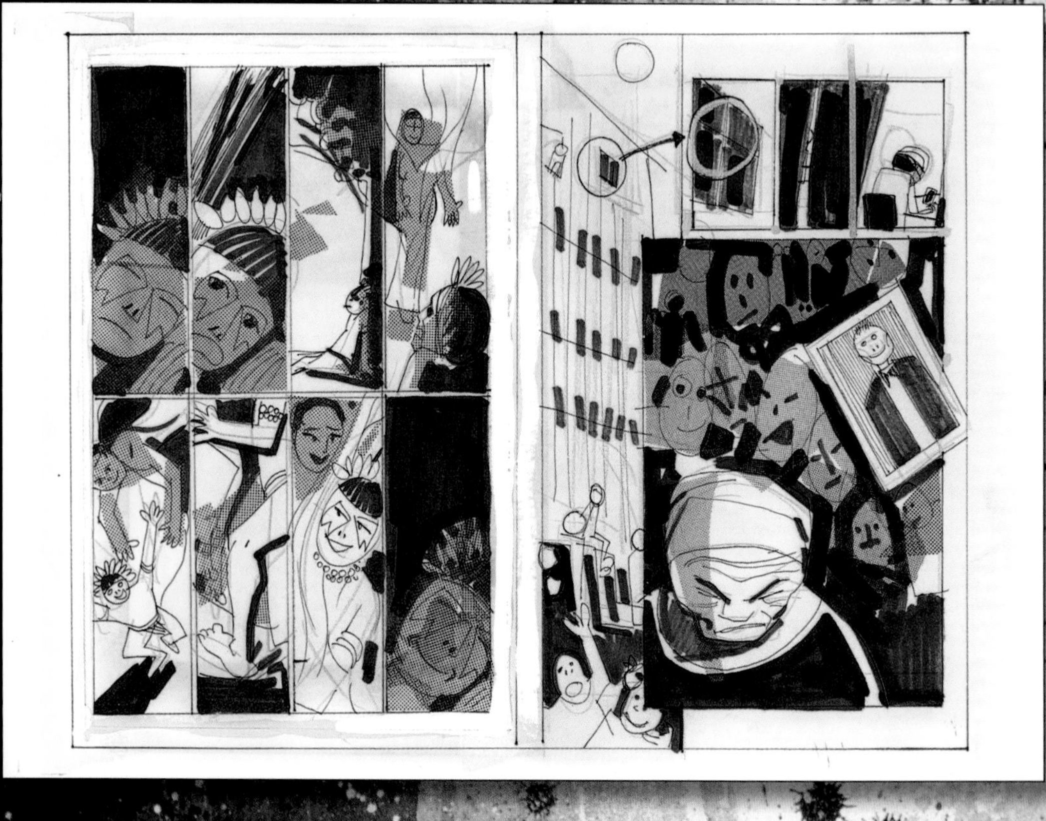

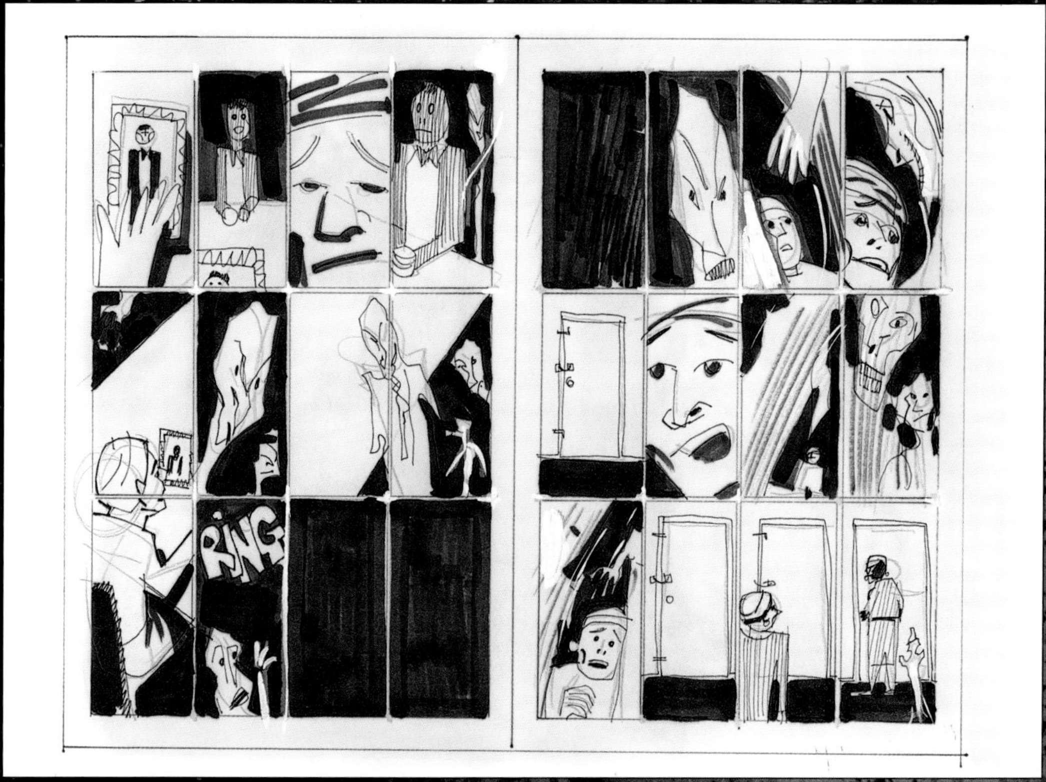
RING
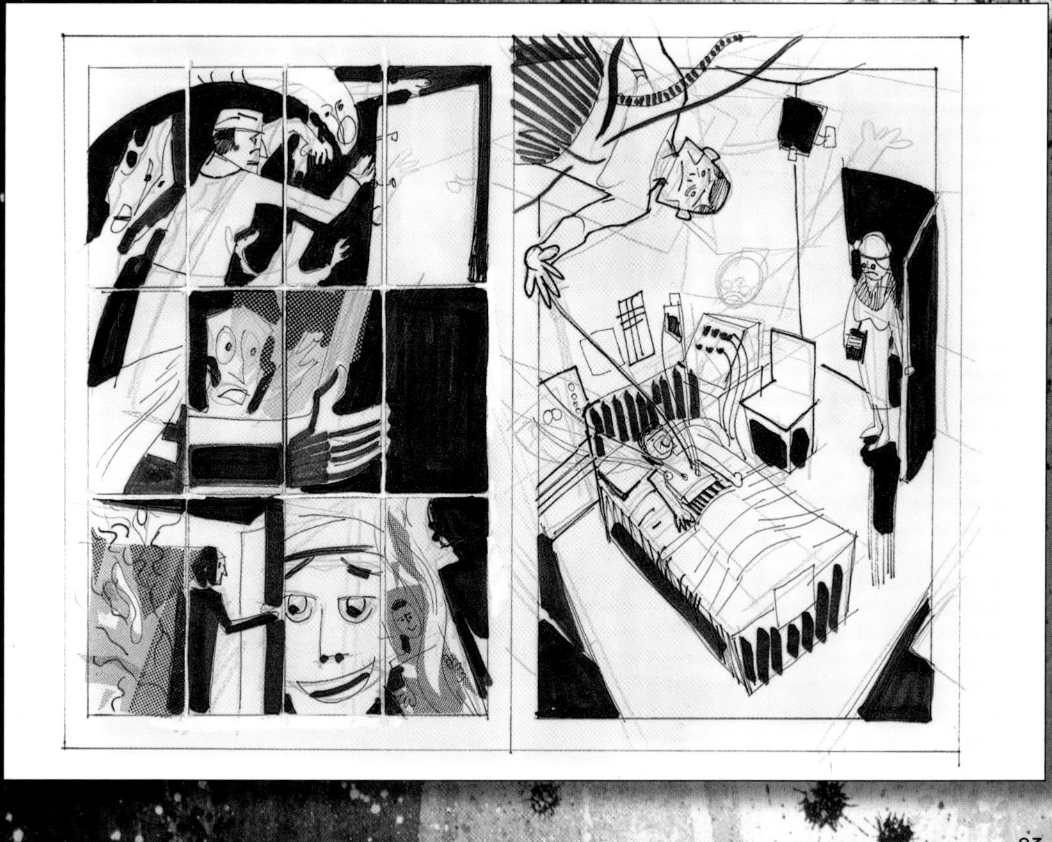

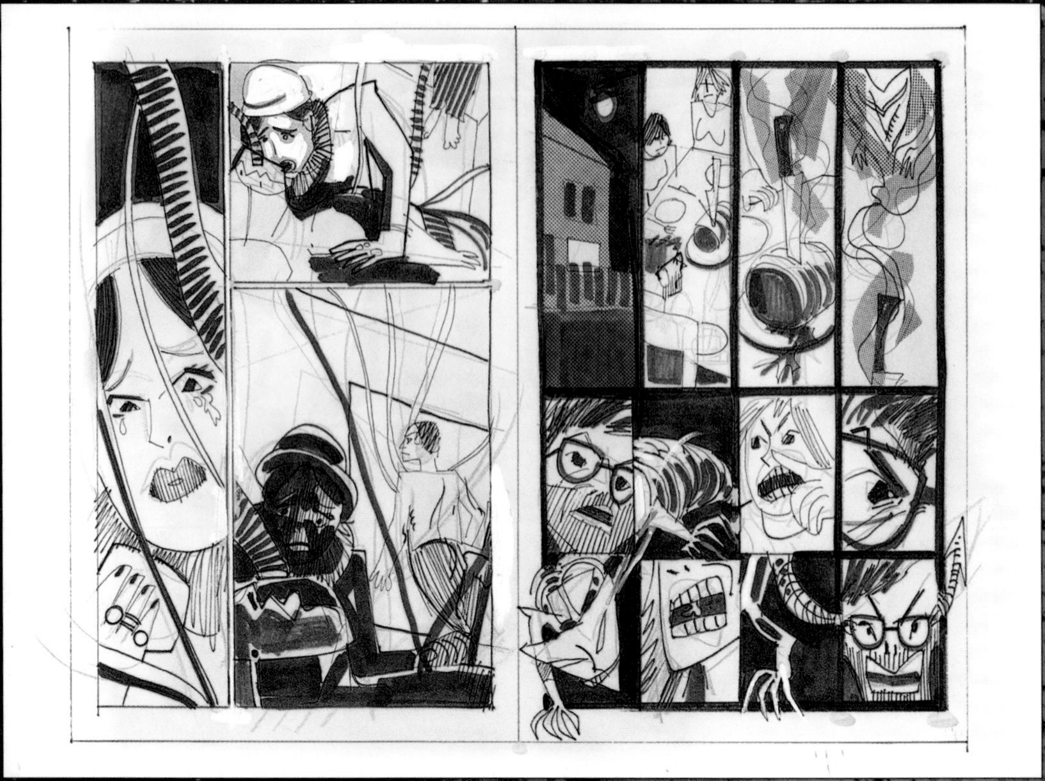

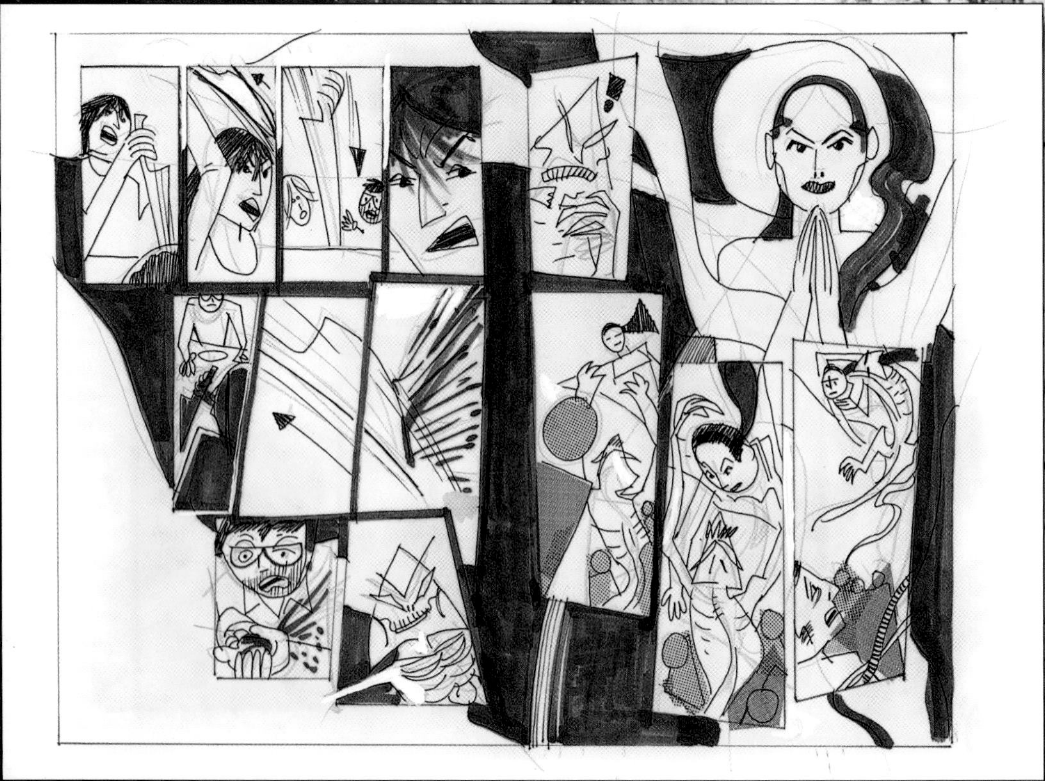

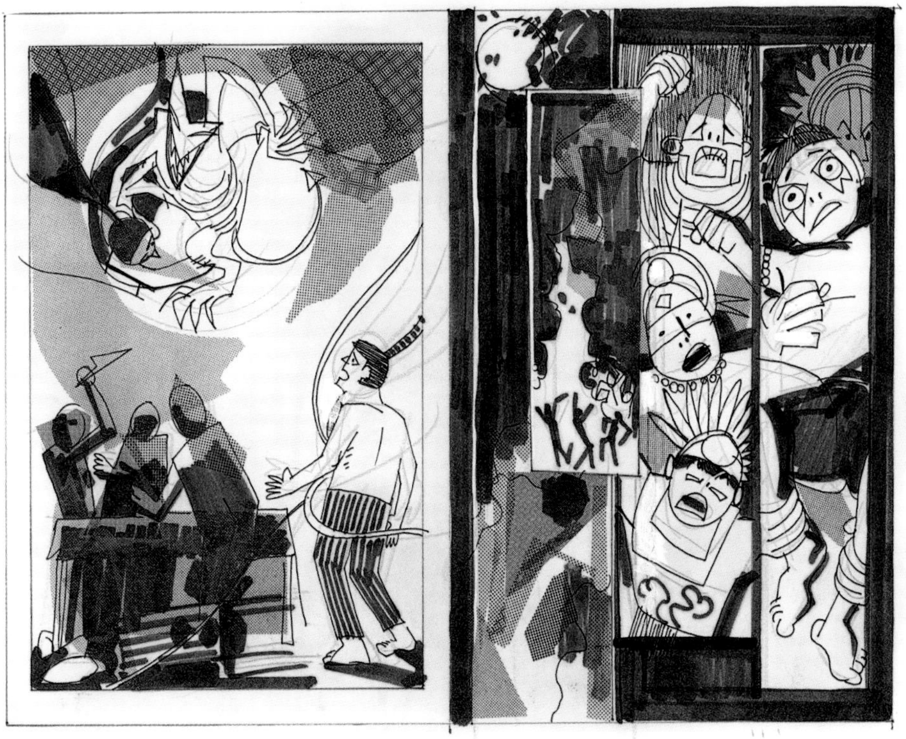

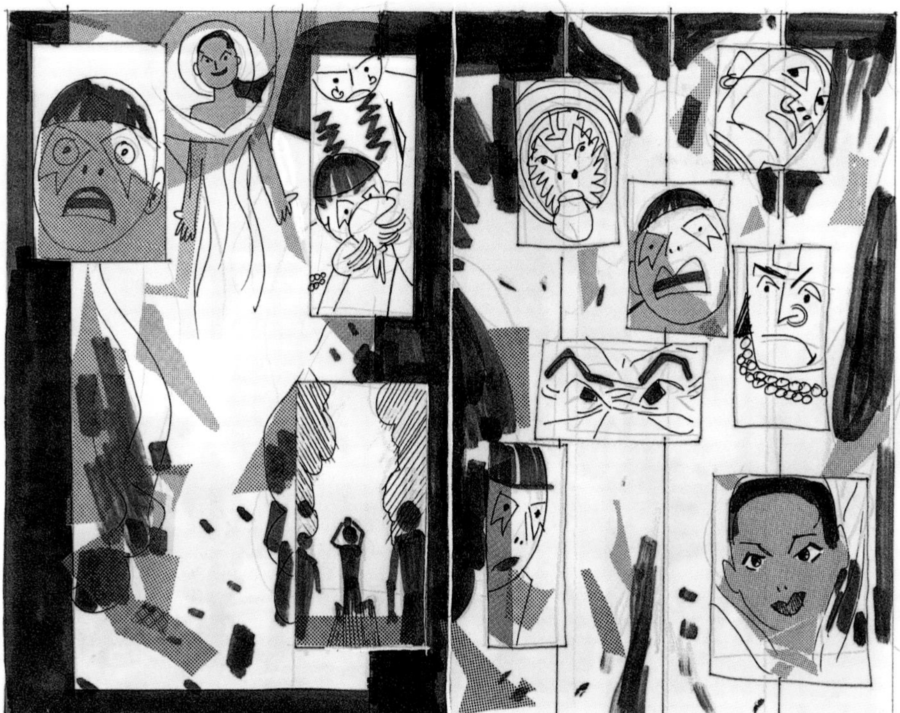

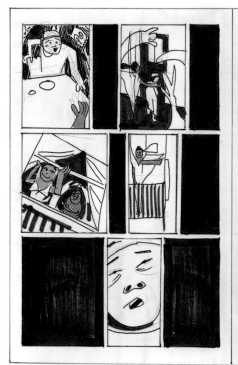
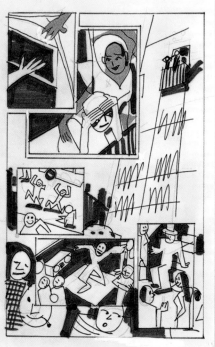

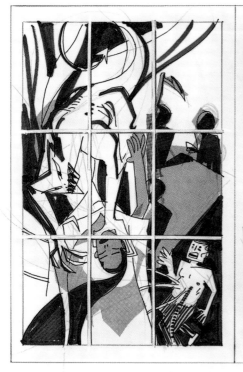
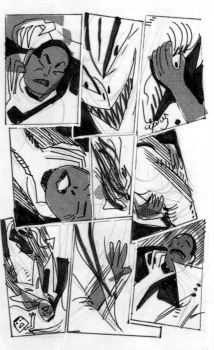

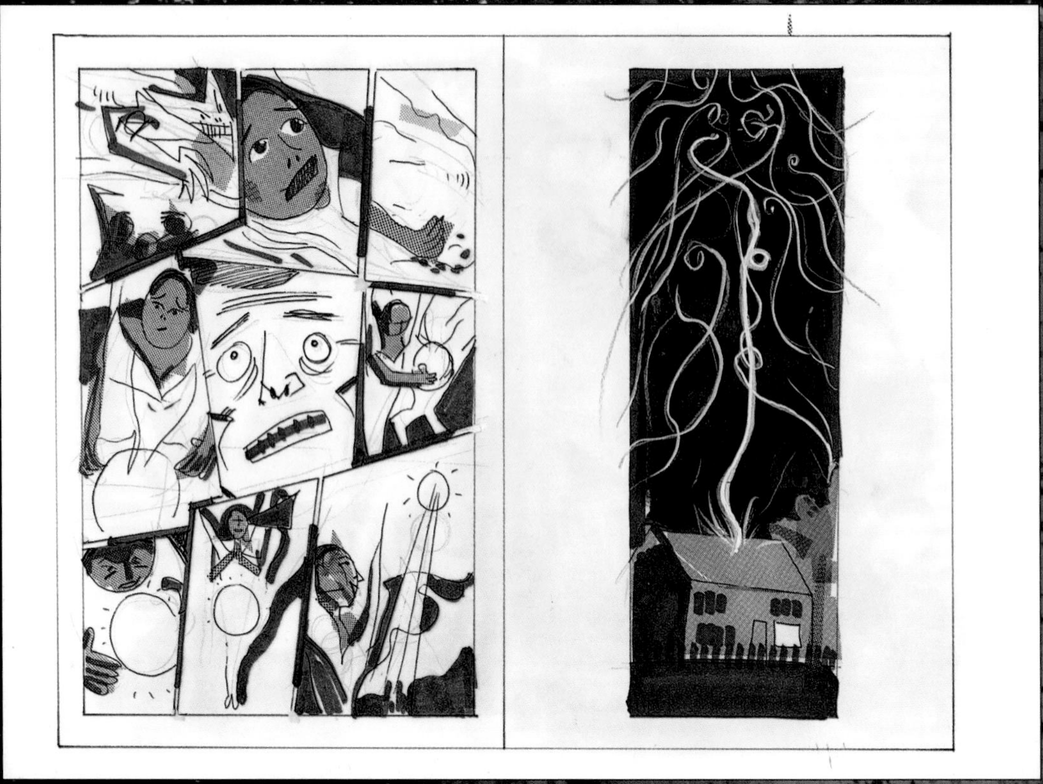

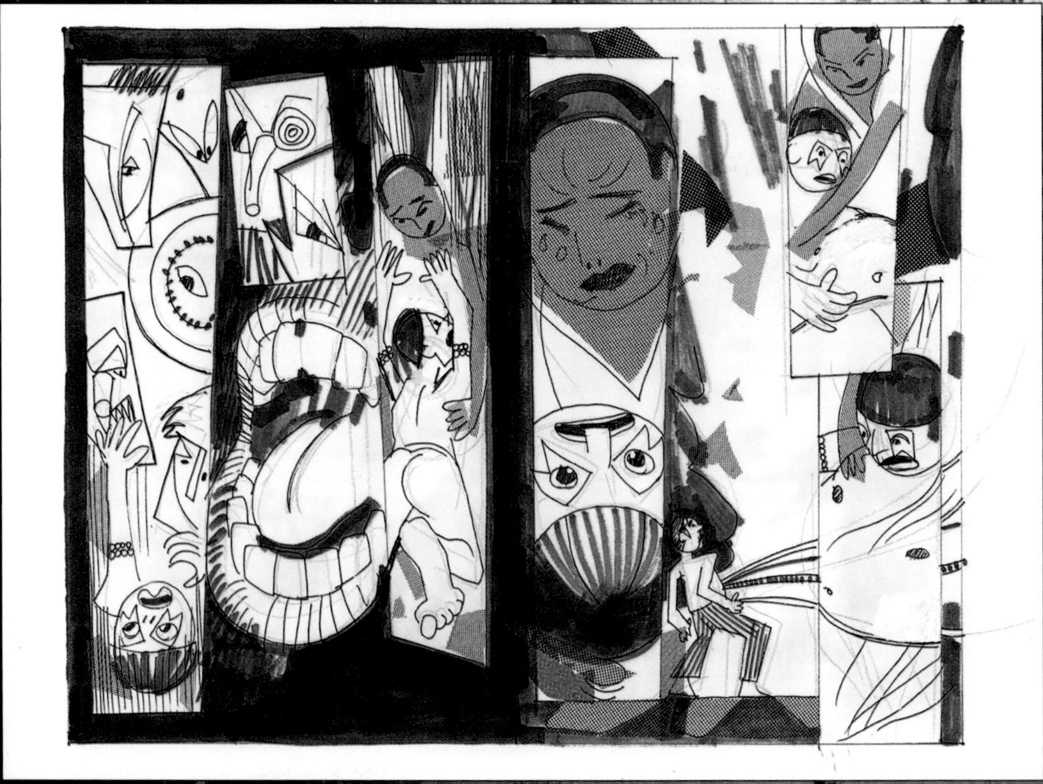

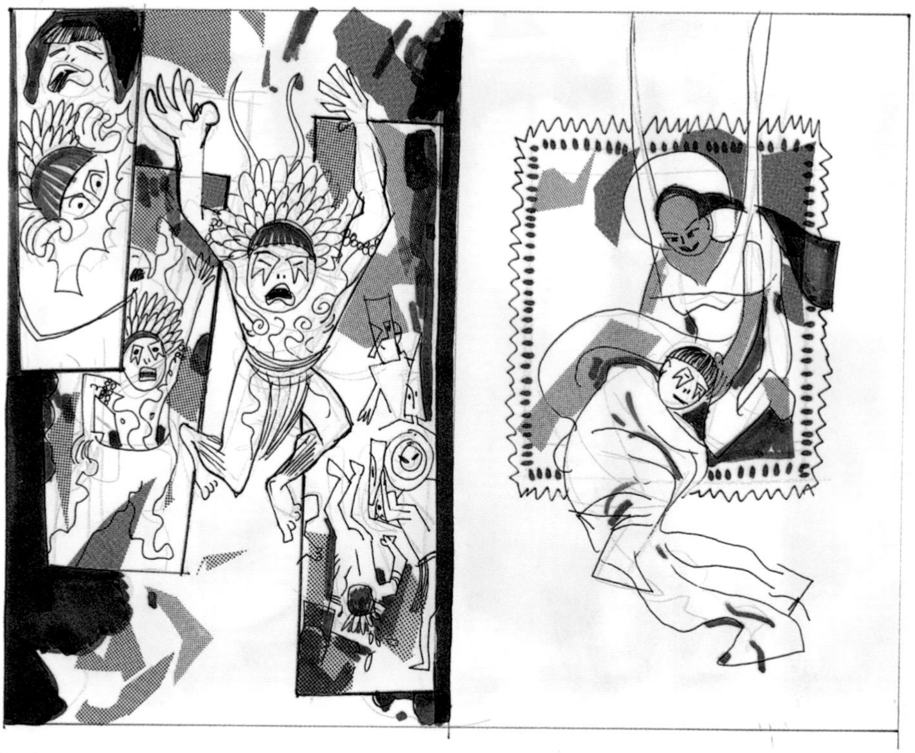

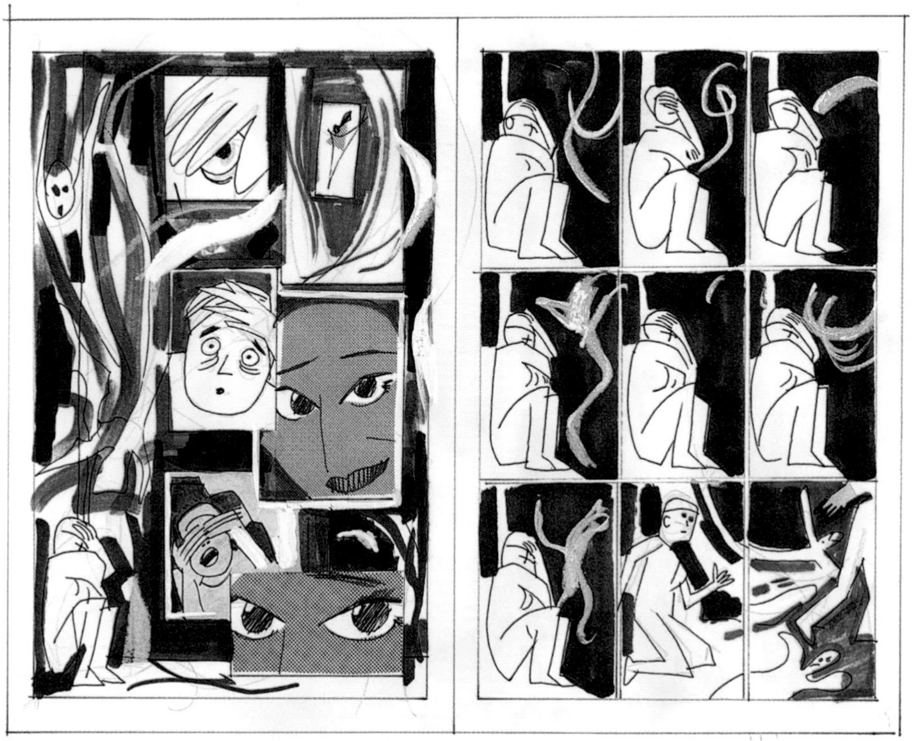

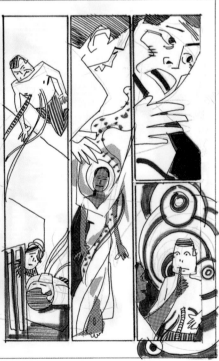

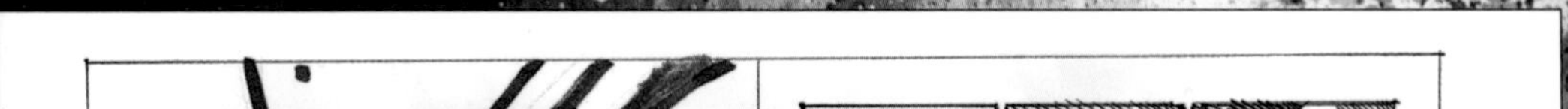

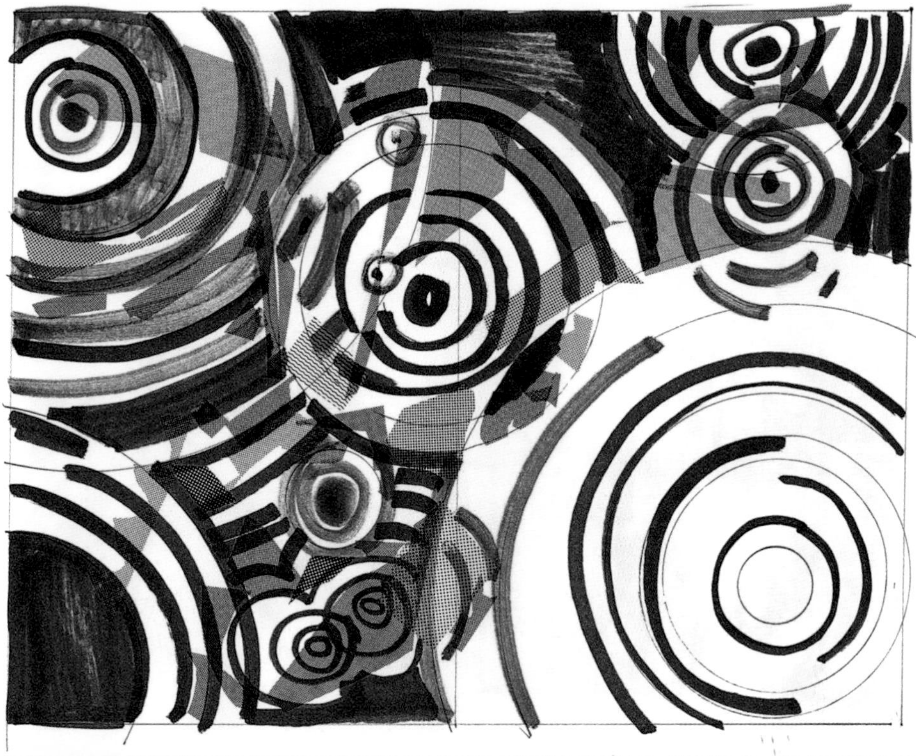

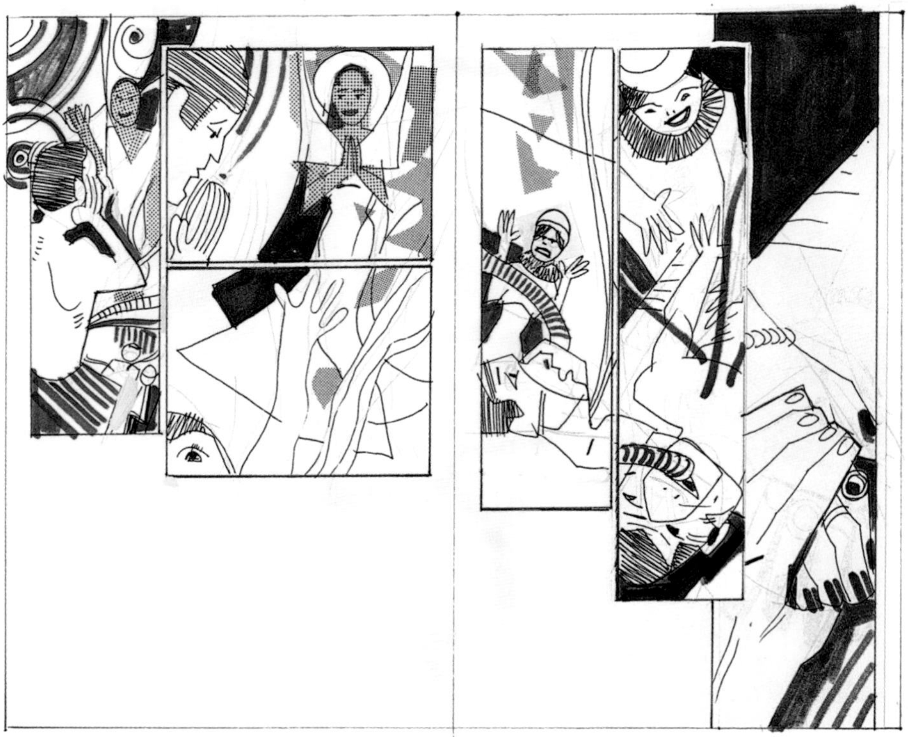

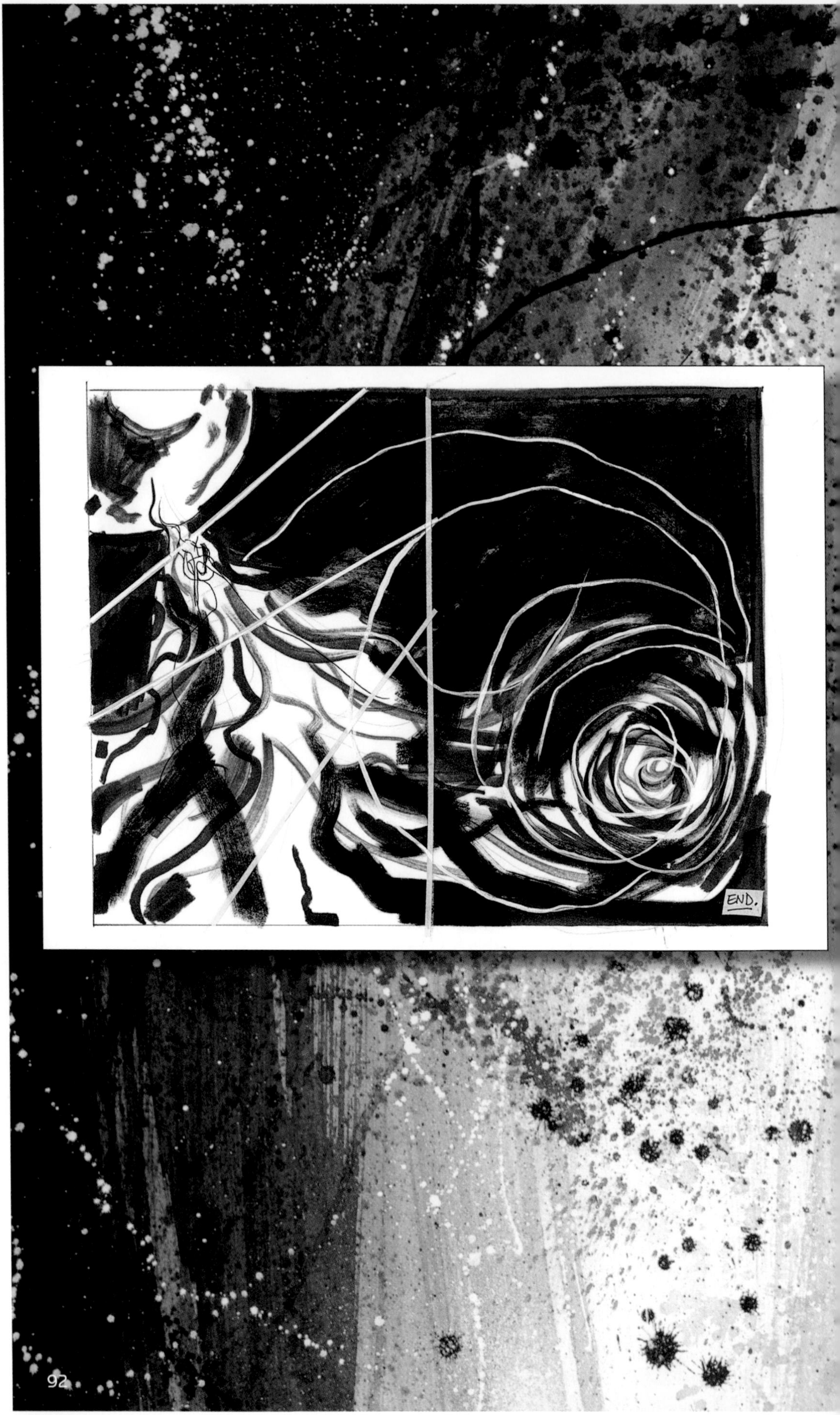
END.

PRODUCTION ART

Mercy: Shake The World

About the Art

The design for the Mercy character went through several stages. An initial idea was that Mercy would be like a universal flame, so we toyed with the idea of having her yellow and naked. I was concerned that that would make her too vague, so we looked at the idea of coloring her blue like the Hindu gods. We wanted to avoid anything that would make her identifiable as coming from one race, and the blue worked well with that idea.

When I got the script I read through it several times to understand the arc of the story and the pacing of individual sequences. I was then able to see how I could break the narrative up using different storytelling techniques—full-page illustrations, lots of panels on one page, double-page spreads, and collages.

Using different panel layouts enabled me to expand or collapse time to heighten the emotion of different parts of the story. Being able to focus the reader's attention is a key skill for a comic book artist.

As I was just working from a "shooting script" (rather than a script with completed dialogue) I had to make sure to leave enough space for Marc's prose, which would be written after the pages were completed.

I laid out the breakdowns (the storyboard) of the comic in as raw a manner as possible. At that point I wasn't really concerned about making things look pretty. It was just about getting to grips with how many panels there would be on a page, if they would be rigidly structured or jumbled, what viewpoint the reader would see the action from, where would the light source would be—that kind of thing. So I ended up with a dummy copy of the book that was only slightly smaller than the printed item would be. That was when the hard work started!

The artwork was produced larger than the printed page—about fifty percent larger. I would draw all the main aspects of the panel in a blue or red waterproof pen. I would then put in all the main tonal differences with a water-based ink. So a whole page might be blocked in with a purple or blue ink under-painting.

I liked using lots of texture, so at this point I might splatter ink on as well, or rough up the surface of the art board. Once that was dry, I could apply local color with a spirit-based marker, which wouldn't smudge the ink. After applying a fixative to seal the surface, I could work over the top with other media—acrylics, colored pencils or gouache—and apply any collage elements.

I liked working on things that were esoteric and spiritual at that time. I've always been interested in what lies between the world as we perceive it and what really exists. This edition carries some of my private art that has never been seen in print before, that draws upon the themes of angels and devils, hiding behind masks, and alchemy.

—PAUL JOHNSON

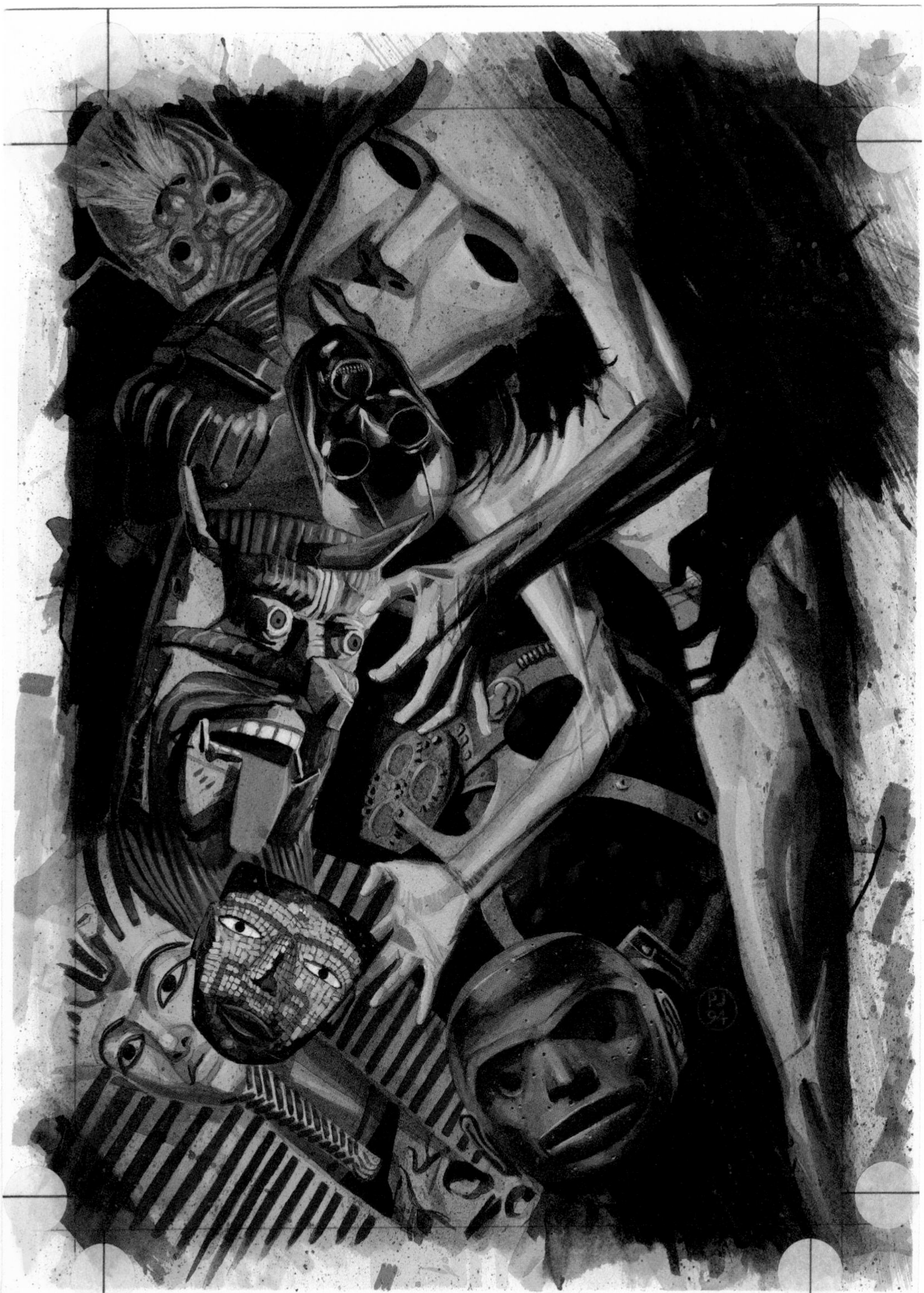

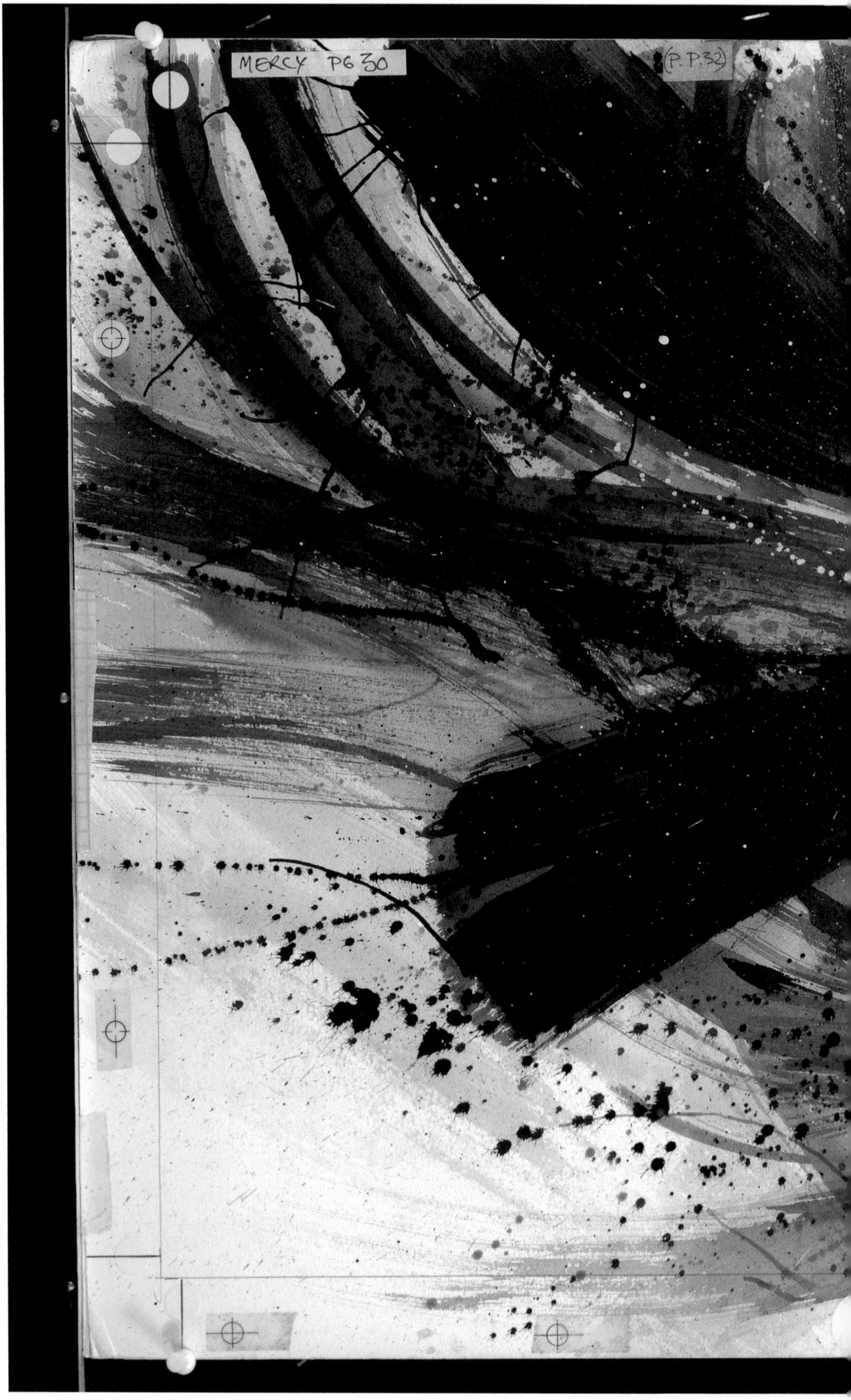
MERCY PG 30
(P.P.32)

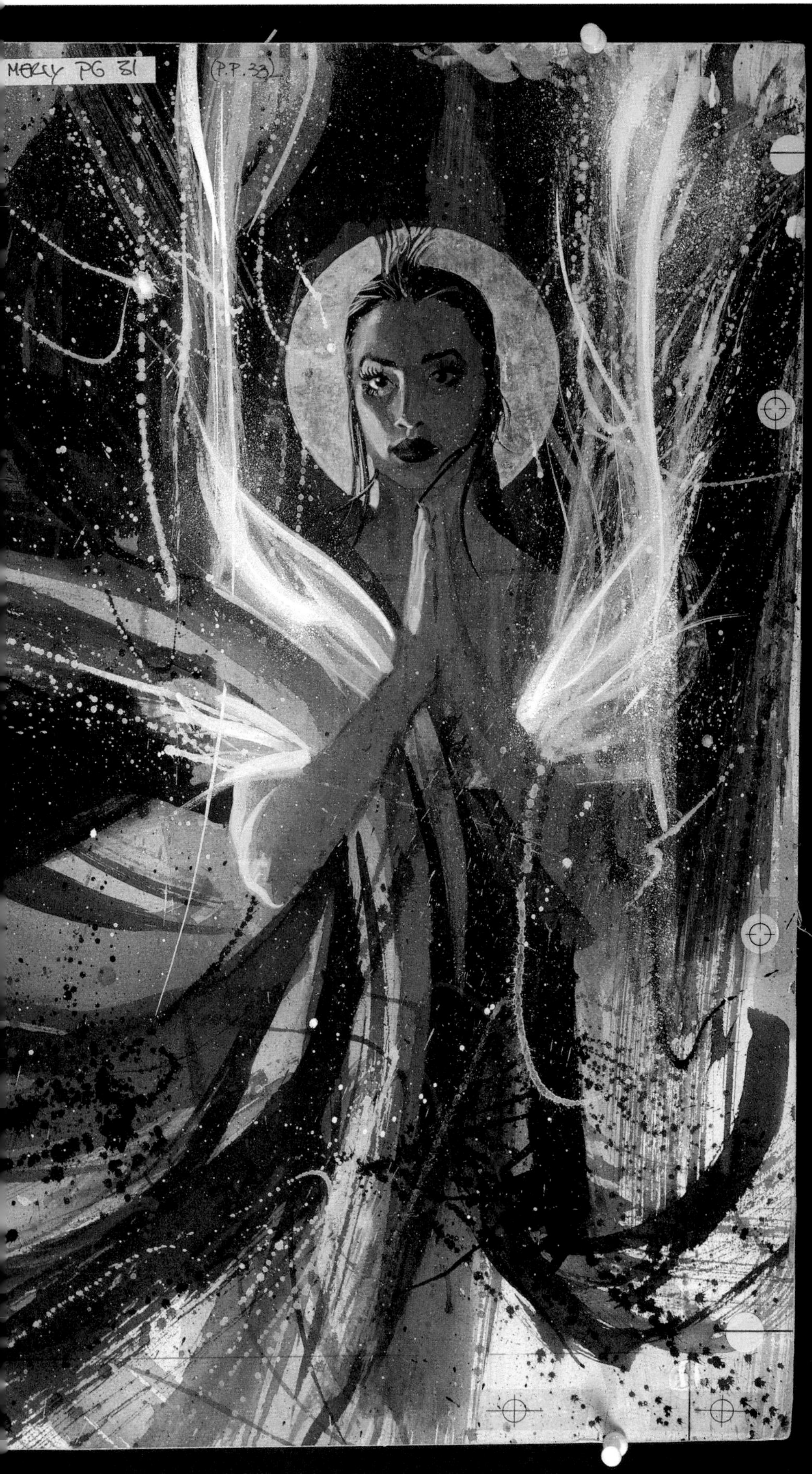
MERCY PG 31
(P.P.33)

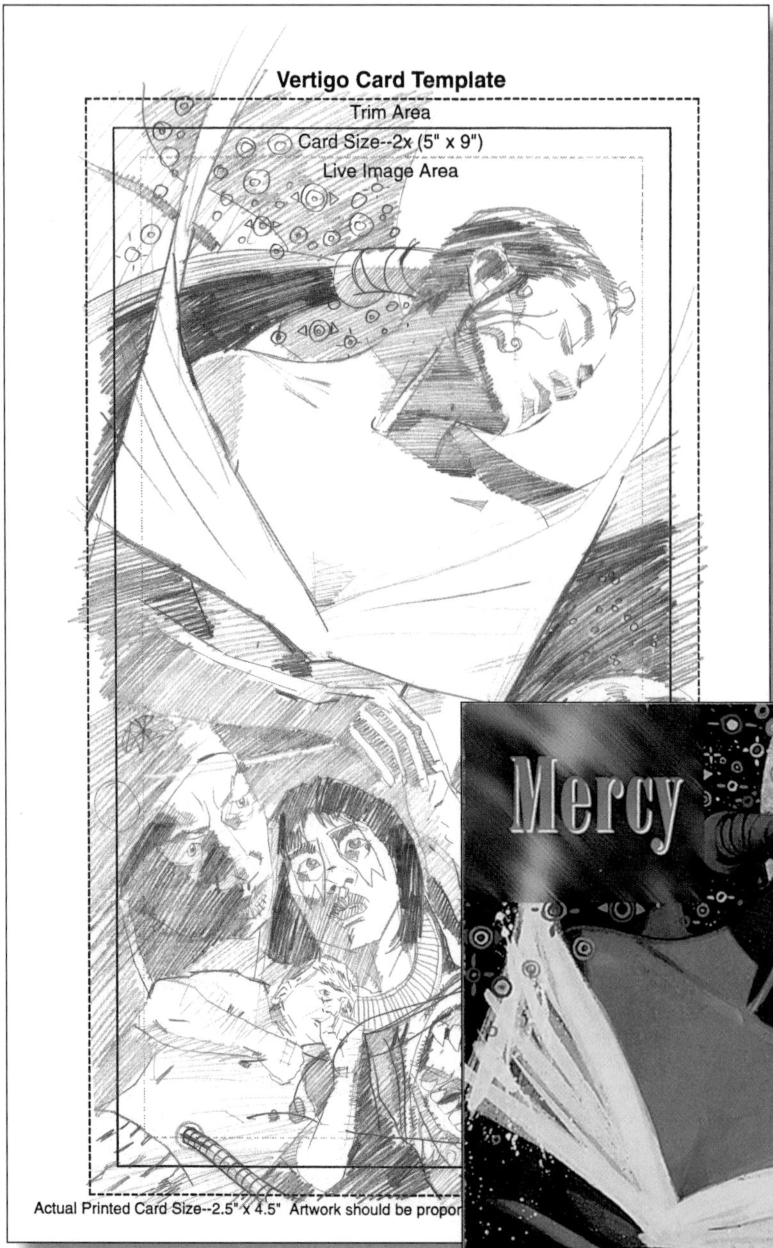
Vertigo Card Template
Trim Area
Card Size--2x (5" x 9")
Live Image Area
Actual Printed Card Size--2.5" x 4.5" Artwork should be propor

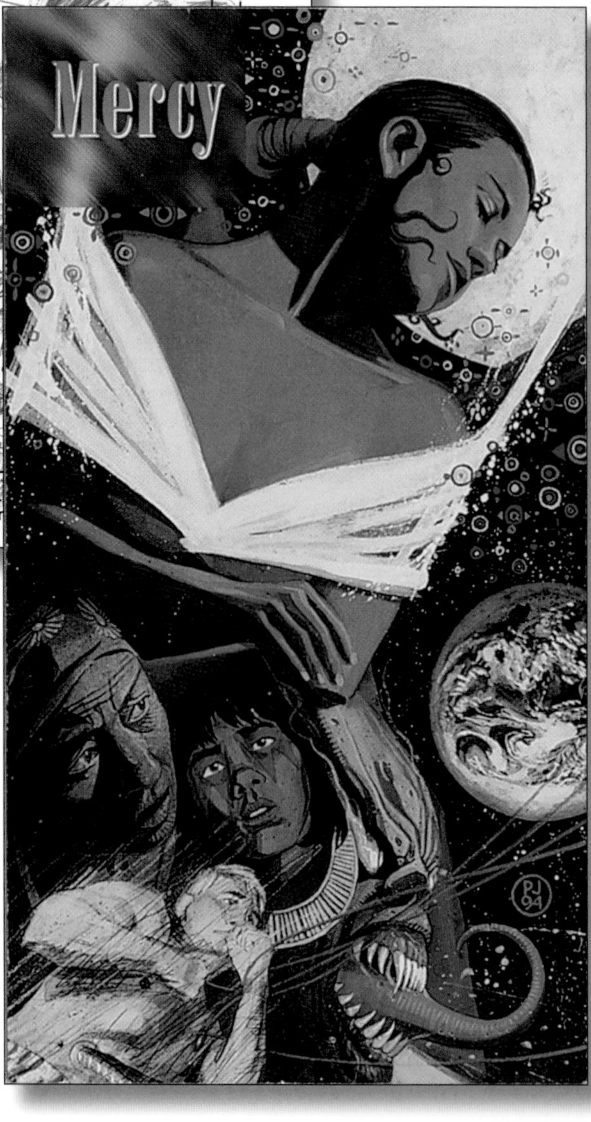
Mercy
PJ 94

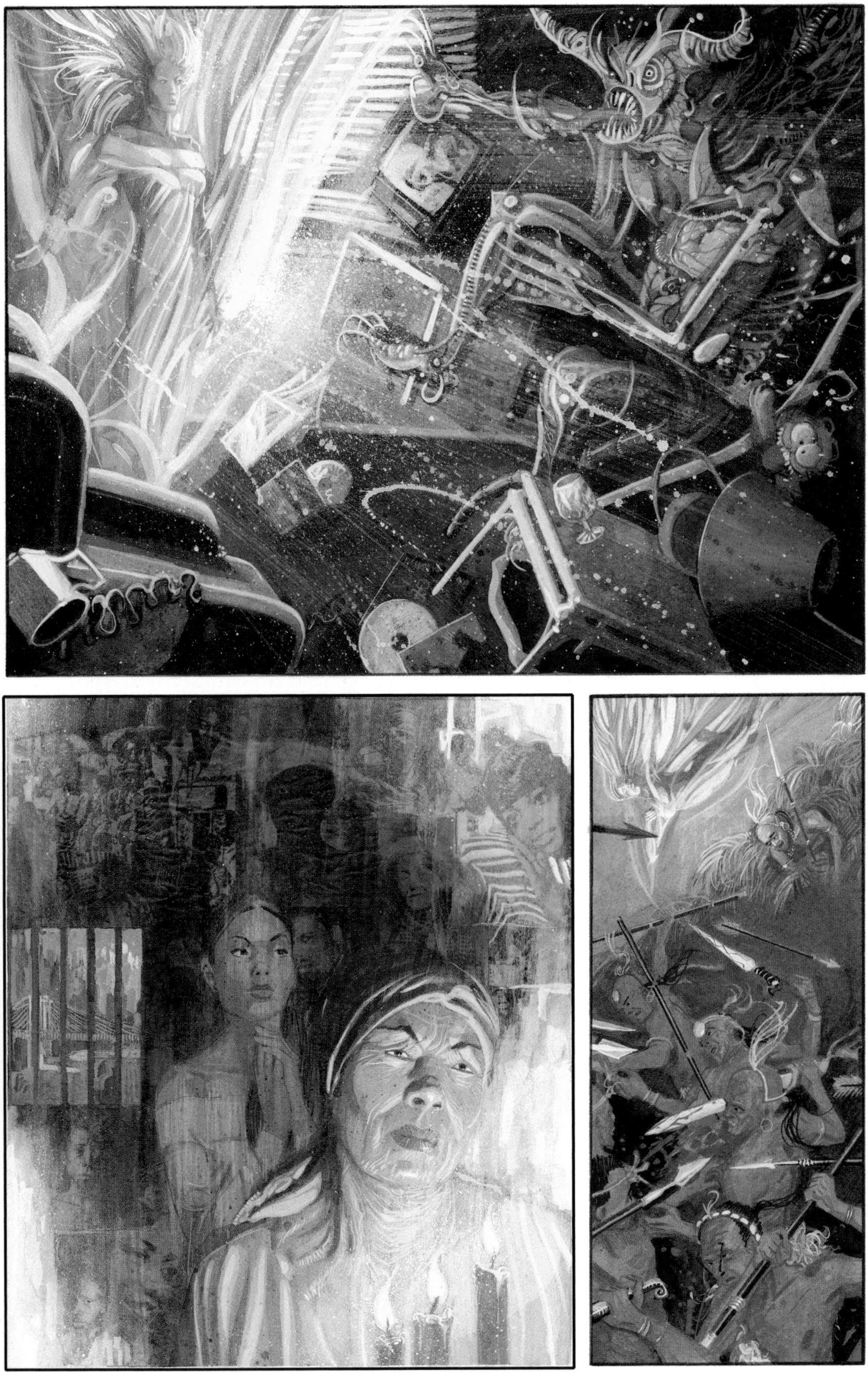

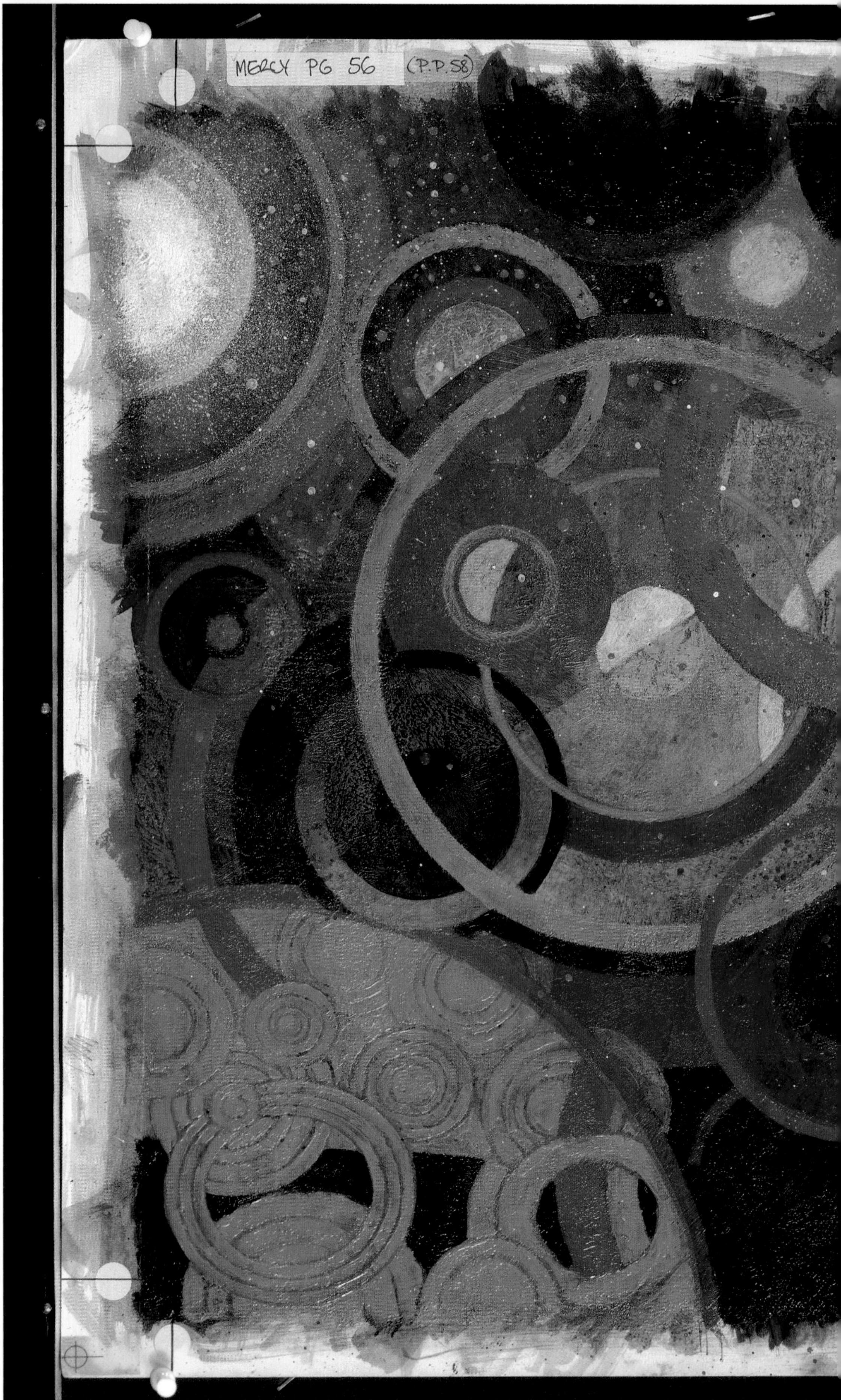
MERCY PG 56 (P.P.58)

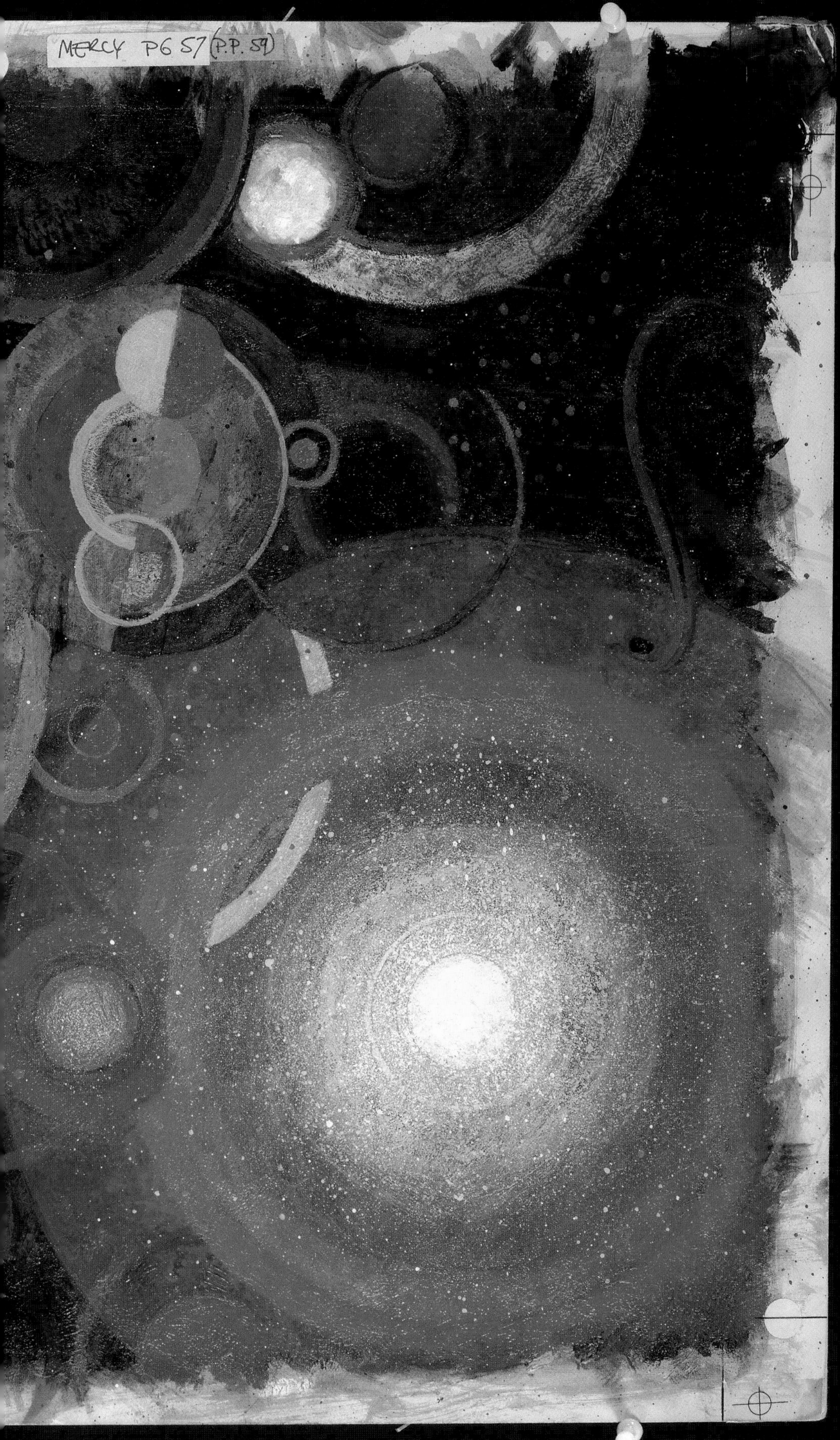
MERCY PG 57 (P.P. 59)

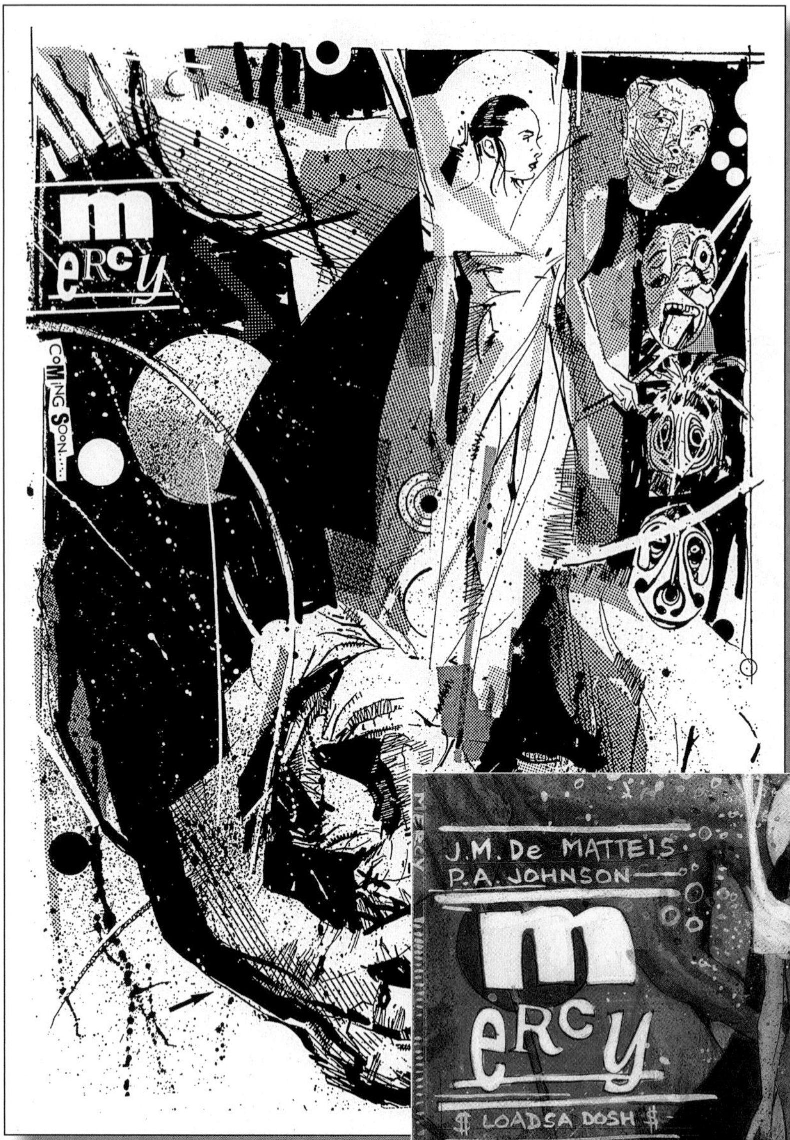
m
eRcy
COMING SOON...

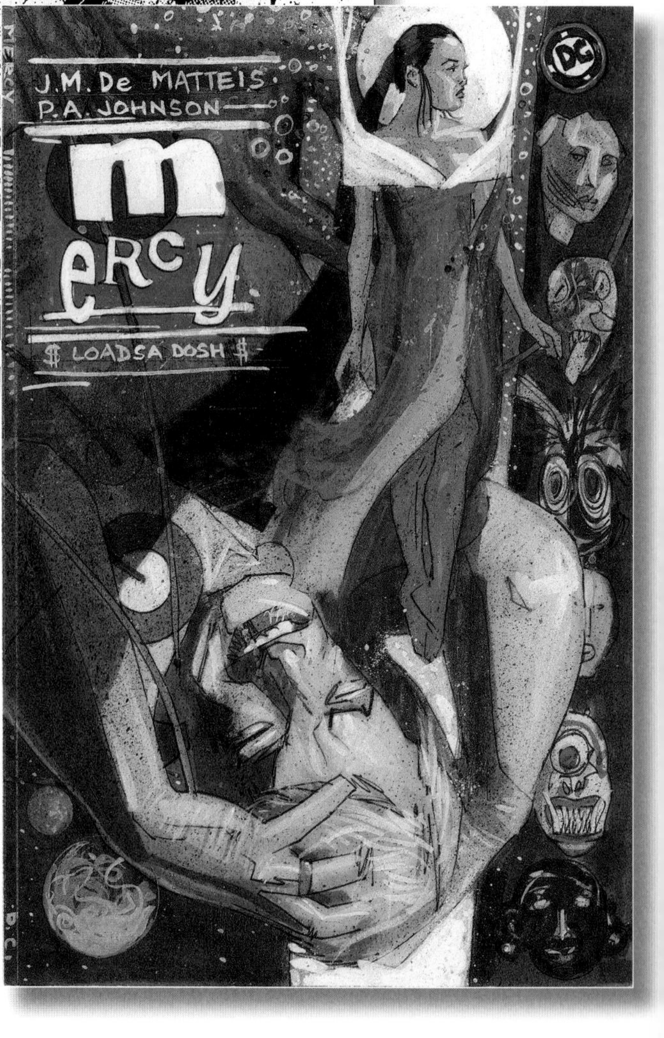
J.M. De MATTEIS
P.A. JOHNSON
m
eRcy
$ LOADSA DOSH $
DC

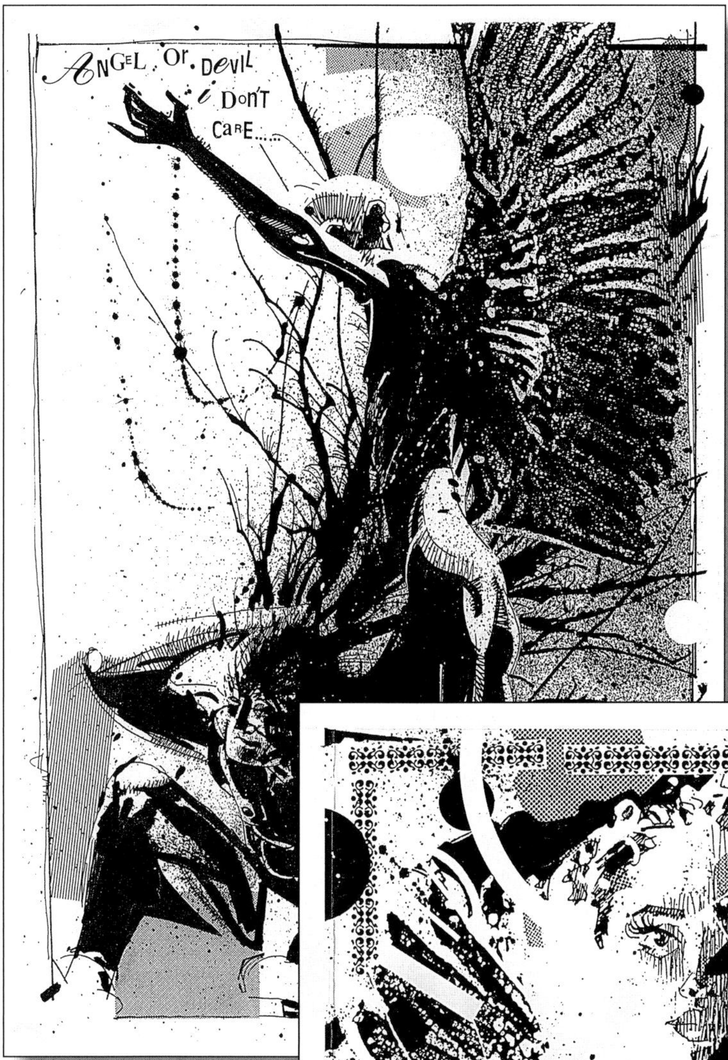
Angel Or Devil
I Don't
Care.....

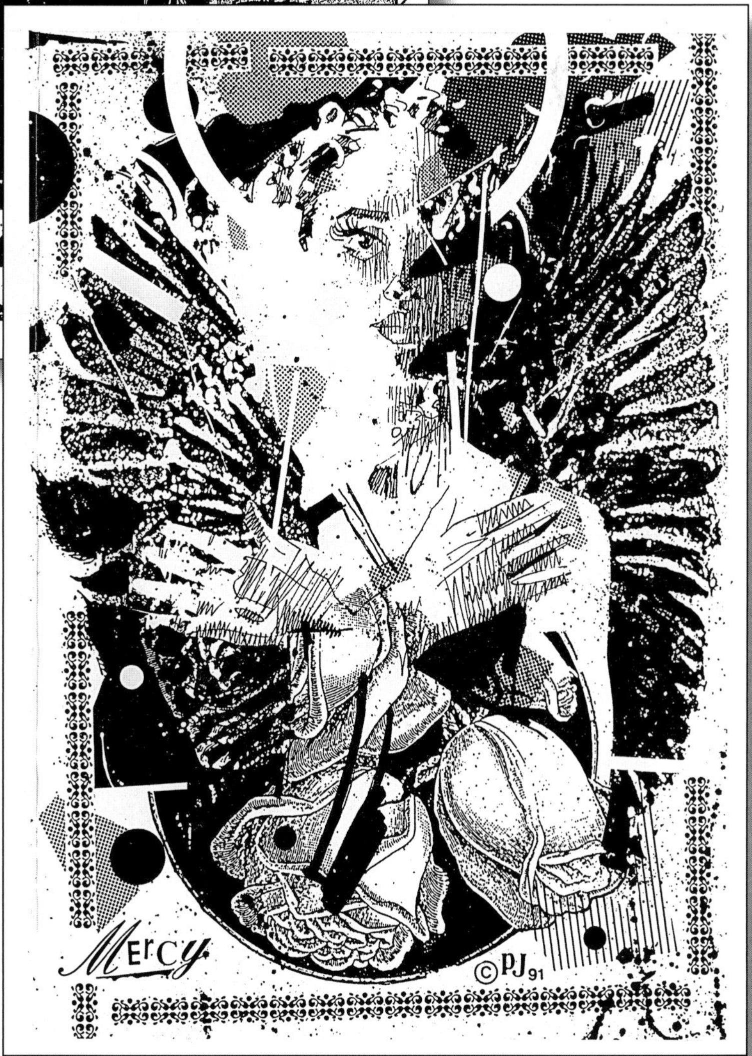
Mercy
© pJ 91

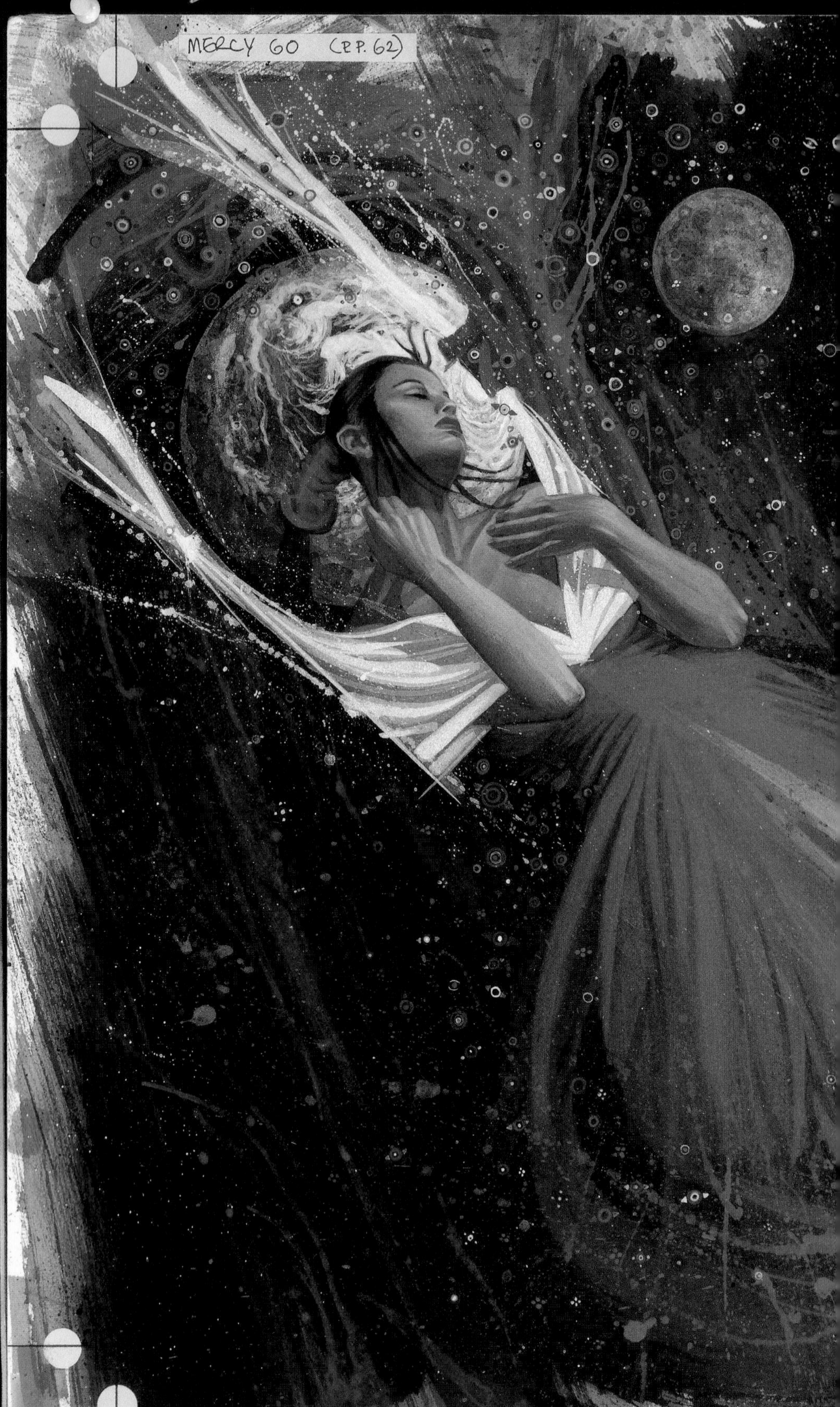
MERCY 60 (P.P. 62)

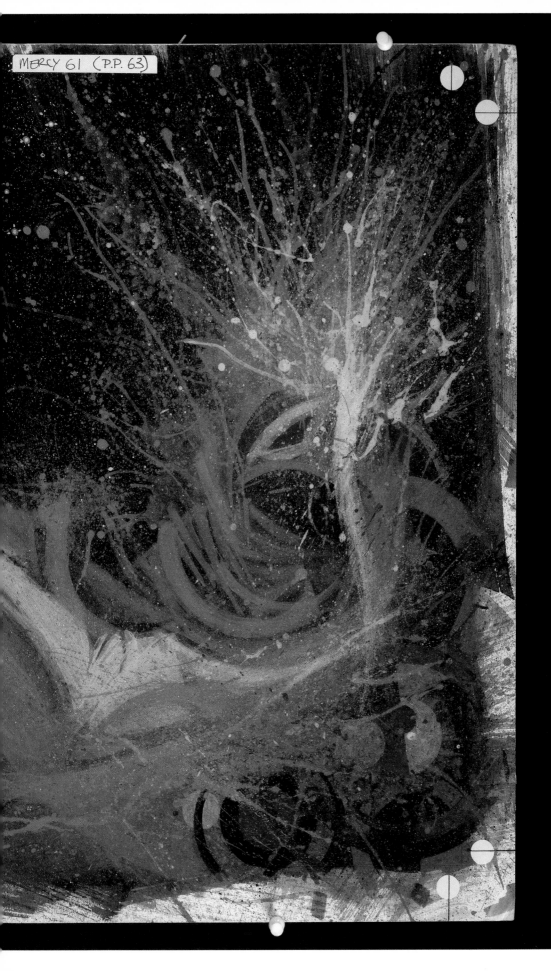

MERCY 61 (P.P. 63)

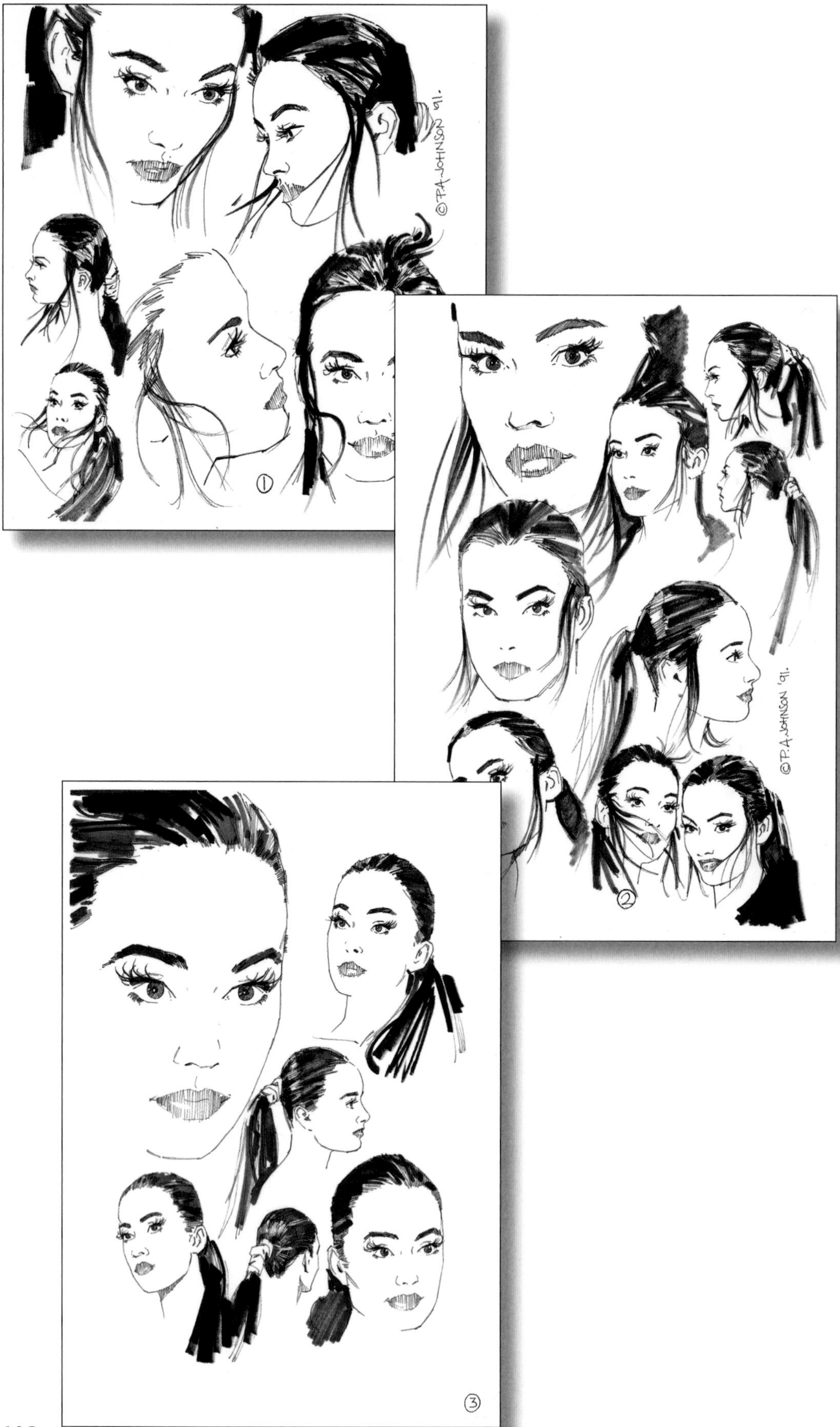
©P.A.JOHNSON '91.
1
©P.A.JOHNSON '91.
2
3

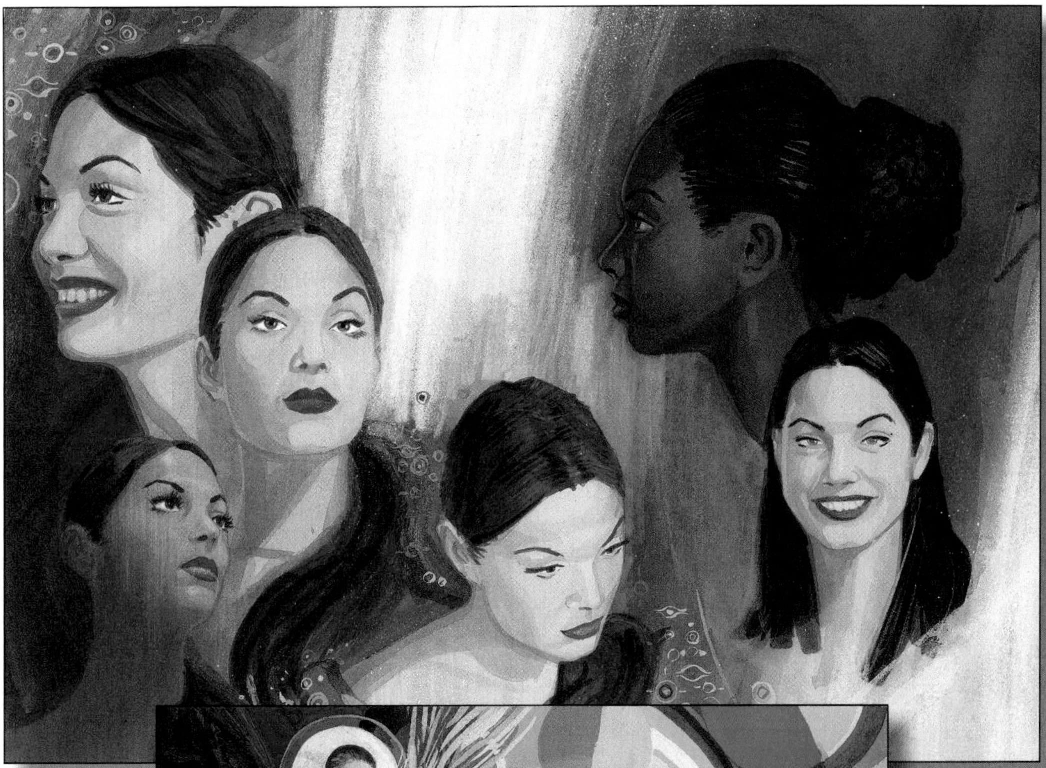

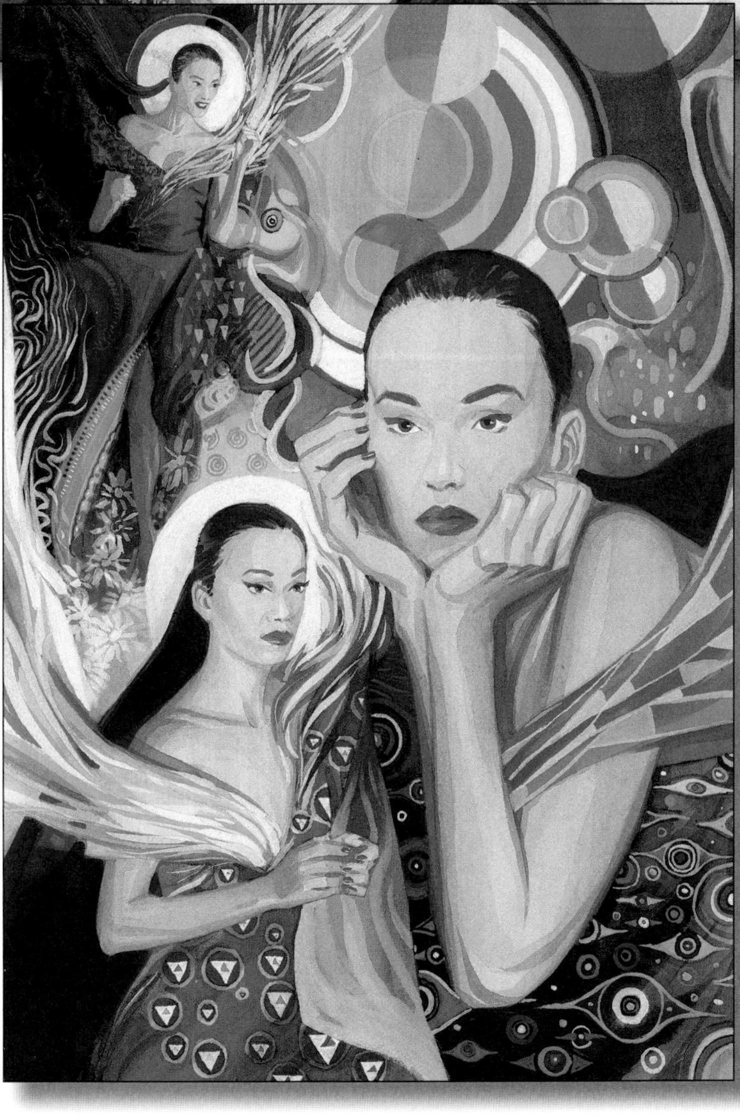

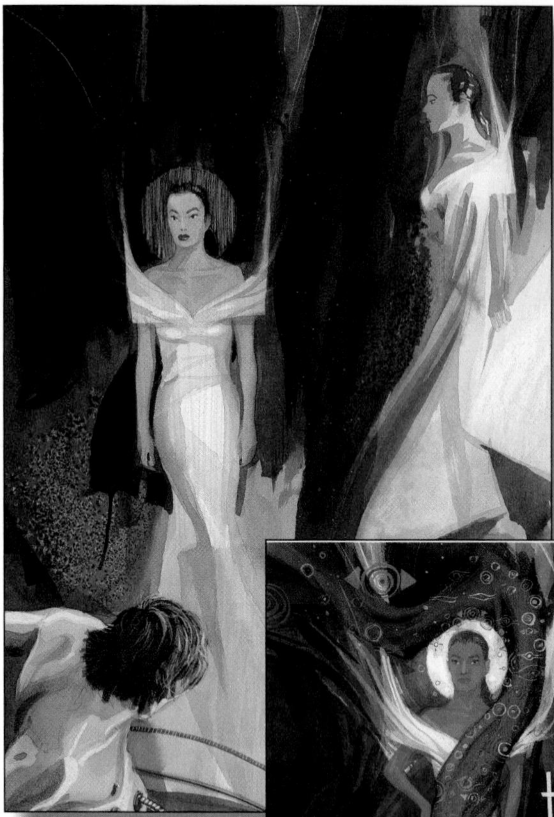

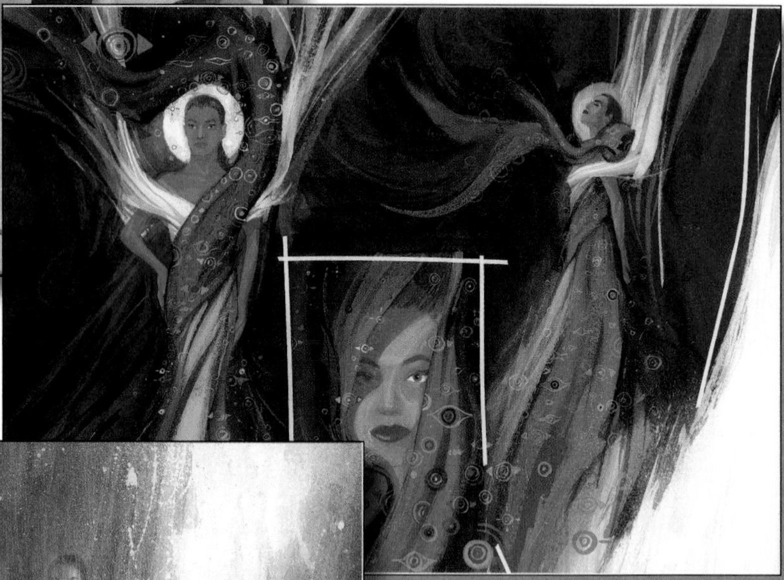

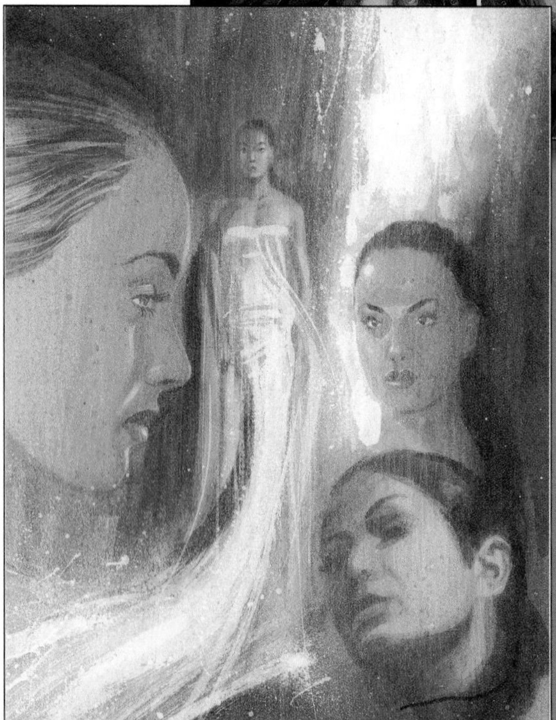

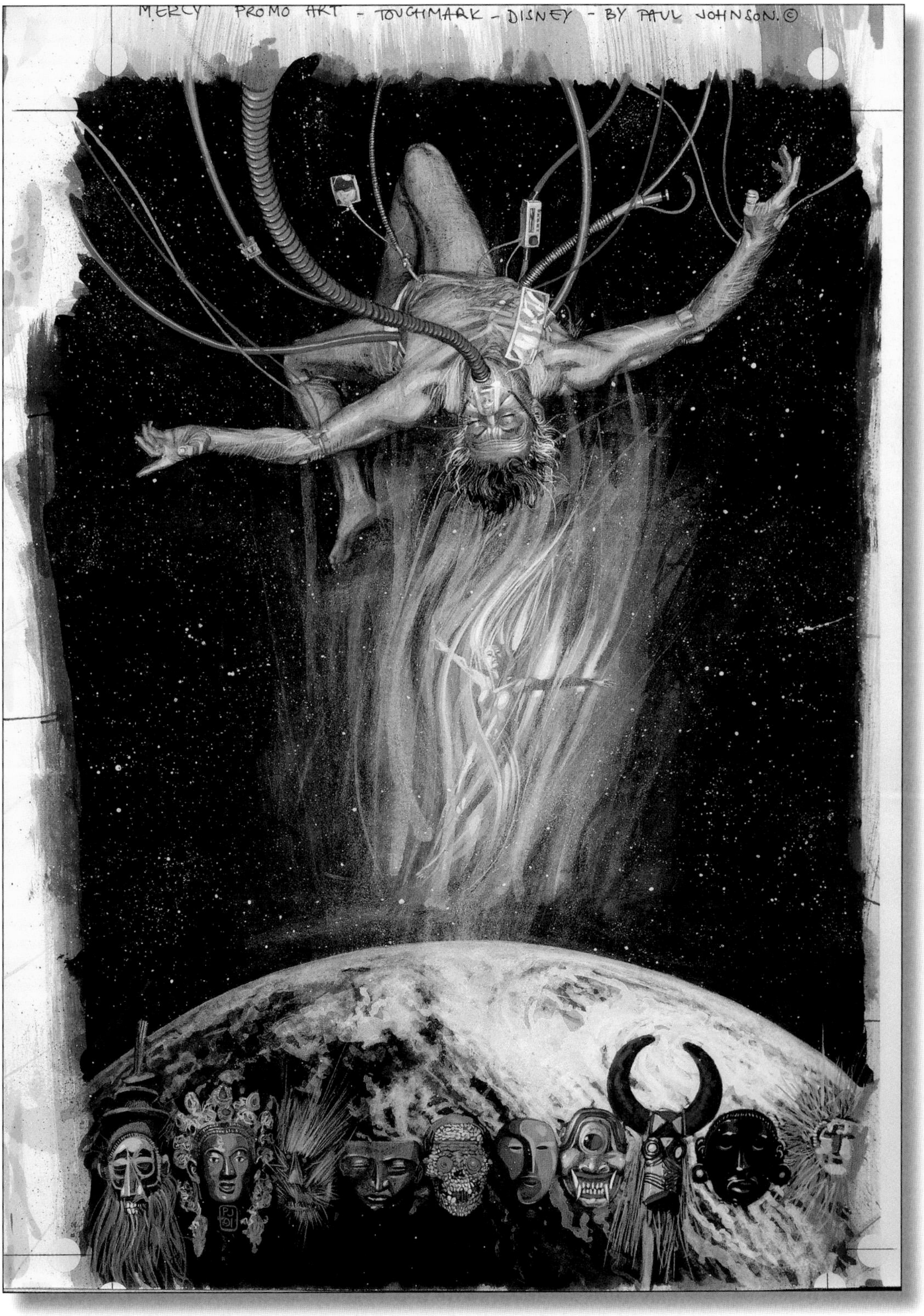
MERCY PROMO ART - TOUCHMARK - DISNEY - BY PAUL JOHNSON.©

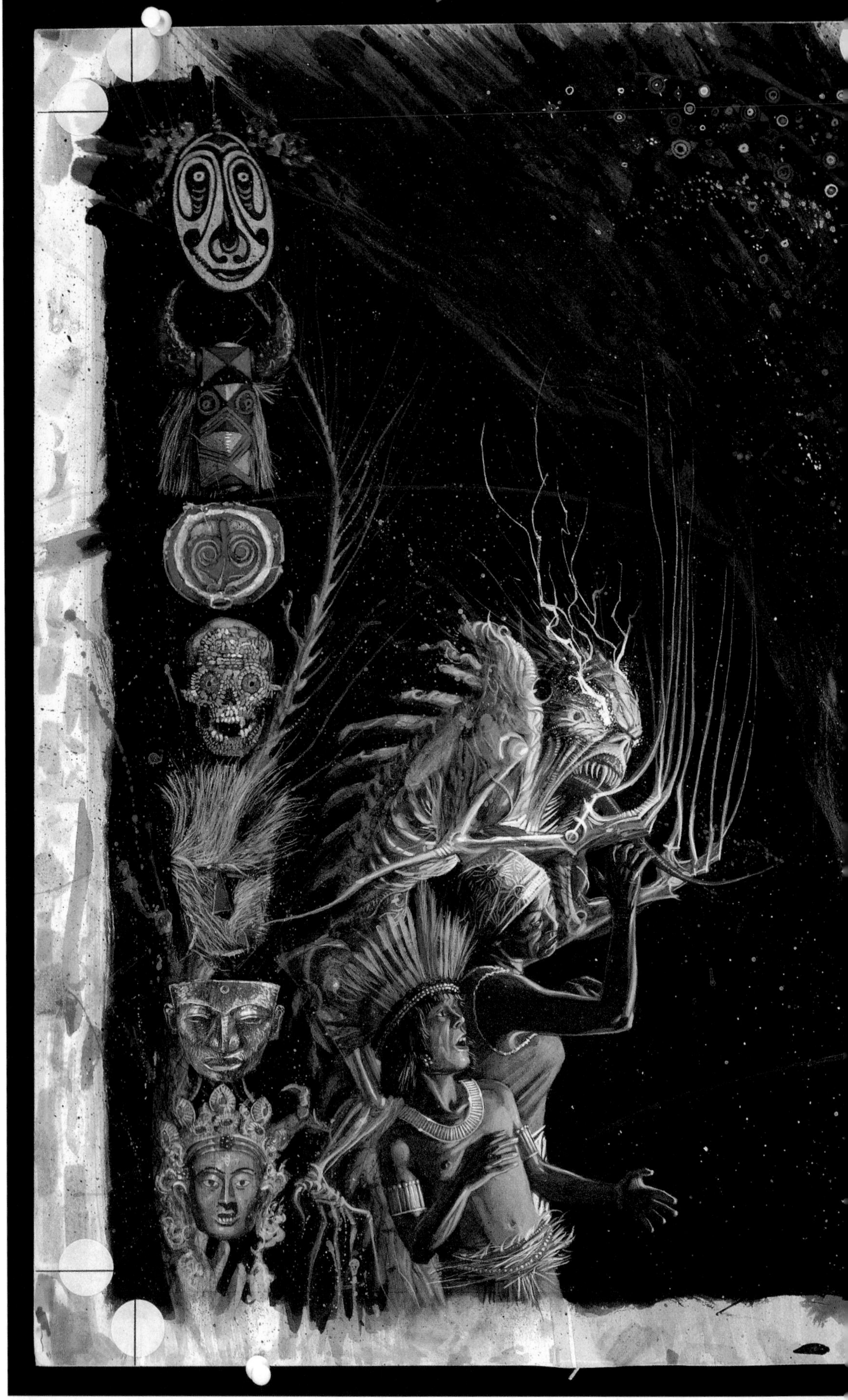

'MERCY' COVER ART.

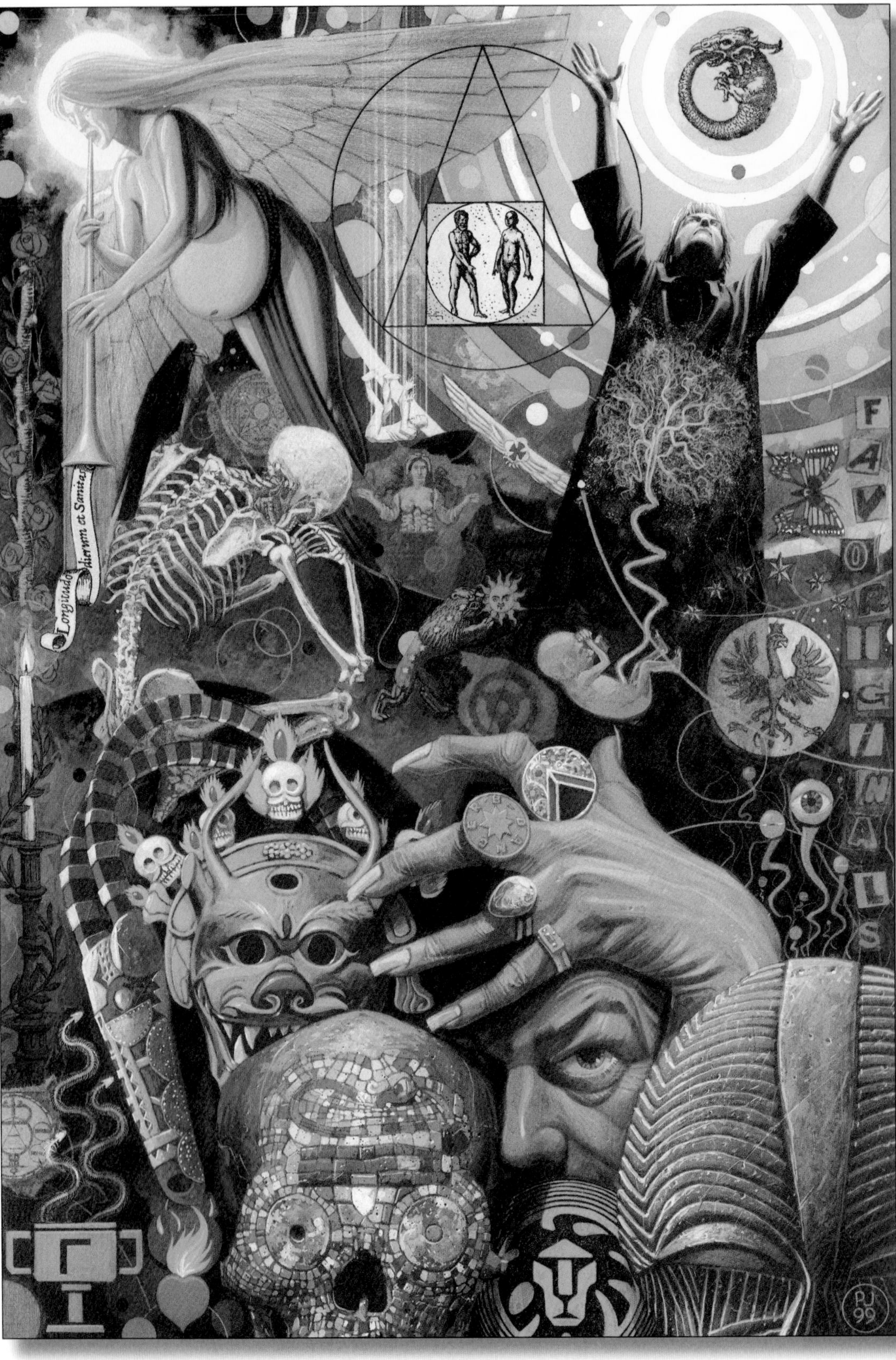
PJ
99

AFTERWORD

The comics writing legend I know as Marc—J.M. DeMatteis to you—
approached me with the idea for *Mercy* because we wanted to work
together again. We had just finished a wild and wacky two-year run on
DC Comics' *Dr. Fate.* (Actually, the subject matter was quite mystical.
Marc is one of the few writers I know—perhaps the only one—who
can be wacky and mystical at the same time.) *Mercy* sounded more
than mystical. It sounded…uplifting. A radical concept for comics at
the time—this was the "grim and gritty" era, and darkness was king.

The year was 1990, and I had just met Paul Johnson at the late,
lamented UKCAC (United Kingdom Comic Art Convention). We hit it
off straight away, and I was also intrigued by his very photorealistic
artwork—achieved by posing human models, photographing them
and then painting the results. (I was to become one of these models
eventually—along with just about everyone else Paul knew!)

One of the most important qualities a comic book editor can
have, I've always thought, is the ability to achieve that "alchemy"
of putting the right writer and the right artist together on the right
project. I thought Paul would be a good fit—both with Marc and for
Mercy. So I sent it to him.

I remember Paul writing me a little note (people actually wrote on
paper back then, kids) saying "Art, why did you send me this?" "Oh
no," I thought—the first thing I've suggested and he doesn't like it.
But then I read on. "It's exactly the sort of project I've been looking
for—how did you know?"

At this point I was no longer at DC in New York. I had been lured away
to Los Angeles by Walt Disney (not him personally, you understand).
Disney had recently launched *Touchstone* and *Hollywood Pictures*
as a way of producing films aimed at adults—rather than children
or families—without "besmirching" the Disney name. They thought
they'd try the same trick in comics, expanding beyond books starring
the famous mouse and duck—and they needed someone to helm
the new enterprise.

They also wanted me to name it. If I'm honest, the responsibility
caused me several sleepless nights. But I eventually came up with
Touchmark (riffing on *Touchstone*)—an obscure term meaning an
official maker's mark. I thought it suited the creator-owned nature of
this new comics line. (I seem to remember then-Disney editor Len
Wein wrinkling his nose with distaste and remarking that the word

sounded like the result of an obscene act. That sealed the deal!) Todd Klein perfectly executed a logo I had in mind for *Touchmark*. He also designed *Mercy's* logo, as well as providing the lettering—masterfully, as always.

I was enormously flattered—and grateful—when it transpired that all the writers and artists I'd worked with at DC were also happy to contribute to this brave new venture. The flagship *Touchmark* titles were to be Peter Milligan and Duncan Fegredo's *Enigma*, Grant Morrison and Steve Yeowell's *Sebastian O*—and *Mercy*. Sharp-eyed readers will have spotted that these three titles actually helped launch DC's *Vertigo* line—but more on that later.

I thought Marc and Paul would be on the same wavelength, and so it proved. Marc's moving, heartfelt script had clearly struck a chord with Paul, who rose to the occasion interpreting it. I remember that whenever a new parcel from Paul arrived, Disney staff would swarm into my office to coo over the beautiful paintings.

So far, so good. But then…upheaval.

Some of their younger-skewed comics suddenly weren't doing so well, and Disney was starting to get cold feet about publishing a "mature readers" line—understandably perhaps, as it wasn't exactly their forte.

By a happy coincidence, back at DC Karen Berger was now in the process of coalescing the more esoteric of her titles into DC's own "mature readers" line: *Vertigo*. But she needed help to do it—and she asked me, her erstwhile assistant editor, to join her.

After all, we worked together well and had similar tastes—it made perfect sense. Besides, the previously mentioned trilogy of *Touchmark* titles would add some much-needed creator-owned series to the nascent *Vertigo*, providing both high-profile names and instant gravitas.

Crucially, the inclusion of *Mercy* in the launch titles showed that the *Vertigo* line needn't be relentlessly dark—something I felt strongly about.

Rereading it today, I'd forgotten how poetic the writing is, how vibrant the art. Needless to say, Marc and Paul were a delight to work with—the fact that they were both immensely enjoying what they were doing was obvious from the start. And I think that shows in the work you're holding in your hands.

Like I said. Alchemy.

ART YOUNG
Editor, *Mercy*